SEEDS AND FOOD

PROCESSING AND STORAGE TECHNIQUES

ENV BOOKS SERIES

SEEDS AND FOOD

PROCESSING AND STORAGE TECHNIQUES

Editors

Dr. Prasann Kumar

Division of Research and Development
Lovely Professional University
Jalandhar - 144 411 (Punjab)
(India)

&

Dr. Pawan Kumar 'Bharti'

Society for Environment, Health Awareness of
Nutrition & Toxicology (SEHAT)
B-225/5D, Top Floor, Subhash Gali, Road No. 7, Block B
Ashok Nagar, Shahdara, Delhi - 110 093
(India)

DPH

DISCOVERY PUBLISHING HOUSE PVT. LTD.

INDIA

Published by:
Namit Wasan
DISCOVERY PUBLISHING HOUSE PVT. LTD.
4383/4B, Ansari Road, Darya Ganj
New Delhi-110 002 (India)
Phone : +91-11-23279245; 23253475; 43596065
E-mail : discoverybooksindia@gmail.com
discoverypublishinghouse@gmail.com
namitwasan9@gmail.com
web : www.discoverypublishinggroup.com

***First Edition:* 2020**

ISBN: 978-93-88854-41-2

Seeds and Food: ***Processing and Storage Techniques***

Printed at:
Infinity Imaging Systems
Delhi

M.S. Swaminathan Research Foundation

M.S. Swaminathan
Founder Chairman
Ex-Member of Parliament (Rajya Sabha)

Foreword

I am very glad to know that a several books are being edited under the aegis of ENVBOOKS series, Delhi, India on various sub-themes of Agriculture and environment like:

'Cultivation Techniques for Agriculture Crops'
'Air Pollution and Control'
'Seed and Food Storage Technologies'
'Heavy Metals and Impacts on Plants'
'Climate Change and Agriculture Production'
'Scientific Writing and Research Methodology'
'Laboratory Management'
'Statistical Tools in Science'
'Advances in Chemistry and Chemical Sciences'
'Irrigation techniques in Crop management' 'Waste Management Practices'
'Vermitechnology, Farm and Fertilizers'
'Animal Science and Pest Control'
'Recent Research in Biochemistry and Molecular Biology'
'Water Management and Sustainability'
'Soil Quality and Agriculture'

I am very happy to learn that a number of editors and authors from different institutions and university of different nations are involved in editing these books. The books are the compendium of screened-in manuscripts received from different countries like UK, Canada, Egypt, Nigeria, Ghana, Ethiopia, China, South Africa, Japan, Guyana, PNG, Nepal, South America, and various parts of India. I am feeling delighted in writing forward to these books and congratulate to Dr. Pawan Kumar Bharti, Editor-in-Chief and founder of ENVBOOKS series and of course his team for their tenacity and hard work in compiling these valuable compendiums.

I hope these books will be beneficial for academician, researchers, industrialist, policy makers and students as study material and will work as reference for further research work.

M.S. Swaminathan

Preface

Seed storage is preservation of seed with initial quality until it is needed for planting. The ability of seed to tolerate moisture loss allows the seed to maintain the viability in dry state. Storage starts in the mother plant itself when it attains physiological maturity. After harvesting the seeds are either stored in ware houses or in transit or in retail shops. During the old age days, the farmers were used farm saved seeds in little quantity, but introduction of high yielding varieties and hybrids and modernization of agriculture necessitated the development of storage techniques to preserve the seeds.

Proper storage of seed is vital to conserving its vigor and vitality. Seeds can last from a few years to centuries, depending on the species and the storage conditions. In general, most seeds stored in cool, dry conditions will survive longer than seeds stored in a wet, warm environment. In many parts of the world, agricultural seeds are stored in bins that are open to the ambient conditions, often resulting in short storage life and poor seed quality in hot, humid regions, as well as losses due to insects and rodents. As the viability period for seeds decreases by half for every 1% increase in seed moisture content or 10°F (~5°C) increase in temperature, sealed bins and controlled environments are used to maintain seed viability for longer periods. A common rule of thumb is that the temperature (in Fahrenheit) plus the relative humidity in the air (in percent) should total less than 100 for satisfactory seed storage.

The present book updates the subject content on seed processing, seed cleaning, seed storage, oil seed significance, seed preservation techniques for shorgum, chilli and other crops. On the other hand a few chapters are highlighting the seed production and hatchery technology for several fishes too.

Thanks are due to publisher and contributors from various institutions and universities.

The book will be helpful for the researchers, academia working in the field of Seed processing, equipments for seed cleaning, grading and upgrading; Major seed oils; Seed storage, seed storage sanitation and maintenance, Physiological Attributes; Seed Preservation Techniques; Hatchery Seed Production Technology; Drying and Measurable Quality Attributes of Chilli; Food and Crop Storage Technology; Packages and Practices of Sorghum.

–Editors

(envbooks@gmail.com)

Contents

Foreword

Preface

Introduction

1. **Seed Processing:** ***Importance, Sequence, Equipments for Seed Cleaning, Grading and Upgrading*** 1-28
Sridevi. R. and G. Gopalakrishnan

2. **Major Seed Oils and their Significance** 29-47
Anubhuti Sharma, Meghna Garg, P.K. Rai

3. **Seed Storage:** ***Importance, Factors Affecting Storage, Seed Storage Sanitation and Maintenance*** 48-82
R. Sridevi

4. **Physiological Attributes of Sorghum** 83-94
Prasann Kumar, Shipa Rani Dey

5. **Advances in Seed Preservation Techniques** 95-127
R. Sridevi

6. **Hatchery Seed Production Technology and Grow-out Farming of Monosex Tilapia** ***Oreochromis Niloticus*** **in North 24 Parganas, West Bengal** 128-141
Subrato Ghosh

7. **Methodology of Drying and Measurable Quality Attributes of Chilli:** ***An Overview of Experiment*** 142-148
Prasann Kumar, Shipa Rani Dey

8. **Seed Production of** ***Notopterus Chitala*** **and other Fishes and Fish Farming in Advanced Recirculatory Aquaculture System in North Bengal** 149-167
Subrato Ghosh

9. **Food and Crop Storage Technology** 168-179
Prasann Kumar, Shipa Rani Dey

10. **Packages and Practices of Sorghum** 180-189
Prasann Kumar, Shipa Rani Dey

Index 191-197

Introduction

There are numerous examples of the use of seeds as food for humans. The seeds may be eaten directly, or used to manufacture flour, starch, oil, alcohol, or some other edible products. The seeds of certain agricultural grasses are especially important foodstuffs, for example, those of wheat (Triticum aestivum), rice (Oyza sativa) maize (Zea mays), sorghum (Sorghum bicolor), and barley (Hordeum vulgare). Other edible seeds include those of the legumes, the second-most important family of plants after the grasses, in terms of providing foods for human consumption. Examples of legumes whose seeds are eaten by people include the peanut (Arachis hypogaea), soybean (Glycine max), lentil (Lens esculenta), common pea (Pisum sativum), and common bean (P. vulgaris). Other edible seeds include those of the coconut (Cocos nucifera), walnut (Juglans regia), pecan (Carya illinoensis), and sunflower (Helianthus annua).

Many other seeds are eaten with their fruits, although it is generally the encasing fruit walls that are the sought-after source of nutrition. A few examples of edible fruits include those of the pumpkin or squash (Cucurbita pepo), bell pepper (Capsicum anuum), apple (Malus pumila), sweet cherry (Prunus avium), strawberry (Fragaria vesca), raspberry (Rubus idaeus), and sweet orange (Citrus sinensis).

An edible seed is a seed that is suitable for human or animal consumption. Of the six major plant parts, seeds are the dominant source of human calories and protein. A wide variety of plant species provide edible seeds; most are angiosperms, while a few are gymnosperms. As a global food source, the most important edible seeds by weight are cereals, followed by legumes, nuts. and then spices.

Cereals and legumes correspond with the botanical families Poaceae and Fabaceae, respectively, while nuts, pseudocereals, and other seeds form polyphylic groups based on their culinary roles.

Cereals

A cereal, also called a cereal grain or simply a grain, is the edible seed of a grass, a plant in the family Poaceae. Cereals can be consumed in a variety of ways, all of which require husking and cooking, including whole, rolled, puffed, or ground into flour. Many cereals are present or past staple foods, providing a large fraction of the calories in the places in which they are eaten. Today, cereals provide almost half of all calories consumed in the world.

Pseudocereals

A pseudocereal, or pseudocereal grain, is the edible seed of a pseudocereal, one of a polyphyletic group of plants that produce seeds that resemble those of cereals. Pseudocereals are used in many of the same ways as cereals.

Legumes

A legume, or pulse, is the edible seed of a legume, a plant in the family Fabaceae. Legumes can be divided into grams, which do not split, and dals, which split.

Although some beans can be consumed raw, some need to be heated before consumption. In certain cultures, beans that need heating are initially prepared as a seed cake.

Nuts

According to the botanical definition, nuts are a particular kind of fruit. Chestnuts, hazelnuts, and acorns are examples of nuts under this definition. In culinary terms, however, the term is used more broadly to include fruits that are not botanically qualified as nuts, but that have a similar appearance and culinary role. Examples of culinary nuts include almonds and cashews.

The seeds of some plants have other uses, including serving as resources for the manufacturing of industrial chemicals, such as grain alcohol (ethanol), derived from a fermentation of the seeds of corn, wheat, or some other plants. The seeds of some plants are used as attractive decorations, as is the case of the Job's tears (Coix lachryma-jobi), a grass that produces large, white, shiny seeds that are used to make attractive necklaces and other decorations, often dyed in various attractive colors.

Seed Storage

Seed storage is preservation of seed with initial quality until it is needed for planting. The ability of seed to tolerate moisture loss allows the seed to maintain the viability in dry state. Storage starts in the mother plant itself when it attains physiological maturity. After harvesting the seeds are either stored in ware houses or in transit or in retail shops. During the old age days, the farmers were used farm saved seeds in little quantity, but introduction of high yielding varieties and hybrids and modernization of agriculture necessitated the development of storage techniques to preserve the seeds.

The practice of storing the seeds starts from the ancient days itself, following simple and cheap techniques eg. Placing the seeds in salt, red earth treatment to red gram etc. But the same practices are not hold good for the present day agriculture, because

- large quantity to be stored
- exchange of varieties and species
- exchange of genes

The type of material to be stored decides the techniques to be followed for safe storage. Now a days storage technique changed from ordinary godown storage to cryogenic tank storage and even gene storage.

Seed Storage/Conservation

Proper storage of seed is vital to conserving its vigor and vitality. Seeds can last from a few years to centuries, depending on the species and the storage conditions. In general, most seeds stored in cool, dry conditions will survive longer than seeds stored in a wet, warm environment. In many parts of the world, agricultural seeds are stored in bins that are open to the ambient conditions, often resulting in short storage life and poor seed quality in hot, humid regions, as well as losses due to insects and rodents. As the viability period for seeds decreases by half for every 1% increase in seed moisture content or 10°F (~5°C) increase in temperature, sealed bins and controlled environments are used to maintain seed viability for longer periods. A common rule of thumb is that the temperature (in Fahrenheit) plus the relative humidity in the air (in percent) should total less than 100 for satisfactory seed storage.

At seed banks that store seeds to preserve genetic diversity, seeds are dried to optimum moisture content, evaluated for quality and genetic purity and sealed in moisture-proof containers. For short-term storage, seeds are dried and placed in sealed containers at 5°C. They are stored at temperatures below freezing for long-term preservation (0°F or -20°C), including the use of cryopreservation, or freezing in or over liquid nitrogen at -180°C, for extremely long-term storage. But when it comes to seed storage, one size does not fit all. Some species have short-lived seeds that do not tolerate dehydration and are therefore difficult to store. Plants producing these recalcitrant seeds must be maintained as living populations, making them vulnerable to loss due to changes in land use or weather patterns.

The vigor and viability of seeds stored even at low temperatures declines over time. The continued maintenance of specific seed lines requires that they periodically be removed from storage and used to produce a new crop of seeds. Seed storage facilities therefore need not only modern storage equipment but also the land, personnel and expertise to periodically grow the stored seeds under conditions that maintain their genetic diversity and purity in order to replenish the original seed stock. Thus, core seed repositories such as the U.S. National Center for Genetic Resources

Preservation in Ft. Collins, Colorado, are complemented by a number of branch stations in different growing environments to store and replenish seed collections of diverse species.

Recalcitrant seeds are seeds that do not survive drying and freezing and therefore cannot be stored for long periods of time. Some plants that produce recalcitrant seeds include avocado, mango, lychee and some horticultural trees.

Seed Enhancement

Seed enhancement refers to various technologies used to increase the consistency of seed performance, thereby improving a crop's harvested yield and quality. Seed enhancement technologies are gaining increasing attention for their potential to confer greater disease resistance in seeds, improve seed vigor and modify seed emergence capabilities.

Seed coating refers to the application of materials to the seed surface, often containing seed protectants such as fungicides. In recent years, film coating, in which the active ingredient is applied in a quick-drying polymer film around the seed, has gained popularity. A major advantage of film coating is reduced loss of active material from the seed during seed transport and handling. Seed pelleting technologies are used to alter seed shape, surface properties, density and size to enable more precise seed singulation and placement in the planting tray or soil. Singulation eliminates clustering of seed that leaves too much or too little space between plants within a row. Seed pelleting is also used to deliver a range of beneficial additives, including micronutrients and plant protection agents.

Seed priming is used to increase germination rate (speed) and uniformity and overcome seed dormancy. In seed priming, seeds are hydrated in a controlled manner to provide enough water to initiate the metabolic processes of germination, but not enough to allow germination to be completed. Subsequently, the seeds are dried, distributed and planted in the usual way. Primed seed usually exhibit more rapid and uniform emergence of seedlings from the soil compared to non-primed seed of the same seed lot. These differences are greatest under adverse environmental conditions in the field, such as cold or hot soils. Primed seed often has a shorter shelf life than non-primed seed, and should be stored under optimal conditions prior to planting.

REFERENCES

http://sbc.ucdavis.edu/About_US/Seed_Biotechnologies/Seed_Storage_Conservation/

https://www.bioversityinternational.org/fileadmin/bioversity/publications/Web_version/188/ch09.htm

http://ecoursesonline.iasri.res.in/mod/page/view.php?id=17880

http://sbc.ucdavis.edu/About_US/Seed_Biotechnologies/Seed_Enhancement/

https://science.jrank.org/pages/6059/Seeds-Seeds-food.html

https://en.wikipedia.org/wiki/List_of_edible_seeds

Pages: 1-28

Seeds and Food: ***Processing and Storage Techniques***

Edited by: **Dr. Prasann Kumar and Dr. Pawan Kumar 'Bharti'**

ISBN: 978-93-88854-41-2

Edition: **2020**

Published by: **Discovery Publishing House Pvt. Ltd., New Delhi (India)**

1

Seed Processing

Importance, Sequence, Equipments for Seed Cleaning, Grading and Upgrading

Sridevi. R.*[1] and G. Gopalakrishnan[2]

INTRODUCTION

New and improved crop varieties become an important agricultural input only when seed of such varieties are available to farmers varietally pure, in a viable condition, free of contaminating weed seed and inadequate quantities at the right place and time. Seed processing is an integral part of the technology involved in transforming the genetic engineering of the plant breeder and geneticist into improved seed. In its broadest sense seed processing encompasses all the steps involved in the preparation of harvested seed for marketing – handling, shelling, preconditioning, drying, cleaning, size-grading, upgrading, treating and packaging. In common use however, the term seed processing refers only to the preconditioning, cleaning, size grading and upgrading of seed.

Seed growers and producers are dependent on the seed processor for preparation of their seed for market. The quality of the final product regardless of its inherent capacity to produce is directly related to the processors ability to remove contaminants and low quality seed, to properly size-grade for precision planting, to treat the seed effectively, and to prevent mechanical mixtures of the seed with those of other varieties or hybrids. In turn, the processors ability to render these services efficiently and effectively is greatly affected by the types of processing and handling

[1] Assistant professor, Imayam Institute of Agriculture and Technology, Department of Seed Science and Technology, Thuraiyur, Trichy - 621 206

[2] Ph.D Research Scholar, Department of Seed Science and Technology, Tamil Nadu Agricultural University, Coimbatore - 641 003, Tamil Nadu (India)

equipment available to him, their arrangement within the plant, and his skill in operating them, and his knowledge of seed characteristics and how they relate to processing.

Seeds are processed to remove contaminants to size-grade for plantability, to upgrade quality through removal of damaged or deteriorated seed, and to apply, seed treatment materials. The demands of the seed producer and seed consumer require that these four objectives be achieved effectively, efficiently and with minimal damage to the seed. A variety of equipment is available for processing seed. They range from the simple winnowing tray - still used in many areas of the world - to complex and highly sophisticated equipment such as the electric sorting machine. Although variable in type and design, all seed processing equipment have one thing in common: the separations they effect are based on differences in physical properties among desirable material (good seed) and undesirable material (contaminants). Some machines separate good seed from contaminants on the basis of differences in several physical properties. More often, however satisfactory removal of contaminating material from seed requires that they be processed in a specific sequence through several machines - each machine removing a certain portion of the contaminating material.

The choice of a machine or sequence of machines for processing seed depends on the kind of seed being processed, the nature and kinds of contaminants (weed seed, other crop seed, inert matter, etc.), the quantity of each in the raw seed, and the quality standards that must be met. Thus, the processor must be as familiar with seed standards and seed characteristics as he is with processing equipment.

SEED PROCESSING

The process of removal of dockage in a seed lot and preparation of seed for marketing is called seed processing. Seed processing may be understood to 'comprise all the operations performed after harvest like preconditioning, cleaning, size grading and upgrading of seeds so as to maximize the seed quality in terms of seed viability, vigour and health'. Seed processing is a vital part of the total technology involved in making available high quality seed. It assures the end users, seeds of high quality with minimum adulteration. In Agriculture, the term seed processing includes cleaning, drying, seed treatment, packaging and storage.

Seed lots received from the field are often at high moisture content and contain trash and other inert material, weed seeds, deteriorated and damaged seeds, off-size seeds, etc. Seed processing is necessary in order to dry the seeds to safe moisture level; remove or reduce to the extent possible the various undesirable material, weed seeds, other crop seeds, deteriorated or damaged seeds.

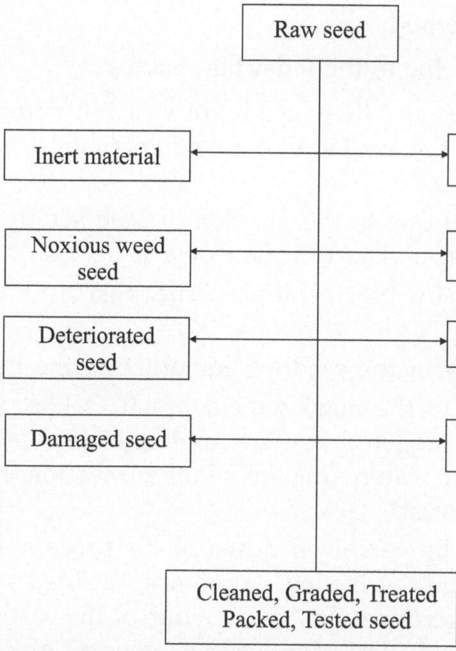

Purposes of seed processing

- To lower the cost of further processes likes storage including transport.
- This is achieved by reducing the bulk of the seed lot by cleaning debris and by removing empty or fractured seed (pre- cleaning)
- To increase the longevity of seeds; by drying seeds to safe moisture content and treating with protective chemicals.
- To reduce the variability in vigour by invigorating the seeds and removing the low vigour seeds.
- To improve the uniformity in seed shape or size by grading or by pelleting.

Principles and objectives

The quality of seed is improved during processing in two ways:

- Separation of other tree seeds or inert matter; and
- Upgrading or the elimination of poor quality seeds.

The ultimate goal of seed processing is to obtain the maximum percentage of pure seed with maximum germination potential. The threshed produce is heterogeneous in nature.

Processing brings homogeneity in the produce. This homogeneity helps in obtaining uniformity in the field. Processing of seeds is carried out in approved (By Director of Seed Certification) seed processing plants. Seed processing is to narrow down the level of heterogeneity of the seed lot by using suitable processing methods.

The seed lot is heterogeneous due to the following reasons:

1. The soil is heterogeneous and there is a lot of variability in the fertility status of the soil due to the availability of nutrients, physical, chemical and biological properties.
2. Variability is introduced due to the position of seed set on the plant/ fruit, time of pollination and fertilization over a period of time.
3. Variability is created by biotic factors like pest and variability infestation.
4. Variability in the ability of the seedling for utilizing the inputs.
5. Variability is also due to the management practices like water, land preparation, leveling, staggered sowing, and uneven distribution of fertilizer and irrigation water, uneven plant protection sprays and uneven maturity at harvest.

This heterogeneity can be narrowed down in the processing of seeds by eliminating the undersized, shrivelled, immature, ill filled seeds using appropriate sieve size. The germinability and vigour of the seed lot can be upgraded by grading the seeds according to size, specific gravity, length and density of the seeds. The inherent qualities such as germinability and vigour are exemplified by certain physical characteristics of the seed i.e., large size, a denser seed, optimum length etc., So, if grading is done to obtain a particular range of size, shape, length and density of the seeds, the quality of the lot is upgraded.

Requirement in seed processing

1. There should be complete separation
2. There should be minimum seed loss
3. Upgrading should be possible for any particular quality
4. There should be have more efficiency
5. It should have only minimum requirement

Types of materials removed during seed processing

- Inert materials
- Common weed seeds
- Noxious weed seeds
- Deteriorated seeds
- Damaged seeds
- Other crop seeds
- Other variety seeds
- Off-size seeds

The flow charts illustrating the types of materials removed from harvested produce during processing:

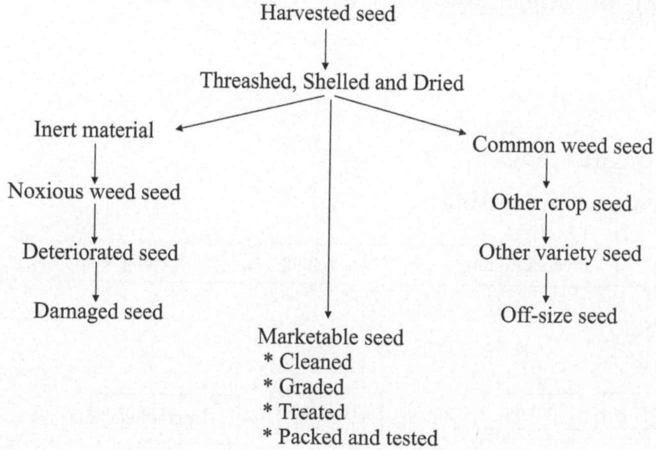

Receiving: The field run produce after threshing is received in the processing plant.

Seed movement/basic steps in seed processing plant

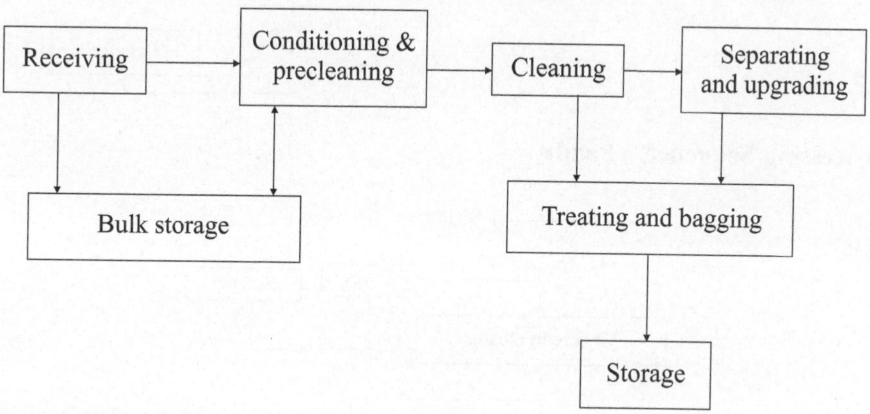

Sequence of Operation in Seed Processing

Sequence of operations is based on characteristics of seed such as shape, size, weight, length, surface structure, colour and moisture content, because each crop seed possesses individually seed structure. Therefore, sequence of operation will be applied proper equipments. However, it is also involved stages following as:

1. Drying
2. Receiving
3. Pre-cleaning

4. Conditioning
5. Cleaning
6. Separating or Upgrading
7. Treating (Drying)
8. Weighting
9. Bagging
10. Storage or Shipping

General sequence of processing

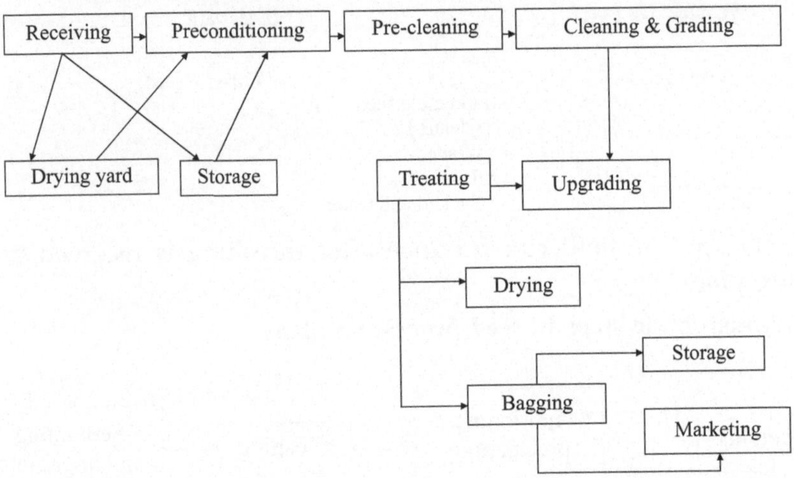

Processing Sequence - Paddy

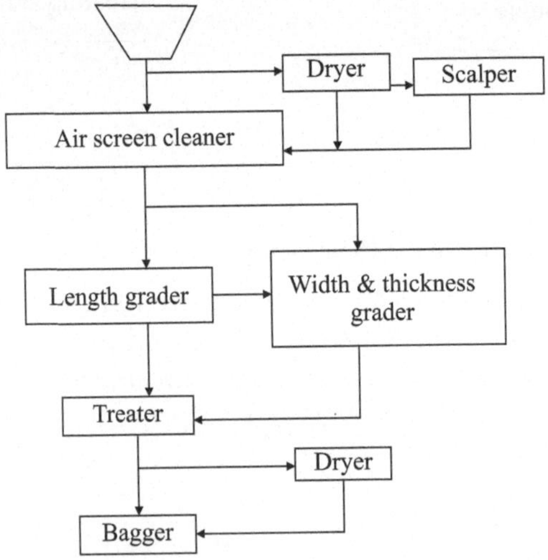

Processing Sequence – Barley

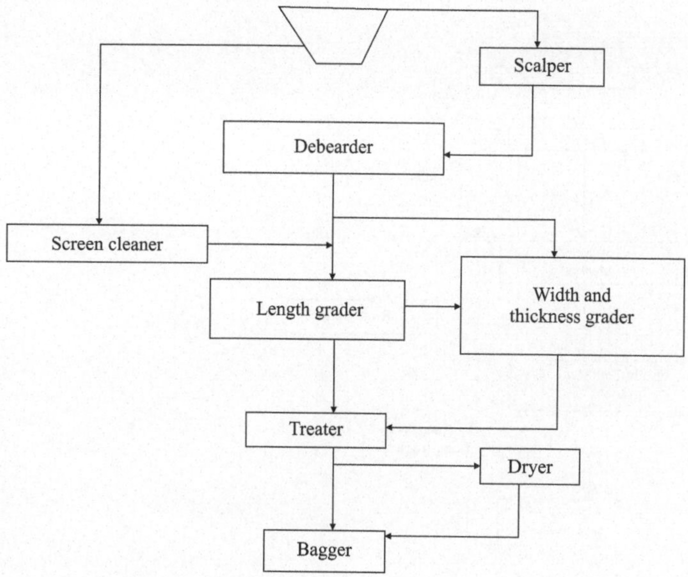

Processing Sequence - Wheat

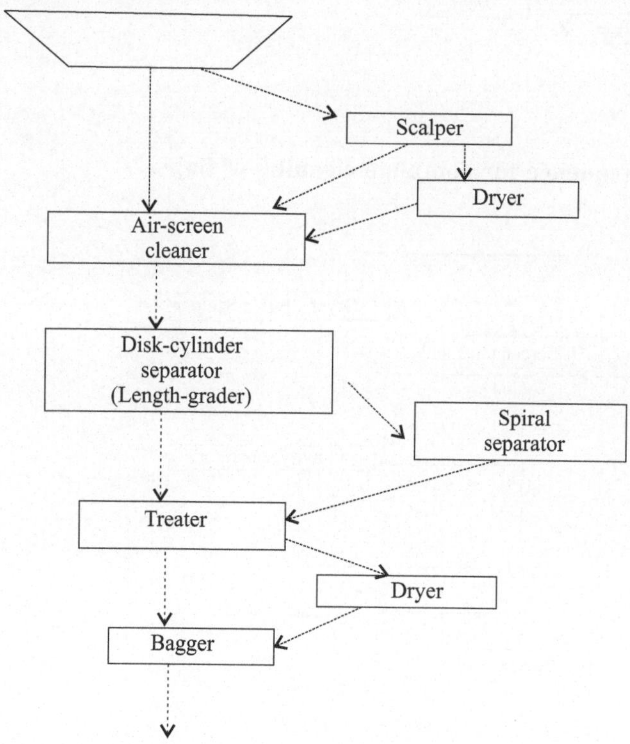

Processing sequence-Maize

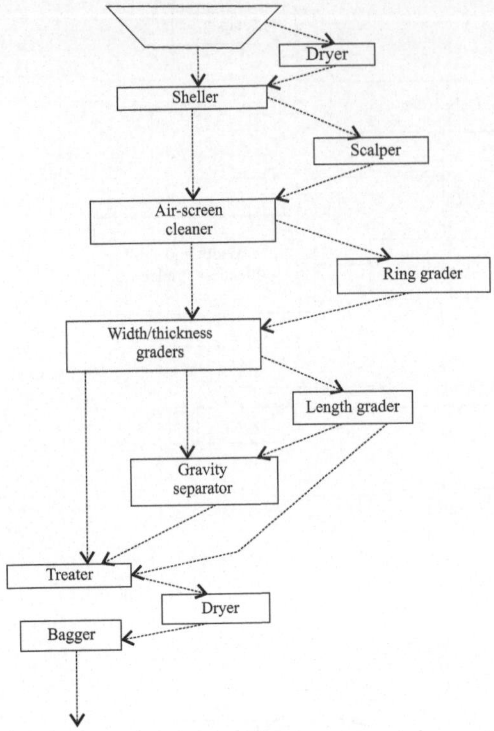

Processing sequence for complete cleaning of bajra

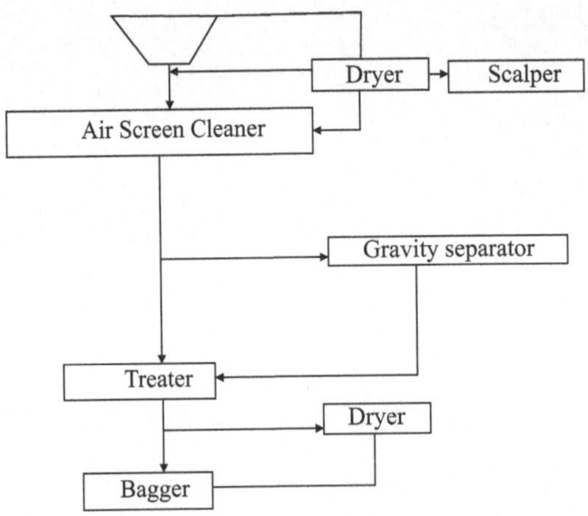

Processing sequence for complete cleaning of Groundnut

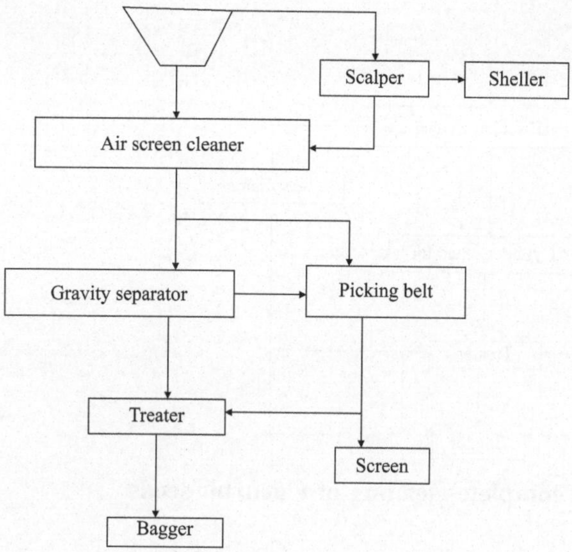

Processing sequence for complete cleaning of Acid-Declined Cotton seed

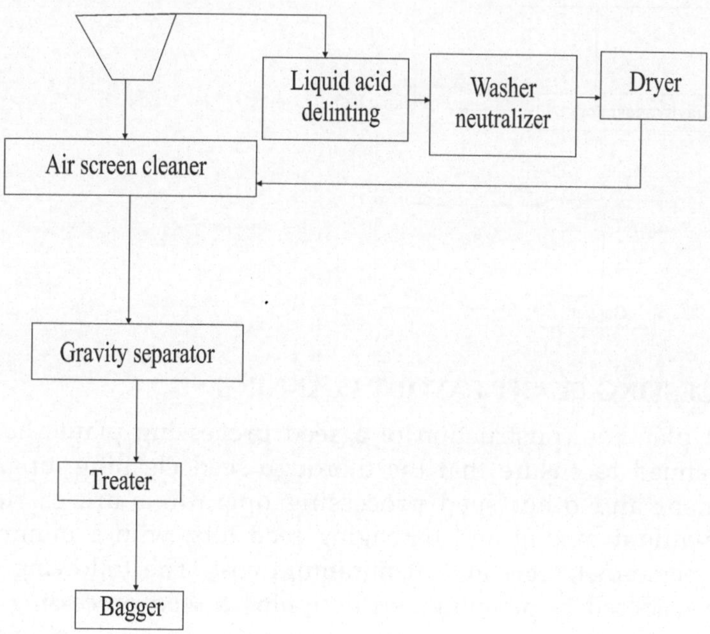

Processing sequence for complete cleaning of Tomato, chilly, carrot

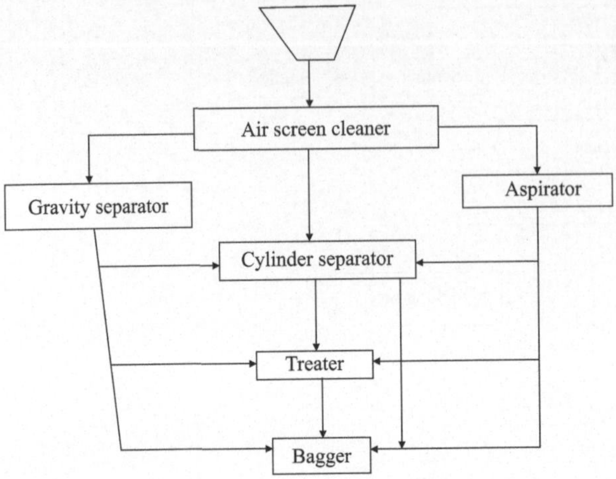

Processing sequence for complete cleaning of Cucurbit seeds

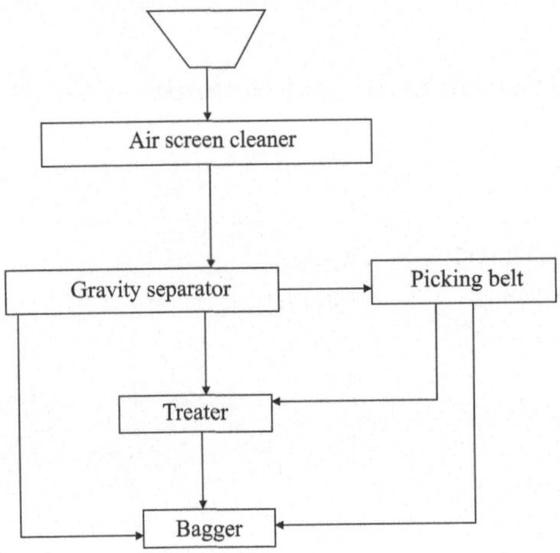

SEED PROCESSING PLANT LAYOUT PLANNING

Layout plan for construction of a seed processing plant should be carefully planned to ensure that the thorough seed cleaning, upgrading, seed treatment and other seed processing operations are carried out efficiently, without mixing and damaging seed lots, with a minimum of equipment, personnel, time and at minimum cost. The following factors should be considered in planning and designing a seed processing plant:

1. Kinds of crop seeds to be handled and kinds of contaminating crop and weed seeds usually present in the seed lots;
2. Size of operation;

3. Whether drying facilities should be required;
4. Selection of suitable equipment;
5. Location of the plant;
6. Source of power for running machinery;
7. System of seed delivery to processing plant; and
8. Availability of labour

The key to efficient plant layout is a thorough knowledge of what needs to be done, and sound planning. First, the general sequence of processes involved between the time seeds enter the processing plant and the time they are cleaned, packaged and ready for shipment, must be charted. The sequence of operations depends upon the kind of crop and the initial quality of seed lot, type of contaminants, moisture content of the seed lot, etc. The layout planner must have an intimate knowledge of the seed to be processed, its physical characteristics, the contaminants in it, and also of the selection of machines used to bring the seed to acceptable marketing standards.

SEED PROCESSING PLANT BUILDING LAYOUT

Seed processing plant building will comprise of following components:

1. Receiving-cum-drying platform
2. Processing area
3. Auxiliary building

RECEIVING-CUM-DRYING PLATFORM

This area will be utilized to receive the raw seed and to sun dry small lots of crop seeds. This area can also be utilized for storage of seeds on wooden palettes. The platform will be connected to processing shed through a rolling shutter.

PROCESSING AREA

The processing area should be situated between the shed and ventilated storage building. The hall should be connected to ventilated flat stores through a covered gallery for easy movement of processed and packaged seed to seed stores. The hall should have a big rolling shutter in the processing plant to permit entry of seed processing equipment into the hall for installation.

Height will be kept to facilitate installation of the seed processing equipment and machinery. Floor of the processing hall should be above the ground level.

The shed should have sufficient provision for natural as well as forced ventilation in order to maintain congenial atmosphere inside the shed. The shed should accommodate seed scalping, seed processing and packaging equipment and will have sufficient space for weighing and packaging.

AUXILIARY BUILDING

In addition to building discussed above, a provision should be made for generator room. Sufficient length of road should be provided to connect various functional buildings with each other and main highway. Boundary wall should be provided all around the complex for security reasons. Entire complex should have a good drainage system.

Provision for firefighting equipment such as extinguishers, water buckets, sand buckets etc. should be made to fight minor fire hazards. The processing plant building should be constructed as per CPWD/PWD norms. It should have tubular trusses, AC sheets pitched hole roof, cement concrete flooring finished with water-proofing cement paint, aerated, ventilated, rat proof and bird protection. Sealed doors should be provided in these buildings. Buildings will be suitably planned to have interconnection for movement of seeds and materials.

Analysis of Operation

(a) **Processing sequence:** After the machines needed have been identified, the next step is to determine the proper processing sequence. The seed separators, elevators, conveyors and storage bins should be so arranged that seeds flow continuously from beginning to end, and yet be flexible enough to bypass a machine or return to a part for re-cleaning.

(b) **Matching capacity:** Equipment size of capacity must be carefully planned to prevent bottlenecks. When the overall operating capacity needs have been determined, all machines must be able to handle that capacity with some reserve capacity for problem lots. Surge bins can handle variations in individual machine capacities. But when differences are great, either larger models, or more than one machine installed in parallel flow, must be used to maintain uninterrupted flow.

(c) **Conveying:** The type of conveying system is also a very important factor. The conveying system must be able to handle the capacity needed in a particular spot. And it must be carefully adapted to the seed handled.

TYPE OF LAYOUTS

There are three main types of processing plant layouts: multistorey, single level and combination.

Multistorey: In this system, seed is carried by elevators to the top floor and emptied into large bins. Cleaning machines are then arranged in a vertical series on the lower floors. Seed flows from one machine down into the next by gravity.

Single level: In the single storey plant, seed is moved from one machine to the next by elevators placed between the machines. A great advantage of the single level system is that one man can supervise the processing line without running up and downstairs. He can thus maintain closer supervision of all operations.

Combined designs: A compromise between the single and multistorey system could also be adapted.

PLANNING

After the proper machines, elevator capacities, cleaning sequences, and lay out design have been selected, detailed layout planning can begin. Careful layout planning can identify and remedy bottlenecks and trouble spots before the plant is built, and thus prevent trouble later.

As the lay out or design develops, it should be drawn on paper. A good method is to draw lines of flow first and then convert these flow lines into machine lines. After appropriate revisions, detailed drawings can be made to show exact locations of equipment and distances. Scale drawings are the most widely used method of layout planning. Scale models and scale templates are also very effective, but are more expensive.

Physical characteristics used to separate seeds are:

1. Size: Based on size it can be separated with air screen cleaner cum grader
2. Length: Disc or indented cylinder separator
3. Weight: Specific gravity separator
4. Shape: Spiral separator or draper separator for round and flat seeds
5. Surface texture: Rough from smooth surface seed- dodder mill
6. Colour: Electronic colour separator
7. Electrical conductivity: Seed differing in their ability to conduct electrical charge can be separated with electronic separator.
8. Affinity to liquid: The seed coat of seed will absorb water, oils etc., which provides a means of separating seed on the magnetic separator.

PROCESSING INVOLVED IN THREE STEPS

Step 1: Pre-conditioning and pre cleaning

Isolation of seed from plant parts with which it was harvested. Removal of external materials like trash, stones, clods which are either in larger size or lighter in weight. No pre cleaning is required for hand harvested and winnowed seeds. It is required to prepare the seeds before the basic cleaning process.

Equipment	Purpose (Uses)
Scalper/Rough cleaner	To remove large trash, twigs and foliage alone
Huller- scarifier	To remove an outer coat or husk and scratching of the seed coat. After hulling and scarification the seeds are moved into a suction chamber where the air sucks and removes the light, fine dust, and the seed discharge at the bottom of the chamber
Debearder	To remove the awns like external features of seeds
Pebble mill	To remove cob-webby hairs from blue grass and similar seeds
Maize sheller	To shell the maize cob.

Pre conditioning: Isolation of seed from plant parts with which it was harvested e.g. Shelling

Pre cleaning

Removal of external materials like trash, stones, clods which are either in larger size or lighter in weight. No pre cleaning is required for hand harvested and winnowed seeds

The machineries involved in this operation are:

Scalper

It removes the larger inert matter from the seeds. If it contains a single sieve it is called as scalpers, two sieves – rough cleaners. The unit consists of a vibrating or rotating screen or sieve having perforation large enough to allow the rough seed pass through readily.

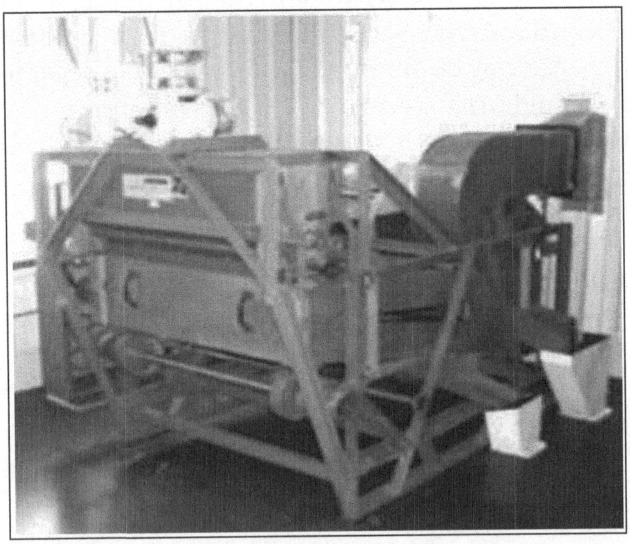

Seed Scalper

Debearders

The machine has horizontal beater with arms rotating inside a steel drum. When the seeds pass through it do the action of rubbing the seeds and clip the seeds of oats, debeard barley, thresh white cap in wheat, remove awns and beards, de hull some grass seeds and polish the seed.

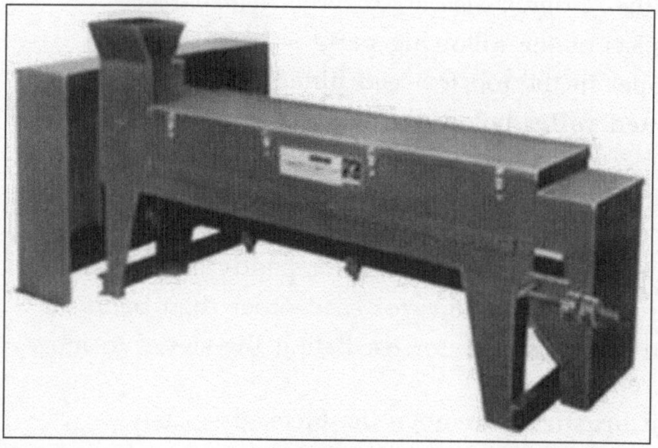

Debearders

HULLER SCARIFIER

Have two rubber faced rough surfaces to rub the seeds. Dehulling (removal of outer coat or husk) and scarifier (scratching the seed coat) can be done simultaneously or separately. Its operations, Seed – rotating disc- centrifugal force – thrown – huller- - suction chamber- removes lighter seeds.

Maize Sheller

1. High capacity power operated shellers - bulk
2. Hand shellers – breeder or nucleus seed.

Step 2: Cleaning

The second stage of cleaning is carried out with air blasts and vibrating screens and is applicable to all kinds of seeds. It is essentially the same as scalping but more refined. It is performed mostly by one machine known as air-screen cleaner.

AIR SCREEN CLEANER CUM GRADER

The air-screen machine is the basic cleaner in most seed processing plants. Almost all seed must be cleaned by air-screen cleaner before specific specifications can be attempted. Machine size varies from small, two-screen farm models to large industrial cleaners with 7-8 screens. Two-screen models are used on farms, in breeder and foundation seed programs and by experiment stations for processing small quantities of seed. In most machines separations are made on the basis of differences in only one physical characteristic.

The dried seeds should be cleaned and graded with help of a cleaner cum grader. For large scale cleaning and grading, the commonly available machine is the *"Crippen Model Seed Cleaner cum Grader"*.

It consists of the following parts

- **A hopper** in the top for seed filling
- **A flutted roller** below the hopper to regulate the seed flow to the screen.
- **Screen (or) sieves**: Perforated metal sheet with specific size of perforation in which there are two types.
  - Rectangular perforations for paddy and
  - Round perforations for seed other than paddy
- **Screen shaking unit**: for oscillating the sieves to move the seeds on the screens
- **Screen brushes** to remove the blocked seeds
- **Air blower** with adjustments for air outlet
- **Collecting outlet**
- **Air duct** for directing the blown up light particles to outside
- **Collecting bins**.

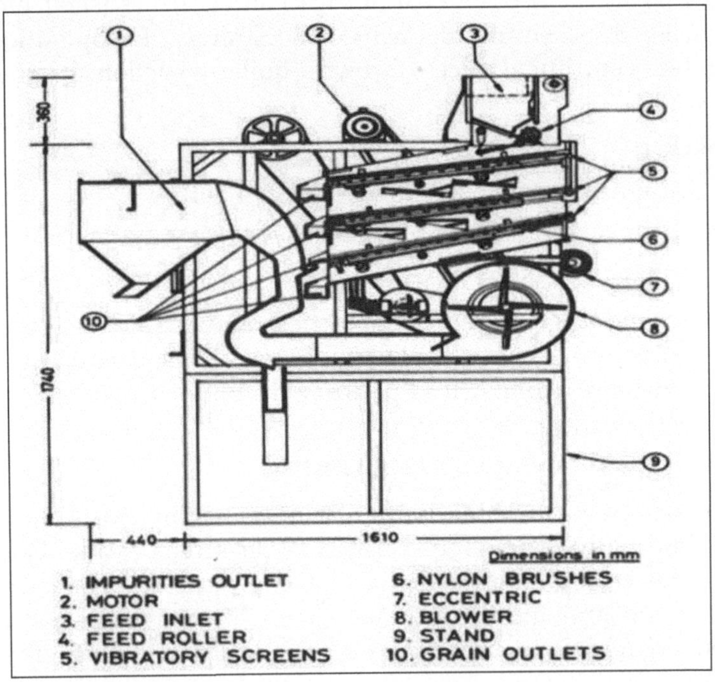

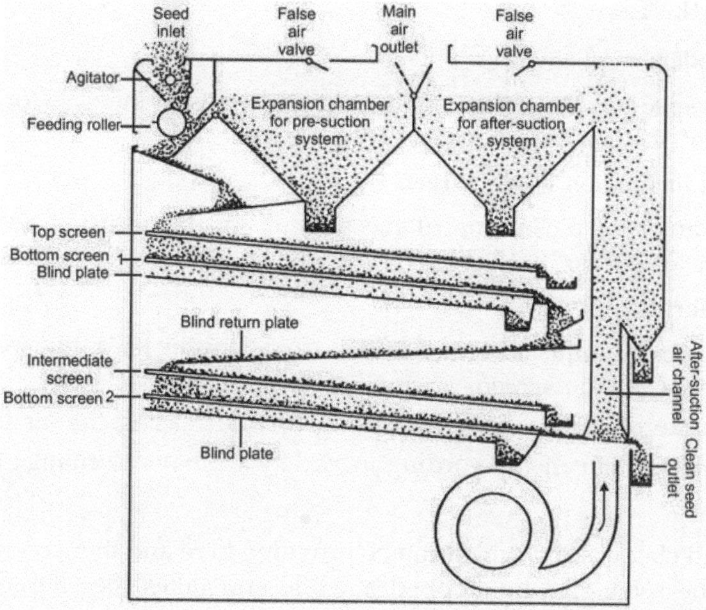

WORKING PRINCIPLE

The air screen machine, however effects separation on the basis of differences in size and weight of seeds. This enables the air screen machine to use three cleaning elements;

Aspiration – in which light weight material is removed from the seed mass

Scalping – in which good seed are dropped through screen openings, but large material is carried over the screen into a separate spout

Grading – in which good seed ride over screen openings, while small particles drop through.

The seeds are fed into the hopper and they are guided to fall on the first sieve. The first sieve is a *scalping screen* which scalps all the foreign materials larger and heavier than seed and the entire quantity of seed passes through the first sieve. The second sieve is a *cleaning sieve* which removes all the unwanted particles larger in size than the seed. The third sieve is actually the *grading sieve* which size grade the seed lot and bring into a uniform size and which also screen the undersized, shrivelled and immature seed, dust and dirt. The seeds are then rolled and passed through air column, where they are relived of the light chaffy and other materials by the blowing air.

ADJUSTMENTS

Flutted roller

The speed of this roller can be adjusted so as to increase (or) decrease the flow of seeds to the hopper of the sieves.

Slope (or) inclination of the screen

The angle of inclination of the screens can be adjusted according to the nature of seeds.

Rate of vibration of sieve

This can be adjusted either to increase or to decrease the speed of the rolling seeds on the screen.

Volume of air flow: By increasing (or) decreasing the air inlet.

Choice of screens: According to variety we have to change the screen

Screen dams

Small check dams, which can be provided here and there on the screens so that the seeds can be stopped a while and takes the charge either to pass or to roll.

Types of seed cleaner cum grader

1. Crippen model cleaner cum grader
2. Clipper model cleaner cum grader
3. Petkas cleaner cum grader

Step 3: Upgrading

Basic cleaning operation done by using air screen cleaner helps to remove the inert materials, physical impurities and small sized seeds. Further processing of seeds is done to separate and remove the low quality seeds based on characteristics such as seed weight, damage or cracks. These operations are called as upgrading techniques.

To obtain quality seed, it is necessary to clean the seed obtained from the farm to get rid of inert materials, weed seeds, other crop seeds, other variety seeds, damaged and deteriorated seed. Different kinds of seeds can be separated when they differ in one or more physical characteristics. Physical characteristics normally used to separate seeds are size, shape, length, weight, colour, surface texture, affinity to liquids, electrical conductivity, etc. The problem lies in identifying the most important property and use the machine that separates seed using the identified property. Some of the identified properties and machines operating by following the properties are listed below:

Name of the Separator	Property followed	Uses
Vibratory separator	Shape and surface texture	Removal of weed seeds
Spiral separator	Shape or the degree of its ability to roll	Separation of damaged/flat and wrinkled seeds from smooth seeds. Separation of mustard, rape, soybean and peas from wheat, flax, oats, etc., and round seeds from flat seeds.
Disk/Indented cylinder separator	Length	Dissimilar material like wheat, rye, mustard, barley from oats
Electrostatic separator	Electrical property	Johnson grass from sesame seed
Electronic colour sorters	Colour/brightness	Separation of off coloured seeds
Inclined draper	Shape and surface texture	Separation of smooth or round seeds from rough flat or elongated seeds
Magnetic separator	Surface texture and stickiness	Removal of contaminating weed seed from clovers, alfalfa seeds and iron metals
Roll mill	Shape and surface texture	Separation of smooth clover seed
Gravity separator or Destoner	Density or specific gravity	Removal of badly damaged, deteriorated, insect damaged crop seed and stones from good seeds.

COLOUR SEPARATOR

The colour separator is used to separate discoloured seed, greatly of lower quality. Separation based on colour is necessary because the density and dimensions of discoloured seed are the same as those of sound seed, so other machines are not effective for separation. Electronic colour separation uses photocells to compare the seed colour with "background" which are selected to reflect the same light as the good seed. Seed that differs in colour is detected by the photo cells, which generate an electric impulse. The impulse activates an air jet to blow away the discoloured seed.

SEPARATING SEED BY COLOUR

The colour sorter uses an electronic eye that can pick up different colours according to the way the machine is adjusted. As seed falls down a shoot, it passes through the electric eye. If the colour of the seed is different than the desired colour, the electric eye will activate a sudden burst of air that pushes that seed into a reject bin while the rest of the seed passes through to another bin.

Many large crop seeds such as peas and beans differ in colour between varieties. Colour variation may also occur due to immaturity or disease. Electronic colour sorting machines can separate such seeds by difference in colour and also remove mud balls and discoloured seeds in the same operation.

The electronic colour sorter views each seed individually with photo electric cells. The seed is compared with a selected back ground or colour range and is discharged from the machine according to its colour. If it is the great desired colour, the seed is discharged through the good seed spout. If it's colour or shade falls within the reject range, a blast of compressed air deflects the seed and sends it in to the reject discharge spout. These are highly sensitive. Since the machine views each seed individually, capacity is low, but the initial cost is high and operating cost is less. The usefulness of machine is greater with large seeded crops.

INDENTED CYLINDER SEPARATOR

The indented cylinder separator is a rotating, almost horizontal cylinder with movable, horizontal separating adjustments which are mounted inside it. Indent lines are there inside the surface of the cylinder. The indented cylinder revolves, turning the seed mass to give each seed a chance to fit into indent. Short seeds are lifted out of the seed mass and are dropped into the lifting and long seeds remain in the cylinder and are discharged out via., a separate spout at the end of the cylinder.

As the cylinder revolves, it creates centrifugal force which helps to hold the seed in the indent. Short seeds are held in the indent until the cylinder turns to the point where the indent is inverted enough for gravity to cause the seed to fall out of the indent. The length, surface texture and size of seeds determine how they fit into the indent, so that it can be lifted out of the seed mass. The speed of the cylinder creates centrifugal force which holds the seed in the indent as it is lifted upward. Thus the shape and size of the seed to cause some seeds to fall out after being lifted only a short distance, while other seeds are lifted closer to the top of the cylinder before they fall out.

As the seeds enter the cylinder, the small, short, easy to separate seeds are quickly removed. The center cylinder section removes the intermediate sizes of seeds still in the cylinder. All indents in a cylinder are the same size, only the progressively declining amount of material to be lifted causes this difference in separating action.

Adjustments

1. Cylinder speed
2. Size of the indent
3. Through setting
4. Tilt of the cylinder
5. Adjustable retarder.

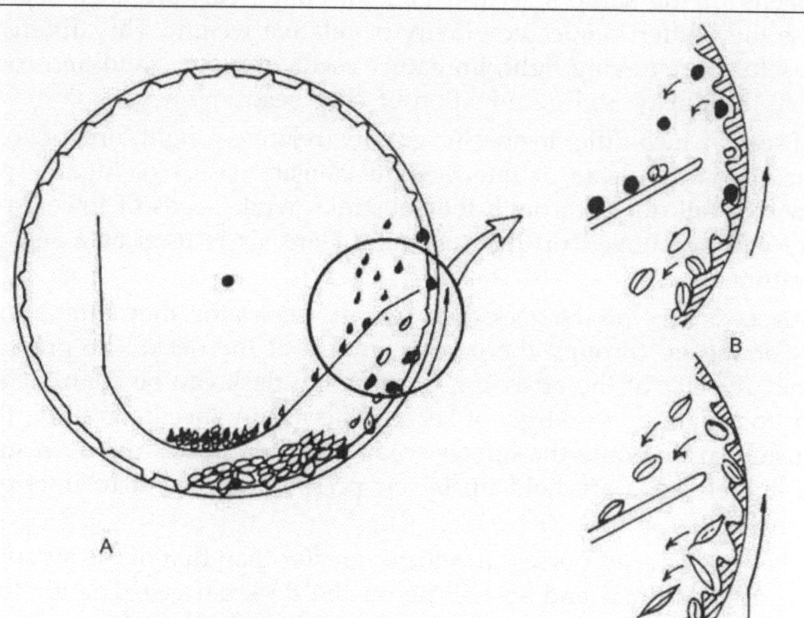

A. Working principle of indented cylinder
B. Round grain application
C. Long grain application

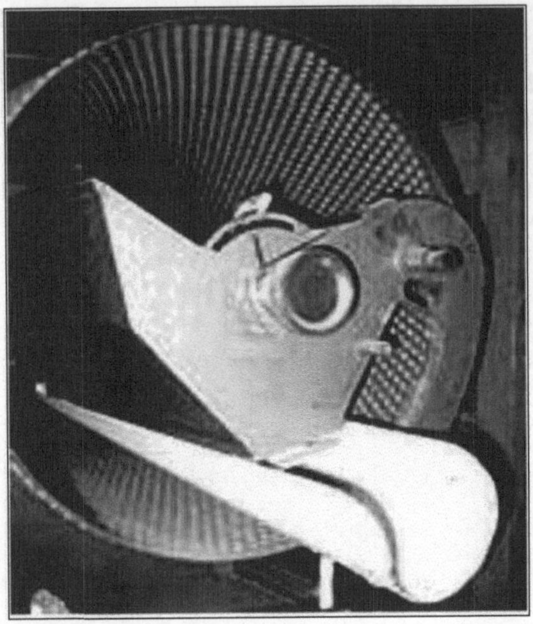

SPECIFIC GRAVITY SEPARATOR

Seeds of the same size and general shape can often be separated because they differ in specific gravity or relative weight. This difference is very useful in removing light, immature seeds or heavy sand and rocks to improve the purity and germination of crop seeds.

If seeds which differ in specific gravity (relative weight/unit of volume) are placed on substrate of intermediate density, seeds of higher specific gravity will fall down through the substrata, while seeds of lower specific gravity will be buoyed up the substrata. Here air is used as a separation substratum.

As seeds flow on the deck of the gravity separator, they enter a column of air coming up through the porous surface of the deck. The pressure of terminal velocity of the air rising through the deck can be controlled very closely to separate two kinds of seeds differing in specific gravity, the air is adjusted so that only the lighter seeds are lifted up off the deck surface. These lighter seeds are held up by air pressure and tend to float on the deck surface.

The heavier seed possess a velocity greater than that of the air columns so they are not lifted and so will lie on the deck surface. The air column thus stratifies the seed mixture into vertical zones of relative weight with the heavier seed lying on the deck and the lighter seeds lifted up to the top of the seed mass.

Adjustments

1. Feed rate
2. Air flow
3. End slope
4. Side slope
5. Deck oscillation speed
6. Deck speed.

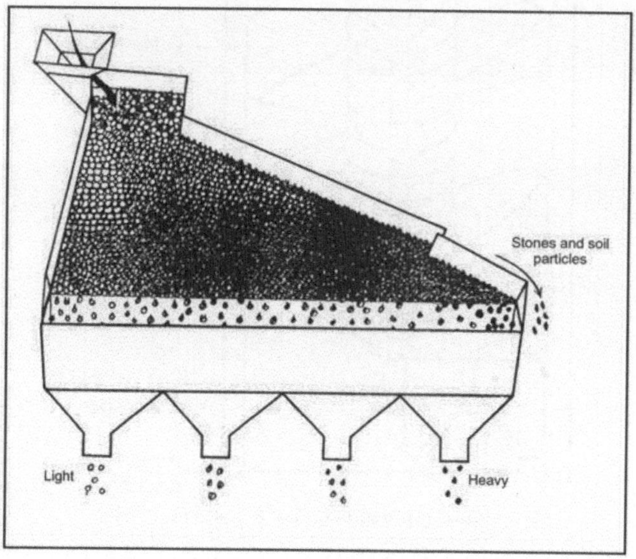

A specific gravity separator with triangular deck showing the different fractions: one light, two intermediate and one heavy fraction. The fifth side outer is used when soil clods are present.

SPIRAL SEPARATOR

The separator, which classifies seed according to its shape and rolling ability, consists of sheet metal strips fitted around a central axis in the form of a spiral. The unit resembles an open screw conveyor standing in a vertical position. The seed is introduced at the top of the inner spiral. Round seeds roll faster down the incline than flat or irregularly shaped seeds, which tend to slide or tumble. The orbit of round seed increases with speed on its flight around the axis, until it rolls over the edge of the inner flight into the outer flight where it is collected separately. The slower moving seed does not build up enough speed to escape from the inner flight. Most spirals have multiple inner flights arranged one above the other to increase the capacity.

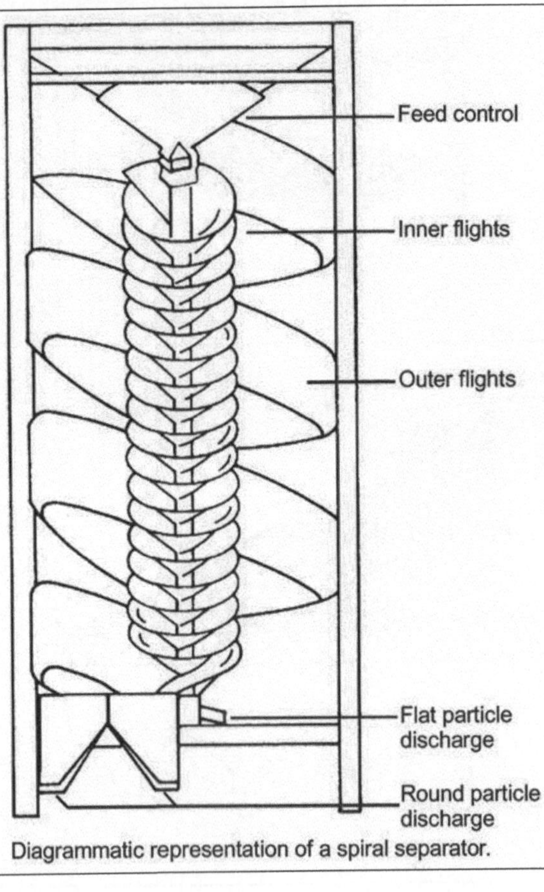

Diagrammatic representation of a spiral separator.

MAGNETIC SEPARATOR

The magnetic separator separates seed according to its surface texture or related seed characteristics. First, seed is treated with iron filings, which adhere to rough surface alone. The treated seed lot is passed over a revolving magnetic drum and separated from smooth, uncoated seed. It may help to add varied amounts of water while mixing seed and powder, depending on the seed type. At any rate, the effectiveness of magnetic separation depends on the components of the seed lot and on the powder and water used in the treating operation. The greater the difference between surface textures of the seed lot's components, more effective will be the separation.

The separation is mainly based on the affinity for liquids which is used for separation. Since seeds contains no free iron and are not attracted by a magnet they must be selectively pretreated with a magnetic material such as finely ground iron powder. Rough seed coats, cracked or broken seed coats, dirt lumps, chaff or seed with a sticky residue on the surface will hold the liquid and become sticky, so that iron powder will adhere to them. Smooth coated seeds will not absorb liquid. So no iron powder will adhere to them.

The seed are then discharged from mixing chamber and brought into contact with a powerful magnet, which removes the iron coated seeds. Most magnetic cleavers pass the seeds over a revolving drum which has a high intensity magnetic field. Seeds with an affinity for liquids which are now coated with iron powder are attracted by the magnet and adhere to the drum until they are removed by a brush or scraper. Seeds which are relatively free of iron powder are not attracted by the magnet and will fall into a separate discharge spout.

The first requisite of magnetic seed separation is that the seed to be separated must possess different seed coat characters. Crop seeds should have a smooth surface, while the seeds to be removed should have a rough surface which will retain liquid and can accept the iron powder. Success in separating the components depends upon the magnitude of seed coat differences and thoroughness with which the moistened seeds and the iron powder are blended.

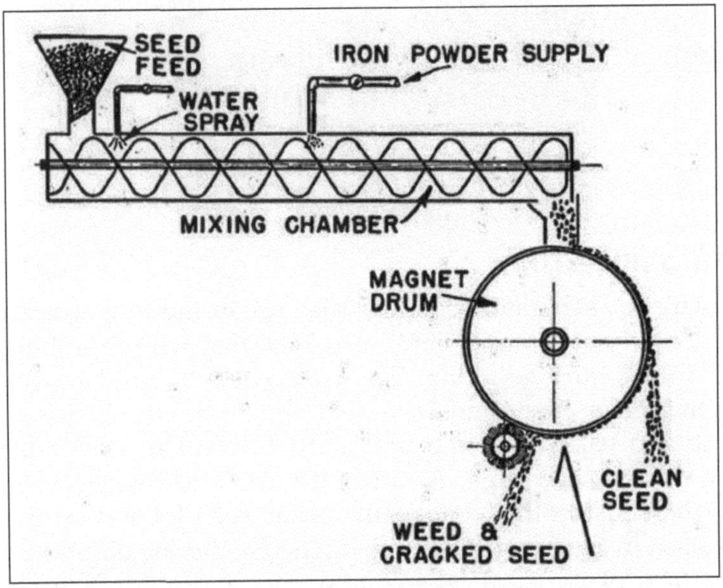

Diagram of a drum-type magnetic seed separator

ROLL MILL OR DODDER MILL OR VELVET ROLL MILL

It is used to separate the seeds based on surface texture and shape. This separator should be used only after the seed has been carefully cleaned and separated from the chaff. These are effective in separating seeds with a rough seed coat or shape angles from smooth seeds.

The roll mill consists basically of two roller, covered with flannel or velvet, placed side by side, so that they touch each other down their entire length. The rollers are mounted on an incline and they turn in opposite directions. A curved adjustable shield is mounted above the rollers.

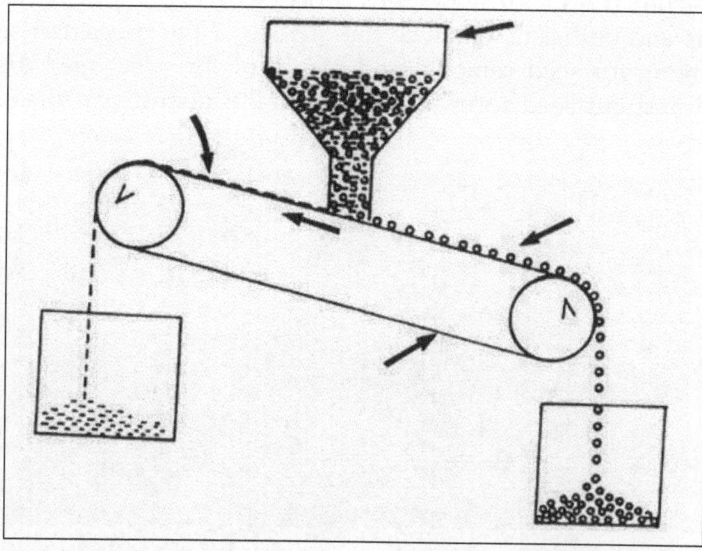

SEPARATING ACTION

The mixture of smooth and rough seeds is fed into the place, where the rollers touch each other, at the high end of the machine. As the rollers turn up and out, seeds that are rough or have sharp or broken edges are caught by the nap of the fabric covering the rollers. These seeds are thrown up against the curved shield. They strike the shield at an angle, bounce back down to the roller and are again thrown up against the shield. Smooth seeds bounce down the inclined position forward between the rollers, and discharge at the lower end of the machine. They are not affected by the fabric roller covering, and are not pitches over the side of the rollers.

Adjustments

1. Rate of feed
2. Speed
3. Clearance between shield and rolls
4. The angle of inclination of rolls.

Needle Separator

It separates seed by sticking a needle or thin steel needle like point into the hole left by an emerging weevil larva. Needles are mounted on the inside of a revolving cylinder. As the cylinder turns, the seeds which are stuck on needles are lifted up and carried out of the seed lot and dropped into a liftings trough.

The needle separator almost 20,000 Stainless Needles and used to separate cotton, pea and bhendi seeds. Needle Sorter is one of the important machines in cotton seed processing. It separates the "Pin Hole" seed and cut seed from the lot of averagely processed seeds. The removal of pin hole seeds and cut seeds enhance the quality of the processed seed. Nylon brush moving for seed removal and conveyor for reject seed disposal. Pin hole seed and cut seed form almost 5% to 7% quantity in the seed lot.

REFERENCES

Agrawal, R.L. (1996). Seed Technology, Oxford & IBH Publishing Co., New Delhi.

Bhaskaran, M., A.Bharathi and K.Vanangamudi. (2013). Text Book on Principles of Seed Production and Quality Control. Kalyani Publishers, New Delhi.

http://ecoursesonline.iasri.res.in/mod/page/view.php?id=17806

http://agritech.tnau.ac.in/seed_certification/seedtech_seed_seedprocessing.html

http://agritech.tnau.ac.in/seed_certification/seed_processing_equipments.html

https://www.indiamart.com/indoamericanequipment/needle-sorter-machine.html

http://ecoursesonline.iasri.res.in/mod/page/view.php?id=17835 (sp gravity)

https://akyurekltd.com/en/Indent-Cylinder-Separator-158s.html

https://www.startraceltd.com/magnetic-separator.html

http://www.marksorter.com/seed-color-sorter-machine.html

http://ecoursesonline.iasri.res.in/mod/page/view.php?id=17844

http://agritech.tnau.ac.in/seed_certification/seed%20processing-importance.html

http://eagri.org/eagri50/GPBR112/pdf/lec28.pdf

Pages: 29-47

Seeds and Food: ***Processing and Storage Techniques***
Edited by: **Dr. Prasann Kumar and Dr. Pawan Kumar 'Bharti'**
ISBN: 978-93-88854-41-2
Edition: **2020**
Published by: **Discovery Publishing House Pvt. Ltd., New Delhi (India)**

2

Major Seed Oils and their Significance

Anubhuti Sharma*, Meghna Garg, P.K. Rai

ABSTRACT

Genetic alterations of fatty acid composition to improve its nutritional, chemical, physical or industrial applications are the major requirement for human being. It can be achieved by improving oilseed crops with various modifications in free fatty acids e.g. production of high polyunsaturated fatty acids, unusual monoenoic fatty acids, reduction in erucic acid, very long chain saturated fatty acids etc. This review focuses mainly on these modifications.

INTRODUCTION

Due to ever increasing industrial interests, there is a continuous need to generate new traits in oilseed crops to get an efficient and sustainable agricultural produce. Present review will focus on the alteration of oilseed crops to improve their nutritional composition and industrial utility.

Though the majority of the researchers are focusing on producing genetically modified (GM) oilseed crops for herbicide tolerant/disease and pest resistant/drought and salinity tolerant, the main potential lies in the genetic alteration of fatty acid composition to improve its nutritional, chemical, physical or industrial applications. Such modifications will include production of high palmitic acid, stearic acid, oleic acid, omega-3 long-chain polyunsaturated fatty acids (LC-PUFAs), arachidonic acid, eicosapentaenoic acid, ricinoleic acid, unusual monoenoic fatty acids, reduction in erucic acid and very long chain saturated fatty acids (VLSFA).

Current understanding of the biochemical, molecular and cellular mechanisms of seed oil synthesis, twosome with the cloning of novel genes, have facilitated the production of novel 'oils' in oilseed crops. Transgenic

ICAR-DRMR, Directorate Of Rapeseed - Mustard Research, Sewar, Bharatpur, Rajasthan, (India)

oilseeds producing novel fatty acids will be a better source for providing renewable raw materials that may compete with, and eventually replace, other non-renewable sources. A detailed description of the lipids and its classes is given below.

LIPIDS

Lipids are one of the most elemental nutrients for humans as they are fundamental mediators of multiple signaling pathways and form indispensable compounds of cell membranes. Fatty acids, or fatty acid residues when they are part of a lipid, are a diverse group of molecules synthesized by chain-elongation of an acetyl-CoA primer with malonyl-CoA or methylmalonyl-CoA groups in a process called fatty acid synthesis.

Fatty acids (FAs) are classified mostly according to the presence or absence of double bonds as:

1. Saturated (without double bonds)
2. Monounsaturated (MUFAs; with one double bond)
3. Polyunsaturated fatty acids (PUFAs; with two or up to six double bonds)

PUFAs are also categorized as n-3 or n-6 PUFAs depending on the position of the first double bond from the fatty acid methyl-end.

The human body cannot synthesize PUFAs with the first double bond on C3 and C6 from the methyl-end because of the absence of appropriate enzymes. Thus, these fatty acids are essential (EFAs) and they have to be obtained from a diet, particularly by the consumption of fish and fish oils (Fig. 2.1). Essential fatty acids (EFAs) have antiatherogenic, antithrombotic, anti-inflammatory, antiarrhythmic, hypolipidemic effects, thus, reducing the risk of serious diseases like cardiovascular diseases, cancer, osteoporosis, diabetes. For e.g., EPA and DHA provides protection against mental disorders like Alzheimer's disease, aging and dementia, chronic daily headache and with attention-deficit hyperactivity disorder in children.

α-linolenic (ALA, 18:3, n-3) and linoleic acid (LA, 18:2, n-6) are fundamental PUFAs from which other important PUFAs are derived. Eicosanoids derived from n-6 and n-3 fatty acids have antagonistic effects. Eicosanoids from the first group promote an inflammation; the latter are much less inflammatory or even anti-inflammatory. Their concentration depends on the fatty acids amounts in diet and is also influenced by the competition between AA and EPA as substrates for specific enzymes—cyclooxygenases and 5-lipoxygenases. Vegetable oils, currently, are being prescribed by the doctors across the world as essential part of a healthy diet due to the high contents and benefits of fatty acids (FAs) and their easy availability as traditional sources, such as fish oil and algae.

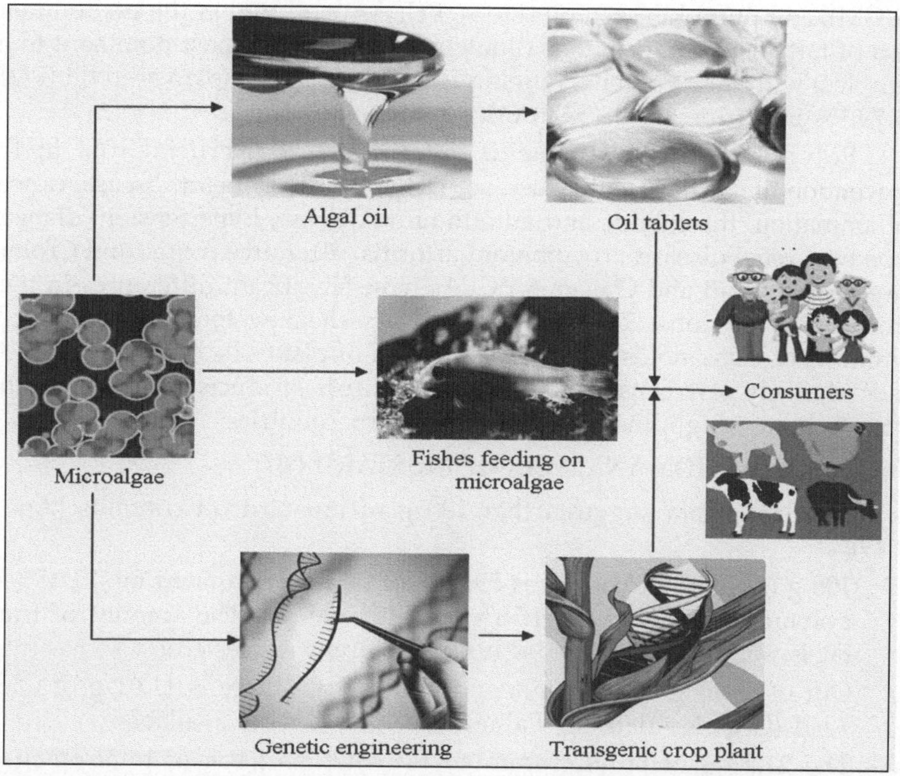

Fig. 2.1: Different sources of LC-PUFAs to the consumers. Microalgae being the major source of VLC-PUFAs, are used directly or indirectly in the form of algal oil or tablets, respectively. Transgenic plants can also serve as an alternative to the oil fishes through genetic engineering.

Natural sources of MUFAs include red meat, whole fat milk products, nuts and high fat fruits (olives and avocados). In general, MUFAs (oleic acid being the most prominent are present in higher proportions than SFAs) in the range from 6.2% to 72.8% in coconut (COC) and rapeseed (RPS) oils, respectively. While analyzing fatty acid compositions of six oils, MUFAs held the highest proportion; 72.8% in rapeseed oil (RPS), 71.1% in peanut oil (PNT), 68.2% in olive oil (OL), 67.9% in almond oil (ALM), 44.0% in rice brain oil (RB), and 42.0% in sesame oil (SES) (Parveez *et al.*, 2015). MUFAs reduce LDL cholesterol, while it might possibly increase high-density lipoprotein (HDL) cholesterol. Oleic acid has also been reported as anti-apoptotic and anti-inflammatory agent.

Algae and marine phytoplankton forms the primary source of PUFAs, especially docosahexaenoic acid (DHA, C22:6, n-3) and linoleic acid (LA, C18:2, n-6). Terrestrial sources includes nuts, seeds, and leafy vegetables.

In seven analyzed oils—safflower oil (SAF), grape oil (GRP), silybum marianum oil (SIL), hemp oil (HMP), sunflower oil (SFL), wheat germ

(WGM), and pumpkin seed oil (PMS), PUFAs presented as the predominant part of fatty acid compositions (linoleic acid being the most dominant in all samples) with their contents ranging from 54.3% in pumpkin seed oil (PMS) to 79.1% in safflower oil (SAF) (McKeon *et al.*, 2016)

Polyunsaturated fatty acids (PUFAs) play a crucial role in the prevention of cardiovascular disease (DVD), coronary heart disease, cancer, inflammation, thrombotic and autoimmune disease, hypertension, diabetes type two, renal diseases, rheumatoid arthritis, ulcerative colitis, and Crohn's disease. Omega-3 and Omega-6 PUFAs have significant differences in their biological functions. The n-6/n-3 ratio is the key factor for balanced synthesis of eicosanoids. High consumption of plant oils rich in n-6 PUFAs and relatively low consumption of marine fish products could cause this ratio to be too high, mainly seen in Western countries.

FAT COMPOSITION ANALYSIS OF MUSTARD OIL

Available data suggests that 100 g of mustard oil contains (Anon, 2019):

1. 100 g of total lipid contains 59.19% of monounsaturated fat, 21.23% of polyunsaturated fat & 11.58% of saturated fat. The amount of trans fat is not available. It does not contain any cholesterol.
2. Out of 59.19 g of total monounsaturated fat there is 11.61 g of Oleic Acid (OA). No data for Palmitoleic Acid (PA) is available.
3. The 21.23 g of polyunsaturated fat contains 5.9 g of total omega-3 fatty acids which is composed mainly of Alpha-linolenic Acid (ALA) (exact value of ALA, however, is unknown). No data is available for the amount of Docosahexaenoic Acid (DHA), Docosapentaenoic Acid (DPA) and Eicosapentaenoic Acid (EPA).
4. Out of 15.33 g of total omega-6 fatty acids, omega-6 Linoleic Acid (LA) is present in maximum amount (exact LA amount is unknown). No data is available for the amount of Arachidonic Acid (ARA), Dihomo-gamma-linolenic Acid (DGLA) and Gamma-linolenic Acid (GLA).
5. Omega-6 is present approximately 2.66 times in higher concentration than omega-3 fatty acids.
6. Out of 11.58 g of total saturated fat there is 3.75 g of Palmitic Acid (PAL), 1.39 g of Myristic Acid (MA) and 1.12 g of Stearic Acid (SA). No data is available for the amount of Caprylic Acid (CA) and Lauric Acid (LAA).

MAJOR OILS WITH SPECIFIC FATTY ACIDS:

1. High Palmitic acid oils

The consumption of saturated fats is controversial. Although many medical authorities, such as the World Health Organization, says dietary intake of saturated fats for e.g., palmitic acid increases the risk of cardiovascular diseases however, in moderation, palmitic acid might not be entirely bad, as it does display mild antioxidant and anti-atherosclerotic properties, at least in animal studies. (Korean study published in a 2010 edition of the "Journal of Medicinal Food")

There is increasing consumption of high palmitic acid oils in both edible and industrial markets, especially in bakery, confectionary items and soaps. To modify palmitate content, β-Ketoacyl-ACP synthetase II (KASII) and FatB thioesterase activity are the two candidate genes for GE approach. Palmitic acid content was increased in soybean oil by suppressing KASII activity with simultaneously increasing FatB thioesterase activity (*5*). In cotton seed oil, KASII activity was also suppressed by RNAi mediated down-regulation of *ghKAS2* (*6*).

2. High stearic acid oils

Stearic acid is found in relatively high percentages in hard oils and butters like cocoa butter (24-37% stearic acid), shea butter (20-50% stearic acid), and tallow (14% stearic acid).

Stearic acid melts at 69.3°C (156.7°F) (higher melting point even than beeswax), thus, making it a very effective hardening ingredient that raises the melting points of the products without adding any waxiness. Stearic acid is a common ingredient in soaps and cosmetics. Chemical synthesis of stearic acid can be achieved by 3 possible ways; Firstly restricting the release of 16:0-ACP (FatB thioesterase activity), then to promote elongation of 16:0-ACP to 18:0-ACP (KASII activity) and lastly detachment of 18:0 from ACP (FatA thioesterase activity). One additional activity can be checked *i.e.* to block the conversion of 18:0-ACP to 18:1-ACP (stearoyl-ACP desaturase activity). These all activities favours synthesis of high stearic acid oils. Overexpression of KASII (*7*), integration of FatA thioesterase gene (*4*) and antisense suppression of stearoyl-ACP desaturase mRNA (*8,9*) resulted in high stearic acid oils.

Increasing the level of stearic acid in soybean oil has been promoted as a means to improve oil stability, as well as to improve utility for baking applications. Mutant alleles that result in elevated levels of stearic acid in the seed are referred to as either fas or st (Pantalone *et al.*, 2004). The first reported elevated stearic acid mutant allele was the fas1-a allele from sodium azide-induced mutant line FA8077/A6 (Hammond & Fehr, 1983).

3. Low very long chain saturated fatty acids (VLSFA) oils

Saturated fatty acids (SFAs) are associated with health risks and are undesirable in higher quantity for oil stability and nutrition. Arachidic acid, behenic acid, and ligonoceric acid are the most common very long chain saturated fatty acids (VLSFA) and found in peanuts, cashew nut, canola oil and macadamia nuts. These fatty acids posses risk to many cardiac diseases and obesity.

Table 2.1: Various oils and their applications

S.No.	Major Objectives	Lipid Number	Purpose/Applications
Saturated Fatty acids			
1.	High palmitic acid oils	C16:0	For the production of bakery, confectionary eatables and soaps
2.	High stearic acid oils	C18:0	For production of margarines and shortenings
3.	Low Very long chain saturated fatty acid (VLSFA) oils	C20:0, C22:0, C24:0	To reduce the risk associated with cardiac diseases
Unsaturated Fatty acids			
4.	High unusual monoenoic fatty acid oils	$C18:1\Delta^{6cis}C20:1\Delta^{5cis}$	For industrial production of cosmetics, surfactants and lubricants
5.	High oleic acid oils	$C18:1\Delta^{9}$	Utility as a stable and healthy vegetable oil for frying purposes
6.	High Omega-3 long-chain polyunsaturated fatty acid (LC-PUFAs) oils	$C20:5\Delta^{5,8,11,14,17}$ and $C22:6\Delta^{4,7,10,13,16,19}$	To avert popularly known as the 'obesity time bomb'
7.	High γ-linolenic and stearidonic acid (GLA and SDA) oils	$C18:3\Delta^{6,9,12}$ and $C18:4\Delta^{6,9,12,15}$	For reducing circulating TAGs and platelet activation
8.	High arachidonic and eicosapentaenoic acid oils	$C18:4\Delta^{5,8,11,14}$ and $C18:5\Delta^{5,8,11,14,17}$	For cardioprotective effects and for correct development of brain and visual function in infants
9.	High erucic acid oils	$C22:1\Delta^{13}$	More suitable for industrial uses
10.	Low erucic acid oils	$C22:1\Delta^{13}$	To prevent growth retardation and pathogenic effects on internal organs
11.	High ricinoleic acid oils	12-Hydroxy-cis-9-octadecenoic acid	As an alternative for oleochemical based industries
Triacylglycerols (TAG)			
12.	TAG assembly	Three esterified fatty acids with a glycerol	To produce high value added lipids with better stability

Scientists are targeting the elongation step of stearic acid for the same. Insertion of the gene encoding antisense RNA of the enzyme namely steroyl–CoA:α-ketoeicosanoyl-CoA synthetase can arrest the chain elongation and thus the synthesis of VLSFA also. High copy number of this gene will strengthen the oleic acid and related O\L ratio which would help in preventing cardiac diseases. For increasing the shelf life of oilseeds like groundnut, high O/L ration is desirable as well. Improved O/L ratio was achieved by seed-specific expression of *AtLEC1* in groundnut with concomitant decrease in erucic acid (*10*). Expression of FAT-5, gene for a membrane-bound desaturase enzyme, was cloned from *Caenorhabditis elegans* and inserted in *Arabidopsis* using a strong seed-specific promoter. This has resulted in reducing the levels of VLSFAs by converting 16:0 to 16:1Δ^9, thus improving the nutritional value as well (*11*).

4. High unusual monoenoic fatty acid oils

Monoenoic fatty acids, i.e. with one double bond, make up a high proportion of the total fatty acids in most natural lipids. Cis/Z-configuration of double bond is more prevalent than trans/E-double bond.

Monoenoic fatty acids with 16/18 carbon atoms are abundant in animal and plant tissues. Few fatty acids with 10 to 36 carbon atoms have also been reported in nature in esterified form. Monoenoic fatty acids have the same name as of their saturated hydrocarbon counterpart except that the final 'ane' is changed to 'enoic'.

A list of common monoenoic fatty acids together with their systematic and trivial names is given in Table 2.2.

Table 2.2: The common monoenoic fatty acids

The common monoenoic fatty acids	
Systematic name	**Trivial name**
Cis-9-tetradecenoic	myristoleic
Cis-6-hexadecenoic	Sapienic acid
Cis-9-hexadecenoic	palmitoleic
Cis-6-octadecenoic	petroselinic
Cis-9-octadecenoic	Oleic
Cis-11-octadecenoic	Cis-vaccenic
Cis-11-eicosenoic	Gondoic
Cis-13-docosenoic	Erucic
Cis-15-tetracosenoic	Nervonic
trans-9-octadecenoic	Elaidic
trans-11-octadecenoic	vaccenic

Oleic acid is far most the most abundant monoenoic fatty acid in plant and animal tissues. It comprises 30 to 40% of the total fatty acids in adipose fats of animals, and 20 to 80% of the seed oils of commerce. Olive oil contains up to 78% of oleic acid, and it is believed to have especially valuable nutritional properties as part of the Mediterranean diet. Esterified forms of oleic acid, oleamide and oleoylethanolamide have especially important biological activities. In plants, it is reported to be involved in defense signalling against bacterial and fungal pathogens by upregulating the expression of genes that regulate nitric oxide production. Oleic acid is the biosynthetic precursor of a family of fatty acids with the (n-9) terminal structure and with chain-lengths of 20 to 24 or more.

Petroselinic acid (6c-18:1) occurs up to a level of 50% or more in seed oils of the Umbelliferae family, including carrot, parsley and coriander, while 10-18:1 (with 8-16:1) is considered specific for methane-oxidizing bacteria.

Attempts to increase the amount of petroselinic acid in transgenic crops through genetic engineering have not gained much success. However, expression of coriander Δ^4-16:0-ACP desaturase in transgenic tobacco resulted in only 4% accumulation of petroselinic acid (*15*). This study revealed that atleast three enzymes need to be cloned for achieving optimum level of the petroselinic acid *viz.* (i) acyl-ACP desaturase, specific for palmitoyl-ACP which is known to introduce double bond at 4th position of the substrate, (ii) 3-ketoacyl-ACP synthase, specific for elongation of cis-4 (l6:1) ACP to cis-6 (18:l) ACP and (iii) acyl-ACP thioesterase, specific for releasing petroselinic acid from ACP so that it can be incorporated into triacylglycerol for storage.

5. High oleic acid oils

Oleic acid (18:1) is highly stable to oxidation and can enhance the activity of antioxidants and antipolymerization agents. In combination with antioxidants like tocopherols, it can be blended with other oils to prevent oxidation. These blends of oleic acid and tocopherols have been reported to have better protective effects than α-tocopherol alone (Lampi and Kamal-Eldin, 1998). It has also been reported that isocaloric replacement of about 5% of energy from saturated fatty acids by oleic acid reduced coronary heart disease risk by 20-40%, mainly via low-density lipoprotein (LDL) cholesterol reduction (Kris-Etherton, 1999). It is generally recognized that higher intakes of oleic acid and a limited intake of saturated fats are beneficial and may help protect against cardiovascular disease.

Olive and canola oil are naturally high in monounsaturated fat, but they are also high in polyunsaturated fats which mean they are not very shelf-stable. In recent years, scientists have developed sunflower (and other) oils that are bred to be high in monounsaturated fats and low in polyunsaturated fats so they can be used in products that need to be shelf-stable.

Food companies have switched from trans fats (increases shelf life and preserve flavor) to high oleic oils or palm kernel oil to make their food last longer for customers. These oils are often used in packaged baked goods (packaged cakes, cookies, etc), as spray coating for cereal, crackers and dried fruit; and in non-dairy creamers as well as many types of frying.

Through mutational breeding, oleic acid was increased from 60% to 71% in oilseed rape (*19*) and later on a patent was also filed by Ian Bancroft and Rachel Wells at the John Innes Centre (JIC), Canada, claiming to increase it up to 86%. In GE-based approaches, the target is the suppression of the Fatty Acid Desaturase-2 (FAD2) enzyme, whose function is to convert oleic acid (18:1Δ^{9cis}) into linoleic acid (18:2 $\Delta^{9cis,\ 12cis}$). Down regulation of FAD2 activity should result in accumulation of oleic acid, and will reduce the levels of PUFAs like linoleic acid. Perhaps, regulation of FAD2 activity was reviewed by Dar *et al* (*20*) and had resulted in many transgenic crops like rapeseed (*21*), soybean (*22*) cotton (*8*) and Arabidopsis (*23*).

6. High omega-3 long-chain polyunsaturated fatty acids (LC-PUFAs) oils

Omega-3 long-chain (≥ C20) polyunsaturated fatty acids (n-3 LC-PUFA) play an important role in the prevention of and decreasing the risk of chronic diseases in humans (Nichols *et al.*, 2014, Walker *et al.*, 2015, Watanabe and Tatsuno, 2017). Consumers have become more aware about the health benefits of dietary n-3 LC-PUFA.

However, Western diets have been reported to be severely lacking in these fatty acids (FA) (Fayet-Moore *et al.*, 2015, Salem and Eggersdorfer, 2015). Although major sources of n-3 LC-PUFA are fish and other marine products, seafood is not a regular part of the traditional diet in many Western countries (Byelashov, Sinclair, & Kaur, 2015). Thus, the ability to increase n-3 LC-PUFA content in other human foods, such as red meat and milk, is required to meet the recommended intakes of these FA.

Additional strategies for increasing the omega-3 fatty acid content of some foods include bio-delivery and biotechnology. Biodelivery involves adding omega-3 fatty acids to animal feed so that their tissues become enriched. Some examples of foods that have been enriched with omega-3 fatty acids in this manner include eggs, beef, and pork products.2 Biotechnology involves cultivating varieties of plants containing greater levels of ALA or fatty acids closer to EPA and DHA. However, these plant varieties are currently in development and have not yet been introduced into the marketplace.

Much of the research has focused on increasing n-3 PUFA content in ruminant products (meat and milk) using feeds enriched in n-3 PUFA (Díaz *et al.*, 2017, Parvar *et al.*, 2017). The richest sources of n-3 PUFA supplied in ruminant diets are fish, algae, forage and oilseeds (Doreau *et al.*, 2009,

Nichols *et al.*, 2010). Flaxseed, canola and their oils, which are rich in alpha linolenic acid (ALA) (Dubois, Breton, Linder, Fanni, & Parmentier, 2007), have been of recent interest in various nutritional studies.

Canola seed, also known as rapeseed, contains about 40-55% oil, 25-38% protein and 15-20% fibre (Carré *et al.*, 2016, Wroniak *et al.*, 2016). Although oleic acid is the main FA in canola oil, ALA accounts for around 10% of the total FA (Baker *et al.*, 2016, Howes *et al.*, 2015).

Ghazani, García Llatas, and Marangoni (2014) stated that canola is one of the most economically important food-oil crops. Production of canola oil is the third highest globally, after soybean and palm oils. Thus, canola oil is the most available terrestrial source of n-3 PUFA. In recent years, canola and flaxseed oils have been investigated as sources of n-3 PUFA in prime lamb feeds (Flakemore *et al.*, 2017, Nguyen *et al.*, 2017, Nguyen *et al.*, 2017).

Primary source for the production of omega-3 LC-PUFA are the microbes, specially microalgae of marine origin, and oily fishes. Due to the over-exploitation of wild fisheries and seafood, there is an urgent need for a complete new source of omega-3 LC-PUFA to meet future demands (Fig. 2.1). Transgenic plants with target fatty acids biosynthetic pathway has come up as a boon to cater the increasing demands (*27*).

Synthesis of LC-PUFA is different from the synthesis of routine saturated and unsaturated fatty acids in plants. It demands a series of alternating steps of desaturation and elongation. Depending on the primary substrate, sequential Δ^6-desaturation, Δ^6-elongation and Δ^5-desaturation steps synthesize either omega-6 (ω-6) or omega-3 (ω-3) fatty acids. These two pathways can then be linked by ω-3 desaturases, which convert ω-6 fatty acid into its ω-3 counterpart. *Tetrahymena pyroformis* and *Acanthamoeba sp.* which lacks Δ^6-desaturation, synthesize LC-PUFA through an alternative Δ8-pathway (*28*).

7. High γ-linolenic and stearidonic acid oils

Two relatively rare fatty acids, gamma-linolenic acid (GLA) and stearidonic acid (STA), have attracted much interest due to their nutraceutical and pharmaceutical potential. STA, in particular, has been considered a valuable alternative source for omega-3 fatty acids due to its enhanced conversion efficiency in animals to eicosapentaenoic acid when compared with the more widely consumed omega-3 fatty acid, alpha-linolenic acid (ALA), present in most vegetable oils. Gamma linolenic acid is an omega-6 fatty acid. It's found in various plant seed oils such as borage oil and evening primrose oil. Recently, transgenic technology has made available a highly enriched GLA seed oil from the canola plant (HGCO: 36% GLA).

GLA is synthesized by a Δ6 desaturase. Here, we report identification of PiD6, a new cDNA from the oleaginous fungus, Pythium irregulare, encoding a 459-amino acid protein that shares sequence similarity to carboxyl-directed desaturases from various species. Expression of PiD6 in yeast (Saccharomyces cerevisiae) revealed that it converts exogenously supplied linoleic acid into GLA, indicating that it encodes a Δ6 fatty acid desaturase. Expression of the desaturase in Brassica juncea under the control of the Brassica napus napin promoter resulted in production of three Δ6 unsaturated fatty acids (18:2–6, 9; 18:3–6, 9, 12; and 18:4–6, 9, 12, 15) in seeds. Among them, GLA (18:3–6, 9, 12) is the most abundant and accounts for up to 40% of the total seed fatty acids.

The first member of the omega-3 family and the parent molecule in this series is alpha-linolenic acid (ALA, 18:3n-3), which is abundant in flaxseed oil and is also present in canola, soybean, and walnut oils, among other commodities (Fig. 2.2). Meanwhile, stearidonic acid (18:4n-3) has been detected in viable amounts in several species of algae, fungi, and animal tissues, as well as seeds of Echium (Boraginaceae). It has also been produced in soybean transgenitically.

In an attempt to maximize the STA content of soybean oil, a borage Delta(6) desaturase and an Arabidopsis Delta(15) desaturase were pyramided by either sexual crossing of transgenic events, re-transformation of a Delta (6) desaturase event with the Delta(15) desaturase or co-transformation of both desaturases.

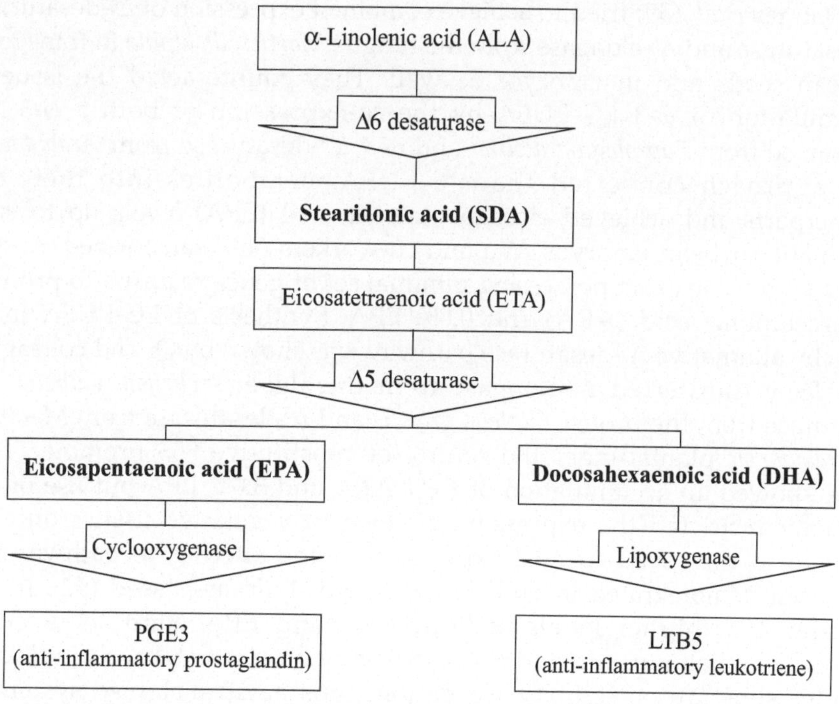

Fig. 2.2: Conversion of ALA to other important fatty acids (Stear *et al.*, 2016)

8. High arachidonic and eicosapentaenoic acid oils

Arachidonic Acid (AA) released from membrane phospholipids by phospholipase A2 during cell activation is the major polyunsaturated fatty acid precursor in mammals for the cyclooxygenase and lipoxygenase pathways. Eicosapentaenoic acid (EPA), a major polyunsaturated fatty acid in fish oils competes with AA for these enzymes. The resulting products from EPA are generally less potent than the corresponding AA metabolites which may explain the beneficial effects of this oil in reducing thrombotic and inflammatory responses.

For the synthesis of LC-PUFA in oilseeds, multiple gene transfer was required, that to a minimum of three sequential non-native enzymatic reactions (e.g. two desaturations and an acyl-CoA mediated elongation). Till date various gene sources have been identified for the above cited enzymes, beginning from algae, fungi to plants and mammals (*38*). Besides knowing the sources and targets, expression of the whole LC-PUFA biosynthetic pathway to seeds is still stands challenging. The reasons for this constraint are low accumulation of desired fatty acid, acceptance of non-native substrates, its specificity (like acyl-CoA for elongases and phospholipid-linked substrates for desaturases), limited expression of the transgenes in seeds, etc.

Kinney *et al*. (*39*) tried to achieve combined expression of Δ^6-desaturase, Δ^5-desaturase and Δ^6-elongase from the fungus *Mortierella alpina* in transgenic soybean seeds and in embryos as well. They counteracted the issue of accumulation of ω-3 LC-PUFA by the co-expression of both a ω-3 Δ^{17}-desaturase from *Saprolegnia diclina* and ω-3 Δ^{15}-desaturase from *Arabidopsis*. This approach converted the ω-6 PUFA metabolites into their ω-3 counterparts and achieved eicosapentaenoic acid (EPA) levels up to 9.3% in somatic soybean embryos. Wu and co-workers (*40*) transformed *Brassica juncea* with a construct possessing minimal set of genes required to produce 7% arachidonic acid (ARA) and 0.8% EPA. Synthesis of LC-PUFA in oil seeds by alternative Δ^8-desaturase pathway was shown by Qi and colleagues (*41*). They transferred Δ^9-elongase from the algae *Isochrysis galbana*, Δ^8-desaturase from the protist *Euglena gracilis* and Δ^5-desaturase from *M. alpina* in *Arabidopsis* plants under the control of constitutive 35S promoter. Leaf tissue showed an accumulation of 6.6% ARA and 3.0% EPA but use of 35S promoter restricted the expression of them to vegetative tissues only. In addition to this, seed-specific expression of the alternative pathway has now been demonstrated in both *B. napus* and *Arabidopsis* seed (*42*). It was revealed that higher levels of both ARA and EPA were achieved in transgenic Indian mustard and soybean than in linseed or tobacco, indicating broader substrate specificity for endogenous acyltransferase system in soybean and *Brassica* sp. as compared to linseed or tobacco.

Nguyen *et al* (*43*) favored genetic improvement of *Camelina*, for developing a high oleic acid oil trait for improved oil oxidative stability. Seed-specific RNAi suppression of *FAD2* was used which controls Δ^{12} desaturation of oleic acid and *FAE1* (fatty acid elongase 1) and mediates oleic acid elongation to LC-PUFAs. Crambe (*Crambe abyssinica*) is also emerging as an industrial oil crop, and is used for metabolic engineering of seed oil traits (*44*).

9. Erucic acid oils

Foodstuff with a high content of erucic acid is considered undesirable for human consumption because it has been linked to myocardial lipidosis and heart lesions in laboratory rats.

Permitted maximum levels established for erucic acid: (range: 0.3-50.8%, limit: 5%)

Rapeseed oil is characterized by a high content of erucic acid which makes it undesirable for human consumption on daily basis.

10. High ricinoleic acid oils

Ricinoleic acid (12-hydroxy-9-octadecenoic acid) is one of the 'exotic' fatty acids which have the potential to replace traditional petrochemicals for oleochemicals production based industries. Castor bean (*Ricinus communis*) oil possess up to 90% of ricinoleic acid. If chemically modified, it brought about myriads of industrially important products like lubricants, Nylon 11, surfactants, plastic films, emulsifiers, encapsulants and many more.

Though the expression of the castor bean hydroxylase gene in transgenic *Arabidopsis* resulted in accumulation of up to 17% of ricinoleic acid in seed oil (*52*) but additional increase in the same requires co-expression of castor bean fatty acyl-CoA ligase and DGAT genes, for the incorporation of ricinoleate into TAGs (*53*).

CONCLUSION

Genetic engineering of economically important fatty acids in oilseed crops represents recent success tales in the area of lipidomics. It is necessary to understand the contributions of different enzymes catalyzing these metabolic pathways in the native species. In addition to it, equal and rather more precise focus is required on down-regulating the non-productive and competing pathways in seeds of the native oilseed crop. The present review shows that palmitate content can be increased by suppressing *KASII gene* while stearoyl-ACP desaturase activity favours high stearic acid oils. RNAi mediated suppression of steroyl–CoA:α-ketoeicosanoyl-CoA synthetase can arrest the synthesis of VLSFA. Desired LC-PUFAs can be obtained by modulating Δ^6-desaturation, Δ^6-elongation and Δ^5-desaturation steps of the synthesis. High erucic acid can be achieved by regulating LEAFY

COTYLEDON1 and LEC1-LIKE genes while it is possible to reduce erucic acid content by altering the expression level of *FAE1* gene. For high ricinoleate oils fatty acyl-CoA ligase and DGAT genes were the candidate genes. 2-GPAT/phosphatase and a bifunctional MGAT/DGAT enzymes were aimed to get desired TAG assembly.

Future of lipidomics rely on more predictable genetic modifications of fatty acid profile in seeds by the use of techniques, such as mass spectrometry-based techniques, CRISPR/Cas9 etc. The ability to gain higher levels of unusual monoenoic fatty acids in non-agronomic crop models like Arabidopsis is still difficult to track down. In spite of this, genetic engineering still provides a reliable, fast and economic way ahead to refurbish important oilseed crops for their nutritional contents and industrial utility. Current and futuristic research endeavors will have to strive for upcoming challenges in the food and nutritional sector.

REFERENCES

1. Simopoulos AP. Human Requirement for ω-3 Polyunsaturated Fatty Acids. Poultry Sci. 2000; 79(7): 961-70.https://doi.org/10.1093/ps/79.7.961
2. Wu G, Truksa M, Datla N, Vrinten P, Bauer J, Zank T, *et al*. Stepwise Engineering to Produce High yields of Very Long-chain Polyunsaturated Fatty Acids in Plants. Nat Biotechnol. 2005; 23(8):1013-7. https://doi.org/10.1038/nbt1107
3. Edem DO. Palm Oil: Biochemical, Physiological, Nutritional, Hematological, and Toxicological Aspects: A Review. Plant Food Hum Nutr. 2002; 57: 319-41. https://www.ncbi.nlm.nih.gov/pubmed/12602939
4. Padley FB, Gunstone FD, Harwood JL. Occurrence and Characteristics of Oil and Fats. In: Gunstone FD, Harwood JL, Padley FB, Editors. The Lipid Handbook. London: Chapman & Hall: 1994. p. 49-170. https://www.worldcat.org/title/lipid-handbook/oclc/12662443
5. Kinney AJ, Knowlton S, Cahoon EB, Hitz WD. Re-engineering Oilseed Crops to Produce Industrially useful Fatty Acids. pp. 623-8 in Sa´nchez, J.; Cerda´-Olmedo, E.; Martinez-Force, E. (Eds) Advances in Plant Lipid Research. Seville, Spain, University of Seville Press. 1998.
6. Liu Q, Guo Q, Akbar S, Zhi Y, El Tahchy A, Mitchell M, *et al*. Genetic Enhancement of Oil Content in Potato Tuber (*Solanum tuberosum* L.) through an Integrated Metabolic Engineering Strategy. Plant Biotechnol J. 2017; 15(1): 56-67. https://doi.org/10.1111/pbi.12590
7. Kinney AJ. β-Ketoacyl-ACP Synthetase II Genes from Plants. US Patent 5500361.1996b.
8. http://www.freepatentsonline.com/5500361.html
9. Liu Q, Singh SP, Green AG. High-stearic and High-oleic Cotton Seed Oils Produced by Hairpin RNA Mediated Post-transcriptional Gene Silencing. Plant Physiol. 2002; 129: 1732-43. https://doi.org/10.1104/pp.001933
10. Parveez GKA, Rasid OA, Masani MYA, Sambanthamurthi R. Biotechnology of Oil Palm: Strategies towards Manipulation of Lipid Content and Composition. Plant Cell Rep. 2015; 34(4): 533-43. https://doi.org/10.1007/s00299-014-1722-4

11. Tang G, Xu P, Ma W, Wang F, Liu Z, Wan S, *et al*. Seed-specific Expression of *AtLEC1* Increased Oil Content and Altered Fatty Acid Composition in Seeds of Peanut (*Arachis hypogaea* L.) Front Plant Sci. 2018; 9: 260. https://doi.org/10.3389/fpls.2018.00260

12. Fahy D, Scheer B, Wallis J, Browse J. Reducing Saturated Fatty Acids in *Arabidopsis* Seeds by Expression of a *Caenorhabditis elegans* 16:0-specific Desaturase. Plant Biotechnol J. 2012; 11(4): 480-9. https://doi.org/10.1111/pbi.12034

13. Broun P, Gettner S, Somerville C. Genetic Engineering of Plant Lipids. Annu Rev Nutr. 1999;19: 197-216. https://doi.org/10.1146/annurev.nutr.19.1.197

14. Uitterhaegen E, Sampaio KA, Delbeke EIP, De Greyt W, Cerny M, Evon P, *et al*. Characterization of French Coriander Oil as Source of Petroselinic Acid. Molecules. 2016; 21:1202. https://doi.org/10.3390/molecules21091202

15. Richter KD, Mukherjee KD, Weber N. Fat Infiltration in Liver of Rats Induced by Different Dietary Plant Oils: High Oleic-, Medium Oleic- and High Petroselinic Acid-oils. Z Ernahrungswiss. 1996; 35(3): 241-8. https://www.ncbi.nlm.nih.gov/pubmed/8896286

16. Cahoon EB, Shanklin J, Ohlrogge JB. Expression of a Coriander Desaturase Results in Petroselinic Acid Production in Transgenic Tobacco. P Natl Acad Sci USA. 1992;89:11184-8. https://www.ncbi.nlm.nih.gov/pmc/articles/PMC50514/

17. Cahoon EB, Marillia EF, Stecca KL, Hall SE, Taylor DC, Kinney AJ. Production of Fatty Acid Components of Meadowfoam Oil in Somatic Soybean Embryos. Plant Physiol. 2000; 124: 243-51. https://www.ncbi.nlm.nih.gov/pmc/articles/PMC59139/

18. Erhan SM, Kleiman R, Isbell TA. Estolides from Meadowfoam Oil Fatty Acids and other Monounsaturated Fatty Acids. J Am Oil Chem Soc. 1993; 70: 461-5. https://doi.org/10.1007/BF02542576

19. von Borcke L. High Oleic Acid Oilseed: Oil Seed Rape FAD2 Mutants with Increased Mono-unsaturated Fatty Acid Content. Patent Literature, International Publication No. WO 2012/117256. US Publication US 2014/0150132 A1. Plant Bioscience Limited, Norfolk, UK. 2014. http://www.pbltechnology.com/technologies/plant-quality-and-composition/10508-high-oleic-acid-oilseed/

20. Schierholt AB, Rücker B, Becker HC. Inheritance of High Oleic Acid Mutations in Winter Oilseed Rape (*Brassica napus* L.). Crop Sci. 2001; 41: 1444-9. https://doi.org/10.2135/cropsci2001.4151444x

21. Dar AA, Choudhury AR, Kancharla PK, Arumugam N. The FAD2 Gene in Plants: Occurrence, Regulation, and Role. Front Plant Sci. 2017; 8: 1789. https://doi.org/10.3389/fpls.2017.01789

22. Kinney AJ. Improving Soybean Seed Quality. Nat Biotechnol. 1996; 14: 946. https://inis.iaea.org/search/search.aspx?orig_q=RN:27028537

23. Graef G, LaVallee BJ, Tenopir P, Tat ME, Schweiger BJ, Kinney AJ, *et al*. A High Oleic Acid and Low Palmitic Acid Soybean: Agronomic Performance and Evaluation as a Feedstock for Biodiesel. Plant Biotechnol J. 2009; 7: 411-21. https://doi.org/10.1111/j.1467-7652.2009.00408.x

24. Stoutjesdijk PA, Singh SP, Liu Q, Hurlstone CJ, Waterhouse PA, Green AG. hpRNA Mediated Targeting of the *Arabidopsis* FAD2 Gene gives Highly Efficient and Stable Silencing. Plant Physiol. 2002; 129: 1723-31. www.plantphysiol.org/cgi/doi/10.1104/pp.006353

25. Logue J, Sattar N. Childhood Obesity: A Ticking Time Bomb for Cardiovascular Disease? Clin Pharmacol Ther. 2011; 90: 174-8. https://doi.org/10.1038/clpt.2011.88

26. Saravanan P, Davidson NC, Schmidt EB, Calder PC. Cardiovascular Effects of Marine Omega-3 Fatty Acids. Lancet. 2010; 376: 540-50. https://doi.org/10.1016/S0140-6736(10)60445-X
27. Beydoun MA, Kaufman JS, Satia JA, Rosamond W. Plasma n-3 Fatty Acids and the Risk of Cognitive Decline in Older Adults: The Atherosclerosis Risk in Communities Study. Am J Clin Nutr. 2007; 85: 1103-11. https://doi.org/10.1093/ajcn/85.4.1103
28. Khan WA, Chun-Mei H, Khan N, Iqbal A, Lyu SW, Shah F. Bioengineered Plants can be a Useful Source of Omega-3 Fatty Acids. Biomed Res Int. 2017; 2017:9. https://doi.org/10.1155/2017/7348919
29. Lees AM, Korn ED. Metabolism of Unsaturated Fatty Acids in Protozoa. Biochemistry. 1966; 5: 1475-81. https://pubs.acs.org/doi/abs/10.1021/bi00869a005
30. Reddy AS, Thomas TL. Expression of a Cyanobacterial Δ^6-desaturase Gene Results in Gamma-linolenic Acid Production in Transgenic Plants. Nat Biotechnol. 1996; 14: 639-42. https://doi.org/10.1038/nbt0596-639
31. Liu JW, Huang S, DeMichele M, Bergana E, Bobik C, Hastilow LT, *et al*. Evaluation of the Seed Oils from a Canola Plant Genetically Transformed to Produce High Levels of γ-linolenic Acid. In: Huang YS, Ziboh VA. Editors. γ-Linolenic Acid: Recent Advances in Biotechnology and Clinical Applications. Champaign, IL: AOCS Press; 2001. p. 61-71.
32. Hong H, Datla N, Reed DW, Covello PS, MacKenzie SL, Qiu X. High-level Production of γ-linolenic Acid in *Brassica juncea* using a Δ^6-desaturase from *Pythium irregulare*. Plant Physiol. 2002; 129: 354-62. https://doi.org/10.1104/pp.001495
33. Sato S, Xing A, Ye X, Schweiger B, Kinnet A, Clemente T. Production of γ-linolenic Acid and Stearidonic Acid in Seeds of Marker-free Transgenic Soybean. Crop Sci. 2004;4 4: 646-52. https://doi.org/10.2135/cropsci2004.0646
34. Ursin VM. Modification of Plant Lipids for Human Health: Development of Functional Land-based Omega-3 Fatty Acids. J Nutr. 2003; 133: 4271-4. https://doi.org/10.1093/jn/133.12.4271
35. Eckert H, La Vallee B, Schweiger BJ, Kinney AJ, Cahoon EB, Clemente T. Co-expression of the Borage Δ^6-desaturase and the Arabidopsis Δ^{15}-desaturase Results in High Accumulation of Stearidonic Acid in the Seeds of Transgenic Soybean. Planta. 2006; 224: 1050-7. https://doi.org/10.1007/s00425-006-0291-3
36. Ruiz-Lopez N, Haslam RP, Venegas-Calero´ n M, Larson TR, Graham IA, Napier JA, *et al*. The Synthesis and Accumulation of Stearidonic Acid in Transgenic Plants: A Novel Source of 'Heart-healthy' ω-3 Fatty Acids. Plant Biotechnol J. 2009; 7: 704-16.https://doi.org/10.1111/j.1467-7652.2009.00436.x
37. Nykiforuk, CL, Shewmaker C, Harry I, Yurchenko OP, Zhang M, Reed C, *et al*. High Level Accumulation of Gamma Linolenic Acid (C18:3$\Delta^{6.9,12cis}$) in Transgenic Safflower (*Carthamus tinctorius*) Seeds. Transgenic Res. 2012; 21: 367-81. https://doi.org/10.1007/s11248-011-9543-5
38. Dong X, He Q, Peng Z, Yu J, Bian F, Li Y, *et al*. Production of γ-linolenic Acid and Stearidonic Acid by *Synechococcus* sp. PCC7002 Containing Cyanobacterial Fatty Acid Desaturase Genes. Chin J Ocean Limnol. 2016; 34: 772-80. https://doi.org/10.1007/s00343-016-4369-x
39. Domergue F, Abbadi A, Ott C, Zank TK, Za¨ hringer U, Heinz E. Acyl Carriers used as Substrates by the Desaturases and Elongases involved in very long-chain Polyunsaturated Fatty Acids Biosynthesis Reconstituted in Yeast. J Biol Chem. 2003; 278: 35115-26. https://doi.org/10.1074/jbc.M305990200

40. Kinney AJ, Cahoon EB, Damude HG, Hitz WD, Kolar CW, Liu ZB. Production of very long Chain Polyunsaturated Fatty Acids in Oilseed Plants. WO 2004/071467 A2. 2004. https://patents.google.com/patent/US20040172682

41. 40. Wu G, Truksa M, Datla N, Vrinten P, Bauer J, Zank T, *et al*. Stepwise Engineering to Produce High yields of very long-chain Polyunsaturated Fatty Acids in Plants. Nat Biotechnol. 2005; 23: 1013-7. https://doi.org/10.1038/nbt1107

42. Qi B, Fraser T, Mugford S, Dobson G, Sayanova O, Butler J, *et al*. Production of very long Chain Polyunsaturated ω-3 and ω-6 Fatty Acids in Plants. Nat Biotechnol. 2004; 22: 739–https://doi.org/10.1038/nbt972

43. Petrie JR, Shrestha P, Belide S, Mansour MP, Liu Q, Horne J, *et al*. Transgenic Production of Arachidonic Acid in Oilseeds. Transgenic Res. 2012a; 21: 139-47. https://doi.org/10.1007/s11248-011-9517-7

44. Nguyen HT, Silva JE, Podicheti R, Macrander J, Yang W, Nazarenus TJ, *et al*. Camelina Seed Transcriptome: A Tool for Meal and Oil Improvement and Translational Research. Plant Biotechnol J. 2013; 11: 759-69. https://doi.org/10.1111/pbi.12068

45. Li X, Fan J, Gruber J, Guan R, Frentzen M, Zhu LH. Efficient Selection and Evaluation of Transgenic Lines of *Crambe abyssinica*. Front Plant Sci. 2013; 4: 162-6. https://doi.org/10.3389/fpls.2013.00162

46. Nath UK, Kim HT, Khatun K, Park JI, Kang KK, Nou IS. Modification of Fatty Acid Profiles of Rapeseed (*Brassica napus* L.) Oil for using as Food, Industrial Feed-stock and Biodiesel. Plant Breed Biotech. 2016; 4(2): 123-34. https://doi.org/10.9787/PBB.2016.4.2.123

47. Qi W, Zhang F, Sun F, Huang Y, Guan R, Yang J, *et al*. Over-expression of a Conserved RNA-binding Motif (RRM) Domain (csRRM2) Improves Components of *Brassica napus* yield by Regulating Cell Size. Plant Breeding. 2012; 131: 614-9. https://doi.org/10.1111/j.1439-0523.2012.01998.x.

48. Tan H, Yang X, Zhang F, *et al*. Enhanced Seed Oil Production in Canola by Conditional Expression of *Brassica napus* LEAFY COTYLEDON1 and LEC1-LIKE in Developing Seeds. Plant Physiol. 2011; 156: 1577-88. https://doi.org/10.1104/pp.111.175000

49. Haslam RP, Ruiz-Lopez N, Eastmond P, Moloney M, Sayanova O, Napier JA. The Modification of Plant Oil Composition *via* Metabolic Engineering — better Nutrition by Design. Plant Biotechnol J. 2013; 11: 157-68. https://doi.org/10.1111/pbi.12012

50. Guan R, Lager I, Li X, Stymne S, Zhu LH. Bottlenecks in Erucic Acid Accumulation in Genetically Engineered ultrahigh Erucic Acid *Crambe abyssinica*. Plant Biotechnol J. 2014; 12(2): 193-203. https://doi.org/10.1111/pbi.12128

51. Kanrar S, Venkateswari J, Dureja P, Kirti PB, Chopra VL. Modification of Erucic Acid Content in Indian Mustard (*Brassica juncea*) by up-regulation and Down-regulation of the *Brassica juncea* FATTY ACID ELONGATION1 (BjFAE1) Gene. Plant Cell Rep. 2006; 25(2): 148-55. https://doi.org/10.1007/s00299-005-0068-3

52. Shi J, Lang C, Wu X, Liu R, Zheng T, Zhang D *et al*. RNAi knockdown of Fatty Acid Elongase1 Alters Fatty Acid Composition in *Brassica napus*. Biochem Biophys Res Commun. 2015;466: 518-22. https://doi.org/10.1016/j.bbrc.2015.09.062

53. Broun P, Somerville C. Accumulation of Ricinoleic, Lesquerolic, and Densipolic Acids in Seeds of Transgenic Arabidopsis Plants that Express a Fatty acyl hydroxylase cDNA from Castor Bean. Plant Physiol. 1997; 113: 933-42. https://www.ncbi.nlm.nih.gov/pubmed/9085577

54. McKeon TA, Lin JT, Stafford AE. Biosynthesis of Ricinoleate in Castor Oil. In: Shahidi F, Kolodziejczyk P, Whitaker JR, Munguia AL, Fuller G. (eds) Chemicals via Higher Plant Bioengineering. Advances in Experimental Medicine and Biology, Vol. 464. Springer, Boston, MA. 1999; 464: 37-47. https://doi.org/10.1007/978-1-4615-4729-7_4

55. Hoffmann M, Wagner M, Abbadi A, Fulda M, Feussner I. Metabolic Engineering of ω-3 very long Chain Polyunsaturated Fatty Acid Production by an Exclusively Acyl-CoA-dependent Pathway. J Biol Chem. 2008; 283: 22352-62. https://doi.org/10.1074/jbc.M802377200

56. Napier JA, Haslam RP, Beaudoin F, Cahoon EB. Understanding and Manipulating Plant Lipid Composition: Metabolic Engineering Leads the Way. Curr Opin Plant Biol. 2014; 19: 68-75. https://doi.org/10.1016/j.pbi.2014.04.001

57. Petrie JR, Vanhercke T, Shrestha P, El Tahchy A, White A, Zhou XR, *et al*. Recruiting a New Substrate for Triacylglycerol Synthesis in Plants: The Monoacylglycerol acyltransferase Pathway. PLoS ONE. 2012b; 7(4): e35214. https://doi.org/10.1371/journal.pone.0035214

58. Cheng D, Iqbal J, Devenny J, Chu CH, Chen L, Dong J, *et al*. Acylation of Acylglycerols by acyl Coenzyme A: diacylglycerol acyltransferase 1 (DGAT1). Functional Importance of DGAT1 in the Intestinal Fat Absorption. J Biol Chem. 2008;283: 29802-11. https://doi.org/10.1074/jbc.M800494200

59. Xu X, Akoh CC. Enzymatic Production of Betapol and other Specialty Fats. In: Gardner HW, Kuo TM. eds Lipid Biotechnology New York. pp. 461-478. (2002) Boca Raton, FL: CRC Press, ISBN: 978-0-8247-0619-7. http://citeseerx.ist.psu.edu/viewdoc/download?doi=10.1.1.513.6109&rep=rep1&type=pdf

60. Xu XY, Yang HK, Singh SP, Sharp PJ, Liu Q. Genetic Manipulation of Non-classic Oilseed Plants for Enhancement of their Potential as a Biofactory for Triacylglycerol Production. Engineering. 2018; 4(4): 523-33. https://doi.org/10.1016/j.eng.2018.07.002

61. Vanhercke T, Divi UK, El Tahchy A, Liu Q, Mitchell M, Taylor MC, *et al*. Step Changes in Leaf Oil Accumulation *via* iterative Metabolic Engineering. Metab Eng. 2017; 39: 237-46. https://doi.org/10.1016/j.ymben.2016.12.007

62. Andrianov V, Borisjuk N, Pogrebnyak N, Brinker A, Dixon J, Spitsin S, *et al*. Tobacco as a Production Platform for Biofuel: Overexpression of Arabidopsis DGAT and LEC2 Genes Increases Accumulation and Shifts the Composition of Lipids in Green Biomass. Plant Biotechnol J. 2010; 8(3): 277-87.https://doi.org/10.1111/j.1467-7652.2009.00458.x

63. Liu Q, Wu M, Zhang B, Shrestha P, Petrie J, Green AG, *et al*. Genetic Enhancement of Palmitic Acid Accumulation in Cotton Seed Oil through RNAi down-regulation of *ghKAS2* Encoding β-ketoacyl-ACP synthase II (KASII). Plant Biotechnol J. 2017; 15: 132-45. https://doi.org/10.1111/pbi.12598

64. Zale J, Jung JH, Kim JY, Pathak B, Karan R, Liu H, *et al*. Metabolic Engineering of Sugarcane to Accumulate Energy-dense Triacylglycerols in Vegetative Biomass. Plant Biotechnol J. 2016; 14(2): 661-9. https://doi.org/10.1111/pbi.12411

65. Fan J, Yu L, Xu C.A Central Role for Triacylglycerol in Membrane Lipid Breakdown, Fatty Acid β-oxidation, and Plant Survival under Extended Darkness. Plant Physiol. 2017; 174(3): 1517-30. https://doi.org/10.1104/pp.17.00653

66. Wang Z, Hobson N, Galindo L, *et al*. The Genome of Flax (*Linum usitatissimum*) Assembled de novo from Short Shotgun Sequence Reads. Plant J. 2012; 72: 461-73. https://doi.org/10.1111/j.1365-313X.2012.05093.x

67. Li-Beisson Y, Shorrosh B, Beisson F, Andersson MX, Arondel V, Bates PD, *et al*. Acyl-lipid metabolism. The *Arabidopsis* Book. 2010;8:e0133. http://dx.doi.org/10.1199/tab.0133

68. Schmutz J, Cannon SB, Schlueter J, Ma J, Mitros T, Nelson W, *et al*. Genome Sequence of the Palaeopolyploid Soybean. Nature 2010; 463: 178-83.https://doi.org/10.1038/nature08670

69. Chan AP, Crabtree J, Zhao Q, Lorenzi H, Orvis J, Puiu D, *et al*. Draft Genome Sequence of the Oilseed Species *Ricinus communis*. Nat Biotechnol. 2010; 28: 951-6.https://doi.org/10.1038/nbt.1674

70. Hajduch M, Ganapathy A, Stein JW, Thelen JJ. A Systematic Proteomic Study of Seed Filling in Soybean: Establishment of High Resolution Two-dimensional Reference Maps, Expression Profiles, and an Interactive Proteome Database. Plant Physiol. 2005; 137: 1397-419. https://doi.org/10.1104/pp.104.056614

71. Bino RJ, Hall RD, Fiehn O, Kopka J, Saito K, Draper J, *et al*. Potential of Metabolomics as a Functional Genomics Tool. Trends Plant Sci. 2004; 9: 418-25.https://doi.org/10.1016/j.tplants.2004.07.004

72. Iyer VV, Sriram G, Fulton DB, Zhou R, Westgate ME, Shanks JV. Metabolic Flux Maps Comparing the Effect of Temperature on Protein and Oil Biosynthesis in Developing Soybean Cotyledons. Plant Cell Environ. 2008; 31: 506-17.https://doi.org/10.1111/j.1365-3040.2008.01781.x

73. Brown AP, Kroon JTM, Swarbreck D, Febrer M, Larson TR, Graham IA, *et al*. Tissue-specific whole Transcriptome Sequencing in Castor, Directed at understanding Triacyglycerol Lipid Biosynthetic Pathways. PLoS ONE, 2012; 7: 1-13.https://doi.org/10.1371/journal.pone.0030100

74. Cahoon EB, Kinney AJ. The Production of Vegetable Oils with Novel Properties: using Genomic Tools to Probe and Manipulate Plant Fatty Acid Metabolism. Eur J Lipid Sci Technol. 2005; 107: 239-43. https://doi.org/10.1002/ejlt.200590020

75. Troncoso-Ponce MA, Kilaru A, Cao X, Durrett TP, Fan J, Jensen JK, *et al*. Comparative Deep Transcriptional Profiling of Four Developing Oilseeds. Plant J. 2011; 68: 1014-27. https://doi.org/10.1111/j.1365-313X.2011.04751.x

76. Sayanova OV, Haslam RP, Calero´ n MV, Ruiz-Lo´ pez N, Worthy C, Rooks P, *et al*. Identification and Functional Characterization of Genes Encoding the Omega-3 Polyunsaturated Fatty Acid Biosynthetic Pathway from the Coccolithophore *Emiliania huxleyi*. Phytochemistry. 2011; 72(7): 594-600.https://doi.org/10.1016/j.phytochem.2011.01.022

77. Raval SS, Mahatma MK, Chakraborty K, Bishi S, Singh AL, Rathod KJ. Metabolomics of Groundnut (*Arachis hypogaea* L.) Genotypes under varying Temperature Regimes. Plant Growth Regul. 2017; 84(3): 493-505. https://doi.org/10.1007/s10725-017-0356-2

78. Anon, (2019). [online] Available at: https://theconsciouslife.com/foods/mustard-oil-04583.htm [Accessed 16 Aug. 2019].https://theconsciouslife.com/foods/mustard-oil-04583.htm

Pages: 48-82

Seeds and Food: ***Processing and Storage Techniques***
Edited by: **Dr. Prasann Kumar and Dr. Pawan Kumar 'Bharti'**
ISBN: 978-93-88854-41-2
Edition: **2020**
Published by: **Discovery Publishing House Pvt. Ltd., New Delhi (India)**

3

Seed Storage
Importance, Factors Affecting Storage, Seed Storage Sanitation and Maintenance

R. Sridevi

INTRODUCTION

Seed storage is preservation of seed with initial quality until it is needed for planting. The ability of seed to tolerate moisture loss allows the seed to maintain the viability in dry state. Storage starts in the mother plant itself when it attains physiological maturity. After harvesting the seeds are either stored in ware houses or in transit or in retail shops. During the old age days, the farmers were used farm saved seeds in little quantity, but introduction of high yielding varieties and hybrids and modernization of agriculture necessitated the development of storage techniques to preserve the seeds.

The practice of storing the seeds starts from the ancient days itself, following simple and cheap techniques eg., placing the seeds in salt, red earth treatment to red gram etc. But the same practices are not hold good for the present day agriculture, because

- large quantity to be stored
- exchange of varieties and species
- exchange of genes

The type of material to be stored decides the techniques to be followed for safe storage. Seeds should have a good storage facility, since seeds are the main genetic linkage between two generations of a plant species. Seeds should be stored in such a manner, that its germination capacity and vigour

Assistant Professor, Imayam Institute of Agriculture and Technology, Trichy, Namakkal - Thuraiyur Rd, Kannanur - 621 206 Tamil Nadu (India)

should not decline. In temperate regions, seeds can be stored at ambient conditions for longer period, whereas in tropical and sub tropical regions parameters such as temperature and moisture should be adjusted as per the requirement to preserve the seed vigour. Nearly 30% of the seeds are lost during storage period due to insects, rodents and microorganisms. The storage period begins right at the time of attainment of the physiological maturity of seeds in the field till it is planted in the next season. Care should be taken to preserve the germination capacity, viability and vigour of the seeds. This manual explains various principles and methods of seed storage.

SEED STORAGE

Seed storage is the preservation of seeds from the time of collection by maintaining with initial quality until it is required for sowing. Maintenance of seed vigour and viability in terms of germination from harvest until planting is of the utmost importance in any seed production programme. Care should be taken at every stage of processing and distribution to maintain the viability and vigour. The harvested seeds of most of the orthodox crop seeds are usually dried and stored for atleast one season until the commencement of the next growing season, except those of the recalcitrant seeds which require high moisture content for safe storage (once dried the viability will be lost. E.g. – Jack, Citrus, Coffee, Cocoa, Polyalthea, etc.,). In such recalcitrant seeds senescence starts in the mother plant itself. The dry weather alters moisture content of the seed, thereby reducing the viability. Some seeds require an after ripening process as in Pinus and Fraxinus. In most of the Agricultural crops ageing starts at physiological maturity, which is irreversible. Hence seeds become practically worthless if they fail to give adequate plant stands in addition to healthy and vigorous plants. Good storage is therefore a basic requirement in seed production.

OBJECTIVE OF SEED STORAGE

To maintain initial seed quality viz., germination, physical purity, vigour etc., all along the storage period by providing suitable or even better conditions. Since the main objective of seed storage is maintenance of an acceptable capacity for germination and emergence, it can only be accomplished by reducing the rate of deterioration to the degree required to maintain an acceptable level of quality for the desired period.

PURPOSE OF SEED STORAGE

Seeds have to be stored, of course, because there is usually a period of time between harvest and planting. During this period, the seed have to be kept somewhere. While the time interval between harvest and planting is the basic reason for storing seed, there are other considerations, especially in the case of extended storage of seed.

The purpose of seed storage is to maintain the seed in good physical and physiological condition from the time they are harvested until the time they are planted. It is important to get adequate plant stands in addition to healthy and vigorous plants.

Seed suppliers are not always able to market all the seed they produce during the following planting season. In many cases, the unsold seed are "carried over" in storage for marketing during the second planting season after harvest. Problems arise in connection with carryover storage of seed because some kinds, varieties and lots of seed do not carryover very well.

Seeds are also deliberately stored for extended periods so as to eliminate the need to produce the seed every season. Foundation seed units and others have found this to be an economical, efficient procedure for seeds of varieties for which there is limited demand. Some kinds of seeds are stored for extended periods to improve the percentage and rapidity of germination by providing enough time for a "natural" release from dormancy.

Regardless of the specific reasons for storage of seed, the purpose remains the same maintenance of a satisfactory capacity for germination and emergence. The facilities and procedures used in storage, therefore, have to be directed towards the accomplishment of this purpose.

- To maintain the seed in good physical and physiological condition from harvested until the time they are planted.
- Seeds are also deliberately stored for extended periods so as to eliminate the need to produce the seed every season.
- Seed suppliers are not always able to market all the seed they produce during the following planting season.

STEPS IN SEED STORAGE

The major steps involved in seed storage are,

- Dry and cool storage conditions.
- Protection from pests.
- Sanitation of seed storage area.
- Drying of seeds before storing.
- Storing well cleaned seeds in the storage godown.

Stages of seed storage

- Storage on plants (physiological maturity until harvest).
- Harvest, until processed and stored in a warehouse.
- In - storage (warehouses)
- In transit (Railway wagons, trucks, carts, railway sheds etc.).
- In retail stores.
- On the user's farm.

1.	Post maturation/Pre harvest segment	Period from physiological maturity to harvest (seed in field).
2.	Bulk seed segment	Period from harvest to packaging (bulk seed in aeration drying bins, surge bins, etc.).
3.	Packaged seed segment	Period from packaging to distribution (seed in Packages in warehouse).
4.	Distribution/Marketing Segment	Period during distributing and marketing (packaged seed in transit)
5.	In retail stores	Period during retailer's storehouse
6.	On-farm segment	Period from purchase to planting of seed (seed in on-farm storage).

Seeds are considered to be physiologically and morphologically mature when they reach maximum dry weight. At this stage dry-down or dehydration of the seed is well underway. Dry-down continues after physiological maturity until moisture content of the seed and fruit decreases to a level which permits effective and efficient harvest and threshing. This stage can be termed as harvest maturity. There is usually an interval of time between physiological maturity and harvestable maturity, and this interval represents the first segment of the storage period. Any delay in harvesting the seed after they reach harvest maturity prolongs the first segment of the storage period – often to the detriment of seed quality.

The second segment of the storage period extends from harvest to the beginning of conditioning. Seed in the combine, grain wagon, and bulk storage or drying bins are in storage and their quality is affected by the same factors that affect the quality of seed during the packaged seed segment of the storage period. The third segment of the storage period begins with the onset of conditioning and ends with packaging. The fourth segment of the storage period is the packaged seed phase which has already been mentioned. The packaged seed segment is followed by storage during distribution and marketing, and finally by storage on the farm before and during planting.

The seed quality can be considerably be affected at any of the stages or segments mentioned above unless sound principles involved in seed storage are practiced and the seeds are properly handled.

STORAGE ON PLANTS

The prevailing environmental conditions from the time seed reaches physiological maturity until harvest, influences the seed quality. Factors such as soil conditions, mineral nutrients, and deficiencies during plant growth, moisture stress, and temperature stress, damage by insects or diseases may deteriorate the seed quality even when the seed is at the mother plant.

STORAGE FROM HARVEST UNTIL PLANTING

During this period the seeds have high moisture content. Transport from field to threshing yard, threshing yard to processing plants involve a certain period of storage during which deterioration can be rapid and serious if the moisture content is above 13 per cent. Moulds may grow on the seed and heating may occur because or respiration.

The higher the relative humidity and temperature, the severe will be the damage. In maize, a condition called the blue eyed seed is frequent because of the infection by *Penicillium* which breaks the dormancy by releasing ethylene. Once the dormancy is broken, the senescence is accelerated (Ecological suicide of seeds). Hence, necessary arrangements for proper aeration and drying of seeds to maintain the seed quality have to be provided.

GENERAL PRINCIPLES OF SEED STORAGE

In view of the various factors affecting seed viability in storage, the following principles emerge as necessary for good storage.

(a) Seed storage condition should be dry and cool.

(b) Effective storage pest control.

(c) Proper sanitation in seed stores.

(d) Before placing seeds into storage they should be dried to safe moisture limits, appropriate for the storage system.

(e) Storing of high quality seed only, i.e well cleaned, treated as well as of high germination with vigour and good pre-storage history.

(f) Determine seed storage needs in view of period or length of storage time, and prevailing climate of the area during storage period.

Long term storage requires more exacting conditions of seed storage than short-term storage. Similarly, the regions with favourable storage climate, i.e one where relative humidity is rather low requiring less sophistication than areas of high relative humidity.

It is considerable importance to decide well in advanced how long it will be necessary to maintain the germination capacity of seed lot. Two types of problems that must be dealt with in seed storage are:

1. Pest Control
2. Environment

As the requirements become more exacting, the cost of storage facility per unit of seed stored increases rapidly.

For most species, the requirements for seed storage are relatively simple. In the regions of no rainfall and low relative humidity, a smooth bare place may be reasonably satisfactory. However, loss from stealing, birds, and rodent s can be considerable and germination capacity can decline, at least in the surface seed, from heat damage and ultraviolet rays. Since it is not possible to have such a favourable climate everywhere, some shelter may be necessary. Such storage facilities can vary greatly. Successful storage structures and methods of storage for meeting the required needs should have following features.

1. Seeds placed in storage must be cleaned to free them of trash which may harbour insects or fungi and prevent free circulation of air.
2. Seeds should be undamaged to minimise decline in vigour and germination.
3. Seeds must be dried to moisture content less than 14 percent for starchy seeds, and less than 11 percent for oily seeds.
4. Storage structure should be constructed so that the rain cannot enter, and that no serious gain in moisture will occur pests of stored seed should be effectively controlled if the following features for constructing warehouses are observed, and the other suggested measures are followed.

Factors affecting seed longevity

1. Biotic factors
2. Abiotic factors

1. Biotic factors

(a) Factors related to seed

- Genetic makeup of seed
- Initial seed quality
- Provenance
- Seed Moisture content

(b) Other biotics

- Insects
- Fungi
- Rodents

2. Abiotic factors

- Temperature
- Relative humidity
- Seed store sanitation
- Gaseous atmosphere
- Packaging material

1. Biotic factors

(a) Factors related to seed

GENETIC MAKEUP OF SEED

The storage is influenced by the genetic make up of the seed. Some kinds are naturally short lived (e.g) onion, soybeans, ground nut etc., As a general rule starchy seeds can be stored considerably for a longer period compared to proteinaceous or oily seeds because of their hygroscopic nature. Based on the genetic make up seeds are classified into:

- Micro biotic - short lived
- Meso biotic - medium lived
- Macro biotic - long lived

INITIAL SEED QUALITY

The seeds of high initial viability are much more resistant to unfavourable storage environmental conditions than low viable seed. Once seed start to deteriorate it proceeds rapidly. The seed which injured mechanically suffered a lot and loses its viability and vigour very quickly. Generally small seeds escape injury whereas large seeds are more likely to be extensively damaged (e.g) bean, lima-bean and soybean. Spherical seeds usually give more protection than flat or irregularly shaped seeds.

Seed lots having plumpy, vigorous undamaged seeds store longer than that of deteriorated. Even seed lots having good germination at the beginning of storage period, may deteriorate at a faster rate depending upon the severity of weathering damage, mechanical injury or otherwise in the field. The low quality seeds should invariably be rejected. Even at best storage conditions, the initial quality of the seed cannot be improved (except for the dormant seed) but can only be maintained.

EFFECT OF PROVENANCE

The place where the seed crop was produced greately influences the storability. (e.g.) Red clover seeds grown in Canada stored for 4 years with 80% germination whereas seeds grown in England and Newzealand stored only for 3 years with 80% germination. This is due to different climatic conditions and soil types prevailing in different places.

The seeds harvested in different climates (or) at different times show differences in viability. Because they would have been subjected to different pre harvest conditions which will have caused different amounts of deterioration by the time, the seeds are harvested.

SEED MOISTURE CONTENT

Most important factor influences the storability. The amount of moisture in the seeds is the most important factor influencing seed viability during storage.

Generally if the seed moisture content increases storage life decreases. If seeds are kept at high moisture content the losses could be very rapid due to mould growth very low moisture content below 4% may also damage seeds due to extreme desiccation or cause hard seededness in some crops.

Since the life of a seed largely revolves around its moisture content it is necessary to dry seeds to safe moisture contents. The sage moisture content however depends upon storage length, type of storage structure, kind/variety of seed type of packing material used. For cereals in ordinary storage conditions for 12-18 months, seed drying up to 10% moisture content appears quite satisfactory.

However, for storage in sealed containers, drying upto 5-8% moisture content depending upon particular kind may be necessary.

Seed moisture content (%)	Storage life
11-13	½ year
10-12	1 year
9-11	2 years
8-10	4 years

It is well known that higher moisture content enhances the biological activity in the seeds and causes excessive heating, besides promoting mould and insect activities. The relationship of moisture content of seeds during post harvest stages furnished below would clearly indicate the role of moisture in the life of seeds in storage.

ROLE AND IMPORTANCE OF MOISTURE CONTENT IN THE LIFE OF SEEDS

35-80% — Moisture content of developing seed, seeds not mature enough for harvest

↓

18-40% — Seeds physiologically mature; respiratory rate high; seed susceptible to field deterioration; heating occurs if seed bulked without adequate ventilation; molds and insects very active; seed susceptible to mechanical damage in harvesting and handling.

↓

13-18% — Respiratory rate still high; can get heating at highest levels; molds and insects can be damaging; seed resistant to mechanical damage.

↓

10-13% → Seeds store reasonably well for 6 to 18 months in open storage in temperate climates; insects can still be a problemn in susceptible seeds; seed susceptible to mechanical damage.

8-10% → Seed sufficiently dry, can be stored for 1 to 3 years open storage in temperate climates; very little insect activity; seed very susceptible to mechanical damage.

4-8% → Safe moisture content for sealed storage.

0-4% → Extreme desiccation can be damaging to seed; hard seededness develops in some kinds of seed.

33-60% → Seeds germinate when they imbibe water to these levels.

The importance of seed moisture content in extending the shelf life of seeds under ideal storage conditions can be well known and understood from the Harrington's thumb rule, that one per cent decrease in seed moisture content nearly doubles the storage potential of the seed. Again this rule is applicable only at a moisture range of 5-14 per cent because moisture content below 5 per cent the physico chemical reaction may take place and at above 14 per cent fungi and insects become active. Another rule given by Harrington states that for every 5°C decrease in storage temperature, the seed life will be doubled. Again this can hold good only in the temperature range of 0-50°C. There are exceptions in this rule in a few crops like chillies, brinjal and bhendi. The safe moisture content again depends upon the period of storage, storage structures, kind and variety of seed and the packaging materials used. For cereals under open storage, seed drying upto 10 per cent moisture content appears quite satisfactory. The storage in sealed containers during upto 4-8% moisture content depending upon the particular kind of seed may be necessary.

(b) *Other biotics*

Microflora, Insects and Mites

The activity of all these organisms can lead to damage resulting in loss of viability. The microflora activity is controlled by Relative Humidity temperature and Moisture Content of seed. Treated seeds with fungicides can be stored for longer periods. Fumigation to control insects will also help in longer period of storage.

Fumigants - (e.g) methyl bromide, hydrogen cyanide, ethylene dichloride, carbon tetra chloride, carbon disulphide and napthalene and aluminimum phosphine.

2. Abiotic factors

RELATIVE HUMIDITY

Relative humidity is the amount of H_2O present in the air at a given temperature in proportion to its maximum water holding capacity. Relative Humidity and temperature are the most important factors determining the storage life of seeds. Seeds attain specific and characteristic moisture content when subjected to given levels of atmospheric humidity. This characteristic moisture content called equilibrium moisture content.

Relative Humidity and temperature are the most important factors determining the storage life of seeds. If there is high RH resulted in increase in seed moisture contentment resulted in faster deterioration of seed quality. Usually at lower humidity seeds can store for longer period. Equilibrium moisture content for a particular kind of seed at a given Relative Humidity tends to increase as temperature decreases.

Equilibrium moisture content for a particular kind of seed at a given Relative Humidity tends to increase as temperature decreases. Thus the maintenance of seed moisture content during storage is a function of relative humidity and to a lesser extent of temperature. At equilibrium moisture content there is no net gain or loss in seed moisture content.

Seeds are hygroscopic. They attain rather specific and characteristic moisture content when subjected to given level of atmospheric humidity at a particular temperature (equilibrium moisture content). The equilibrium moisture content for a particular kind of seed at a given relative humidity tends to increase as temperature decreases and the deterioration starts.

Equilibrium moisture content varies among seed kinds. In general, the equilibrium moisture content of "oily" seed is lower than that of "starchy" seed at the same relative humidity and temperature. This phenomenon can be accounted for by the fact that fats and oils do not mix with water. Thus, in a seed with 50% oil content, the moisture has to be concentrated in half the seed, while in a seed containing 10% oil, the moisture is distributed throughout 90% of the seed.

Thus the maintenance of moisture content of seed during storage is a function of RH and to a lesser extent of temperature. At equilibrium moisture content there is no net gain or loss in seed moisture content when seed is placed in a new environment with RH higher or lower than that of the seed, the seed will gain or lose moisture till it reaches a new equilibrium moisture content at this particular new environment.

TEMPERATURE

Temperature also plays an important role in life of seed. Insects and moulds increase as temperature increases. The higher the moisture content of the seeds the more they are adversely affected by temperature. Decreasing temperature and seed moisture is an effective means of maintaining seed quality in storage. The following thumb rules by Harrington are useful measures for assessing the effect of moisture and temperature on seed storage.

Harringtons Thumb Rule

1. For every decrease of 1% seed moisture content the life of the seed doubles. This rule is applicable between moisture content of 5-14%.
2. For every decrease of 5°C in storage temperature the life of the seed doubles. This rule applies between 0°C to 50°C.
3. Good seed storage is achieved when the% of relative humidity in storage environment and the storage temperature in degrees Fahrenheit add upto one hundred but the contribution from temperature should not exceed 50°F.

GAS DURING STORAGE

Increase in O_2 pressure decrease the period of viability

N_2 and CO_2 atmosphere will increase the storage life of seeds.

SANITATION IN STORAGE

There are several other recognized procedures for good seed storage that most seeds men already know. Seeds should be stored in a seed warehouse, not a fertilizer, chemicals, herbicide, or feed warehouse. Good sanitation should be a continuous practice. It will minimize storage insect infestations. If storage insects are a problem, the judicious use of insecticides and fumigants, combined with sanitation, will alleviate the problem. The best procedure is not to place insect infested lots in storage with other lots unless all the insects have been killed by fumigation or insecticide treatment.

In warehouse with concrete floors, seed bags should be stacked on wooden pallets to keep them from contact with the floor as considerable moisture can be transmitted through concrete floors. Seed warehouses should also be adequately ventilated (unless they are conditioned) and protected against rodents.

Seed storage godown should be clean and dry. Godown should be sprayed periodically once in a week or fortnightly with Malathion 50 EC (1 : 300 Chemical : Water) @ 5 lit. sq. m^{-1} or 0.25% Nuvan @ 1 lit. Seed lots can be fumigated with Aluminium phophide @ 3 gm/cu.m in air tight condition for 7 days. This can be done as propylatic measure and on minimum infestation by insects.

PACKAGING MATERIAL

Depending upon the cost, availability and the period of storage, the packaging materials are to be selected. Normally cereal seeds are being packed in cotton, jute and paper bags. Moisture vapour penetrates in these containers and they offer no protection against high relative humidity. In high humidity locations with inadequate seed storage facilities, consideration should be given to methods of packaging which can protect the seed from moisture vapour. Such moisture vapour proof containers include paper aluminium foil pouches, polyethylene bags of over 700 guage thickness, sealed tins and gasketed rigid plastic containers. The costs of these are high. Polyethylene bags have been regarded as the most attractive, because of their relatively low cost, compared to other kinds of sealed containers. Rigid plastic containers and sealed tins offer some possibility for hybrid seeds of cotton and vegetables, if the quantity needed is not great.

DRY, COOL CONDITIONS DURING STORAGE

The general prescription for seed storage is a dry and cool environment. At this point, the question naturally arises: How dry and how cool? It is difficult to answer this question unless three factors are known: (1) kind(s) of seed to be stored; (2) desired period of storage and (3) physiological quality of the seed.

Seed of most grain crops, e.g., corn, wheat, sorghum, barley, rye, oats, rice, will maintain germination for the 8-9 months period from harvest to planting at moisture content of 12-13% and normal warehouse temperature except possibly in Southern coastal areas. For maintenance of vigour as well as germination, moisture content should not exceed 12% (relative humidity below 60%) and temperature in the warehouse should not exceed 65° F. In the case of carry-over seed, which means a storage period of 20-21 months, the moisture content of seed of grain crops should be less than 11% and temperature should not exceed 65° F. Since the period of carry-over storage encompasses atleast one summer period, temperatures and humidity control during the period is most important.

Cotton seed stores about as well as seed of grain crops, and the conditions mentioned above are applicable. Soybeans and peanut seed are poor storers. For one year's storage (actually 8-9 months), moisture content should be 11 to 12% and the warehouse temperature should not exceed 65°F. Shelled peanuts may have to be stored in a cold room. Carry-over storage should not be attempted unless conditioned storage facilities are available: 65°F and 50% relative humidity or better. Seed of most forage grass and legume crops will store well for one year at moisture content of 10-11% at normal warehouse temperatures. When "carried-over", moisture content should be about 10% and temperature should not exceed 65%.

Vegetable seed vary considerably among kinds in their storage requirements. Generally, however, most kinds will store well for one year at a moisture content of 9-11% and a temperature that does not exceed 65°F. When a storage period longer than 19-21 months is required, conditioned storage is essential for all kinds of seed. Most kinds of seed will maintain quality for 2-3 years when stored at 60°F and 50-55% relative humidity or better. For storage longer than 3 years, conditions should be 50° F and 50% relative humidity or better.

THE ACTIVITY OF ORGANISMS ASSOCIATED WITH SEEDS IN STORAGE

The bacteria, fungi, mites, insects, rodents and birds may do harm to seeds in storage. The general limits of temperature and relative humidity for the multiplication of the various biological agencies infesting stored seeds are:

Organism	Temperature		Relative humidity
	Range for multiplication	Optimum range	
Insects	21-42°C	27-37°C	30-95%
Mites	8-31°C	19-31°C	60-100%
Fungi	8-80°C	20-40°C	60-100%
Microbes	8-80°C	26-28°C	91-100%

It is also interesting to note that the favourable limits of temperature and RH for germination are 16-42°C and 95-100 per cent respectively.

TYPES OF SEED STORAGE

Based on storage behaviour (Roberts and Ellis)

- Orthodox seeds
- Intermediate seeds
- Recalcitrant seeds

Orthodox Seeds

The seeds able to tolerate moisture loss (desiccation) and low temperature i.e. decreased moisture increased storage period. Eg. Rice, sorghum and most of the agricultural species.

Orthodox seeds are long-lived seeds and can be successfully dried to moisture con-tents as low as 5% without injury and are able to tolerate freezing. Orthodox seeds are therefore, also termed as desiccation tolerant seeds. In-fact, the life span of orthodox seeds can be prolonged with low moisture content and freezing temperatures. The longevity or life span of orthodox seeds may vary from over a year to many hun-dred years depending upon the particular species and storage conditions.

Recalcitrant Seeds

Seeds not able to tolerate moisture loss and low temperature. Required high moisture for viability maintenance. Eg. Mango, Coffee, rubber, cocoa, jack

Recalcitrant seeds are remarkably short-lived which cannot be dried to moisture con-tent below 20-30% without injury and are unable to tolerate freezing. Recalcitrant seeds are therefore, also termed as desiccation sensitive seeds. Recalcitrant species belong to trees and shrubs of mostly tropics and also of temper-ate areas which are moist and some plants which grow in aquatic environment. Some com-mon examples of plants that produce recalcitrant seeds (which are generally larger than orthodox seeds) include, avocado, cacao, coconut, jackfruit, lychee, mango, rubber, tea, some horticultural trees, and several plants used in traditional medicine. The longevity or life span of recalcitrant seeds is remarkably very short. Seeds of Acer saccharinum, Zizania aquatica, Salix japonica and S. pierotti lose their viability within a week if kept in air. Seeds of several other species remain viable only for a few weeks and months to less than a year.

Intermediate Seeds

Some of these seeds may have a limited desiccation tolerance but are sensitive to freezing temperatures.

It has been observed by many scientists that certain seeds do not conform fully either to ortho-dox or recalcitrant category. Some of these seeds may have a limited desiccation tolerance but are sensitive to freezing temperatures. For these seeds, an intermediate category has been suggested by Ellis (1991). Citrus and Coffee seeds may fit this intermediate classification.

Based on period of storage

- Storage of Commercial seeds (8-9 months)
- Storage of Carry over seeds (12-18 months)
- Storage of Endorsement seed stocks (3-5 years)
- Storage of Germplasm seeds (months to years)

STORAGE OF COMMERCIAL SEEDS

This storage of commercial seed requires the largest storage need from harvest until planting. The storage period ranges from 8-9 months. Seed must be dried to 14 per cent moisture content for starchy seed and 11 percent for oilseeds.

CARRYOVER SEEDS

About 20-25 per cent of stored seed may have to be carried over through one season to the second planting time. The storage period may range 1-1½ year. Storage of seeds in metal bins with tight fitting lids or in a moisture proof bag will solve the problems of moisture penetration, provided the seeds are already dry enough for sealed storage.

FOUNDATION STOCK AND ENFORCEMENT SEED SAMPLE

It is desirable to store foundation and enforcement seeds for several years since genetic drift are minimized by reproducing foundation or stock seeds. Since the quantity of seeds involved is not large, the storage room is only a small part of the total storage area and in fact, is often a small room within a large warehouse. Relative humidity and temperature combination has to be provided for maintaining the viability. A combination of 25 per cent RH at 30°C temperature or less or a RH of about 45 per cent at 20°C or less will be ideal. The required RH can be achieved by making the room moisture proof and by using a dehumidifier.

GERMPLASM SEED STORAGE

Germplasm seeds are required to be kept for many years, perhaps very long periods. Basic requirements for such long term storage are the coldest temperature economically possible and seed moisture is in equilibrium with 20-25 per cent RH. Germplasm storage built up so far have rooms which can be maintained at 5°C to 10°C and 30 per cent RH. In addition, the stored samples are dried to perfect moisture level.

Based on Environment

- Open storage
- Controlled storage

BULK (OPEN) STORAGE

It is preferred over bag storage for the following reasons

- Large quantities of food grain can be stored
- No difficulty in loading and unloading of grain
- No need to purchase storage containers like gunnies
- Insect incidence is less than bag storage, even this can be eliminated by fumigation in situ
- Avoids waste from leaking bags
- Easy inspections- save labour and time.

CONTROLLED STORAGE

The use and manipulation of natural components of the atmosphere, e.g. oxygen, N, CO_2, to preserve the food is referred as controlled atmospheric storage. An atmosphere in which oxygen, carbon dioxide and nitrogen concentrations as well as temperature and humidity are regulated.

Use of controlled atmosphere is either in the form of hermetic storage or in the form of use of externally generated inert gas to displace the intergranular atmosphere of the stored grain. The use of hermetic storage which is very ancient in practice, involves sealing the grain in air-tight containers. Due to the respiration of the grain and due to the metabolic action of insects on their food, oxygen is consumed leaving CO_2. The quantity of carbon dioxide found is dependent on the ratio of head space to grain volume and the sorptive capacity of the structure. Ultimately, the level of oxygen falls raising the level of carbon dioxide and when the level falls to 2%, the insects die due to anoxia. The death is due to lack of oxygen compounded by the toxic action of CO_2. Use of nitrogen or carbondioxide to displace the intergranular air and to maintain the nitrogenous or carbondioxide enriched atmosphere is being experimented and the results revealed a good control of stored product insects. All stages of most of the common major pests are exterminated in this lethal-oxygen poor (less than 2%) atmosphere while the quality of the commodities stored remains much better than of those preserved by chemical methods normally operating in oxygen ambient.

STORAGE CONDITIONS

Since seed moisture content and ambient relative humidity are in equilibrium during storage, maintenance of a "safe" moisture content requires an average level of relative humidity in the storage environment no higher than that in equilibrium with the "safe" or desired moisture content. This favorable situation can be achieved in only three ways: (1) location of the storage facility in a region where relative humidity does not rise – on the average – above the critical level; (2) maintenance of the relative humidity at the desired level by packaging seed in moisture vapor proof containers; or (3) dehumidification of the storage room atmosphere to the desired level. The desired level of relative humidity for successful storage of seed depends, of course on the kind of seed, the duration of the storage period, and the temperature.

SEED PACKAGING IN RELATION TO SEED STORAGE

In reality the seed package is a small storage container. The kind of container needed is affected by several factors including:

(a) The quantity of seed desired in each package

(b) The protection desired

(c) The cost of the package

(d) The value of the seed

(e) The storage conditions into which the container is to be placed and

(f) The facilities for drying the seeds

Depending upon the cost availability and the period of storage, the packaging materials are to be selected. Normally cereal seeds are being packed in cotton, jute and paper bags. Moisture vapour penetrates in these containers and they offer no protection against high relative humidity. In high humidity locations with inadequate seed storage facilities, consideration should be given to methods of packaging which can protect the seed from moisture vapour. Such moisture vapour proof containers include paper aluminium foil pouches, polyethylene bags of over 700 gauge thickness, sealed tins and gasketted rigid plastic containers. The costs of these are high, for the package of cereal seeds. Polyethylene bags have been regarded as the most attractive, because of their relatively low cost, compared to other kinds of sealed containers. Rigid plastic containers and sealed tins offer some possibility for hybrid seeds of cotton and vegetables, if the quantity needed is not great.

CLASSIFICATION OF PACKING MATERIALS OR CONTAINERS

1. Moisture and vapour pervious containers

These containers allow entry of water in the from of vapour and liquid. These are suited for short term storage. The seeds in these containers will attain seed equilibrium moisture with the surrounding atmosphere (eg) cloth bags, gunny bags, paper bags etc.

2. Moisture impervious but vapour pervious containers

These allow entry of water in the form of vapour and not in liquid. The seeds in the containers can't be carried over for long period in hot humid conditions (.g.) polythene bags of <300 gauge thickness and urea bags.

3. Moisture and vapour proof containers

These containers will not allow entry of moisture in the form of liquid or vapour. These are used for long term storage even in hot humid conditions if the seeds are sealed at optimum m.c. eg. Polythylene bags of >700 gauge thickness, aluminium foil pouches, rigid plastics etc.

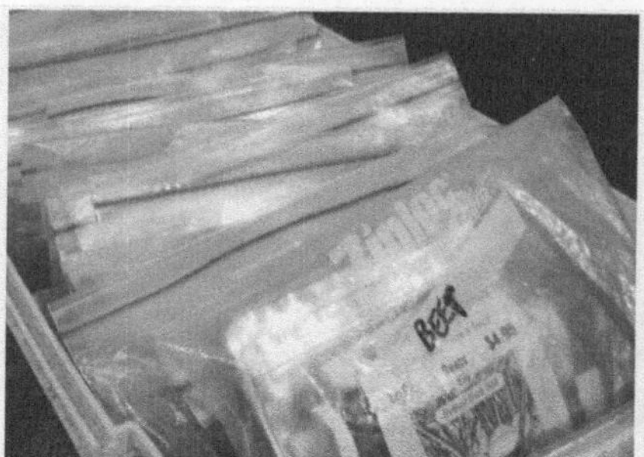

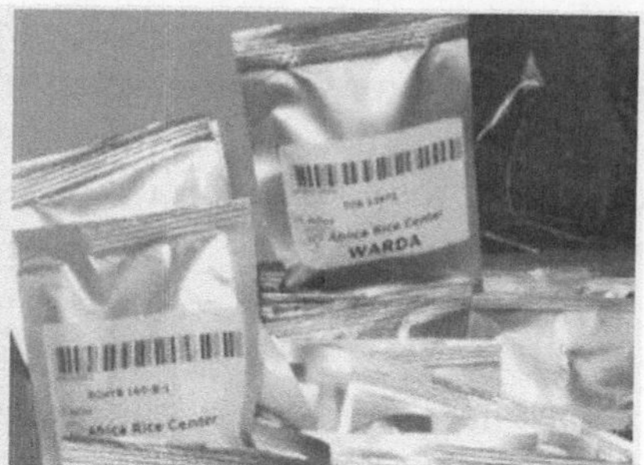

Certified seeds of cereals, pulses and oil seeds are normally packed either in gunny bags or cloth bags. However, paper bag, aluminium foil pouches and polyethylene bags are used for packing flower and vegetable seeds.

SEED STORAGE IN RELATION TO SEED DETERIORATION

The purpose of seed storage has been previously stated, *viz.*, to preserve or maintain the physiological quality of seed for the period desired through minimization of the rate of deterioration. Since seed storage is basically concerned with "control" of deteriorative processes, some knowledge of these processes is essential for successful seed storage operations.

DETERIORATIVE CHANGES IN SEED AND THEIR CONSEQUENCES

In our consideration of some of the characteristics of deterioration in seed, another might have been added that deterioration is characterized by change. Indeed, in our context, deterioration and change – detrimental change – are almost synonymous. For deterioration is identifiable only in terms of observable or measurable changes in the response reactions of the seed. Conversely, detrimental changes, e.g., loss of germination or vigour, are said to be the result of deterioration.

In the sequence of deteriorative changes it can be readily seen that during deterioration, the "performance potential" of seed becomes progressively impaired (reduced) until they lose their capacity to germinate, at which time "performance potential" is zero. Since loss of the capacity to germinate is the last practically significant consequence of deterioration, the design and evaluation of storage conditions only in terms of "maintenance of germination" is not sufficient. The "lesser consequences" of deterioration must also be considered because collectively they determine the "vigour" level of the seed. And, the vigour of seed determines how well they germinate, emerge, grow, and develop in the farmer's field.

LONGEVITY OF DEED IS A CHARACTERISTIC OF THE SPECIES OR VARIETY

Some kinds of seed are inherently long-lived, others are short-lived, while others have an "intermediate" life span. Differences in storability extend even down to the variety level. It has been known, for example, the certain inbred lines of corn are "poor storers" and that this characteristic is inherited.

Inherent differences in seed longevity are facts, the seeds man must accept and contend with as best he can. Among the vegetables, onion seed are notoriously short-lived, radish seed are intermediate in longevity, and watermelon seed are relatively long-lived. Soybean and peanut seed do not store well as compared to seed of wheat, corn, cotton, sorghum and rice. In some cases, seed kinds which have very similar chemical and physical properties differ substantially in longevity. Tall fescue and annual ryegrass seed are similar in structure, chemical composition, and yet, ryegrass seed store better than tall fescue seed.

POSSIBLE SEQUENCE OF CHANGES IN SEED DURING DETERIORATION

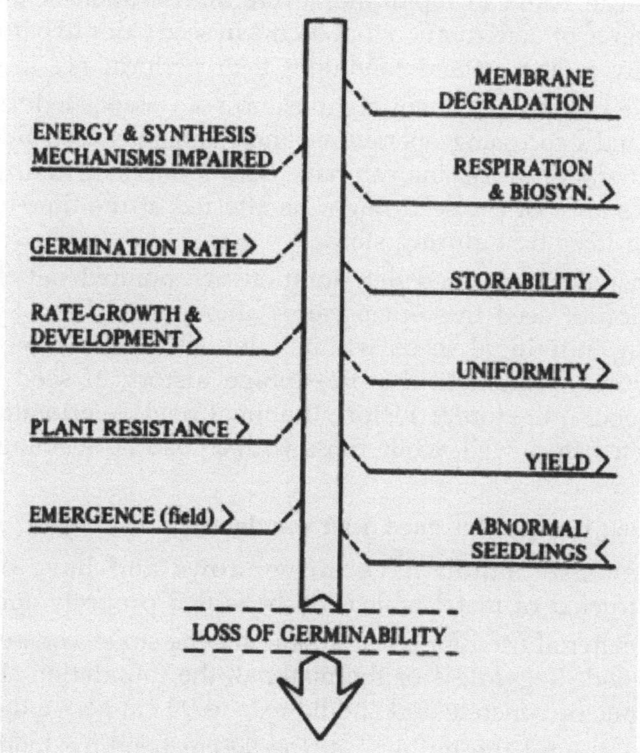

Seed selection for extended storability

- Store well mature seeds.
- Store normal coloured seeds
- Seeds should be free from mechanical injury
- Seeds should not have met with adverse conditions during maturation
- Seeds should be dried to optimum moisture content.
- Seeds should be treated with fungicides before storage.
- Suitable packaging materials should be used for packing.

HIGH QUALITY SEED STORE BETTER THAN LOW QUALITY SEED

The storage potential of seed is greatly affected by their quality at the time they enter storage, or their pre-storage history. The pre storage history of a seed lot encompasses all the "events" in the "life" of the seeds from the time functional maturity is reached until they are placed in storage.

Seeds are highest in quality at the time functional maturity is attained. Since most kinds of seed reach maturity at moisture contents too high for mechanical harvest, the seeds are subjected to the field environment from maturation to harvest. The post-maturation pre-harvest period normally ranges from 1 to 4 weeks for the different kinds of seed. Adverse climatic conditions can result in rapid and severe deterioration of the seed, and so on. The degree of deterioration that occurs in seed prior to harvest determines their quality at harvest and conditions their performance in storage.

In like manner, mechanical, abuse to seed associated with harvesting, handling and processing operations, and damage caused by inadequate or improper aeration or drying can have both immediate and residual effects, i.e., performance of the seed might be affected at the time of injury or not until some later time during storage.

In characterizing seed deterioration, we pointed out that the rate of deterioration of seed in storage varies among seed lots of the same kind and among individual seeds within a lot. These variations in storability are, of course, related to the pre-storage history of seed lots. Seed lots with a "good" pre-storage history (minimal field deterioration, mechanical damage, etc.) store well, while those with a "bad" pre-storage history store poorly.

Construction features for good seed warehouse:

(a) Warehouse should have no windows and have only one door constructed of metal which can be sealed properly and locked.

(b) The material used for construction may be stone, concrete, brick, metal or wood. Regardless of the material, the foundation should be made of stone or concrete and should extend 90 cm above the ground level.

(c) A lip around the building at the 90 cm height extending out 15 cm should also be constructed. Such construction makes entrance by rodents virtually impossible, as long as the foundation remains uncracked.

(d) The floor must be paved and any cracks that may develop must be repaired.

(e) Construction of the floor, walls and ceiling of the storage should be such that no cracks exist which can harbour insects. All cracks around openings, E.g Electric conduits, ventilation openings, and doors should be thoroughly sealed.

(f) Ventilation openings should be screened against birds and insects.

STORAGE GODOWN AND THEIR MAINTENANCE

Seeds undergo deterioration due to aging in storage. This is accelerated by climatic factors and external biotic factors like insects and pathogen. In addition to seed borne pathogen and storage insects, seeds are damaged by birds and rats for their feed. Clean and hygienic godowns protect the seed from external insects and preserve the seed. Hence care should be taken in construction of godown. The points to be noted are as follows.

- Seed godowns should not be constructed in areas near seashore. Since the high RH of atmospheric air accelerate the deterioration of seed.
- Seed godown should be in a place where transport facilities are easily available.
- Seed godown should not be constructed in low lying water stagnating areas.
- Seed godown should be constructed in places where atmospheric RH is low, free circulation of air is possible, sunlight is adequate and elevated in nature.
- The ventilators should be at bottom for free air circulation.
- Ground moisture should not reach the floor.
- Should be rat proof with wire mesh
- Should not be near industries as smoke is injurious

In maintenance of seed in godown following points are to be considered.

1. Godown should be clean and dry
2. Seed bags should not be stacked directly on floor. Should be stacked on wooden ballets.
3. The height of the stack should not be more than 6-8 bags.
4. Different seed lot should be kept separately.
5. Godown should be sprayed periodically once in a week or fortnightly with Malathion 50 EC (1 : 300 Chemical : Water) @ 5 lit. sq. m-1 or 0.25% Nuvan @ 1 lit. 100 m^{3-1}.
6. Altering the chemicals at weekly intervals will give better control.
7. Seed lots can be fumigated with Aluminium phophide @ 3 gm/cu.m in air tight condition for 7 days. This can be done as propylatic measure and on minimum infestation by insects.
8. Seed lots should be periodically (once in month) tested for seed quality.
9. Based on seed testing result, seeds can be dried under sun for the removal of moisture. It reduces insect and pathogen infestation.
10. New seed lots should be kept away from old seed lots to avoid secondary infestation of insects.
11. Seeds should be treated with combination of fungicide and insecticide (eg.) Thiram @ 2 g kg-1 + carbaryl @ 200 mg kg-1.
12. Frequent supervision of each and every lot is must.
13. Seed bag should be restacked once in 3 months for free aeration.
14. Instead of gunny bags low cost interwoven polythene bags should be used to prolong the life of seed.
15. Pesticides, fungicides, fertilizers, rejects should not be stored with seed.

16. Each lot should be labeled accurately and registers for stocks should be maintained.
17. Per acre or per hectare packing (small) is preferable for easy handling and effective supervision.

Storage godown sanitation

- Storage environment should be free from insects and rodents.
- Storage room should be kept clean, cool and dry.
- Use wooden pallets for arranging the bags in cris-cross manner for effective ventilation on all sides of the bags.
- Seed bags should be stacked upto 6-8 tires depending upon density of seeds.
- Restacking once in 3 months or less is important for prolonging seed viability.
- Disinfect the godowns by spraying malathion 50% E.C. @ 5 lit /100 m^{-2} area or 0.25% Nuvan @ 1 lit. 100 m^2
- Seeds should be treated with combination of fungicide and insecticide (eg.) Thiram @ 2 g kg-1 + carbaryl @ 2 g kg-1.
- Seed lots can be fumigated with Aluminium phophide @ 3 gm/cu.m in air tight condition for 7 days.
- Fumigants - Phosphine and Methyl Bromide, dichlorvos, Ethylene oxide and HCN.
- Seed lots should be periodically (once in month) tested for seed quality.
- Pesticides, fungicides, fertilizers, rejects should not be stored with seed.
- Reduce the moisture content of seed to prevent insect build up (usually below 10%).
- Cracks and crevices around corners have to be brushed to eliminate hiding pests.
- Provision of wire meshes to doors, ventilators, gutters, drains to prevent entry of rats, squirrels, birds, etc.
- Previously used bags, bins, etc. should be dried in the sun repeatedly.

CARE AND PREPARATION BEFORE STORAGE

Seeds should be dried to optimum moisture level, less than 12% for starchy seeds and less than 9% for oily seeds. Seeds should be cleaned thoroughly and should be free from trash, insect and microbial damage. If the relative humidity is low or maintainable, then the seeds can be stored in paper envelopes. Storage containers should be reasonably inexpensive, airtight with low thermal conductivity. Storage containers should be moisture proof which includes sealed tins or aluminium cans, glass jars with gasket lids.

SELECTION AND MAINTENANCE OF STORAGE GODOWN

Storage area should be easily accessible for loading and unloading operations. The storage area should be relatively moisture proof which is necessary for the maintenance of seed moisture content. The godown should be clean and dry. Storage area should be termite and rodent proof. There should not be any cracks or holes in the wall and floor of the storage godown. Disinfestation is done by spraying neem oil solution - 200 ml of neem oil should be mixed with 2 litres of water. It is recommended for a single storage room of 200 square feet. After spraying neem oil solution, the rooms can be fumigated with the powder of sweet flag rhizome *(Acorus calamus)*. Before stacking the seeds or grains, the storage godowns or rooms and storage structures or receptacle should be cleaned and made free from insects.

FUMIGATION OF THE GODOWN

For fumigation of the storage area, the following things are required:

Vessel with a wide mouth made of iron, aluminium or mud, rope, coal, *Vaividangam*/sweet flag, leaves of *Vitex* (five - leaved chaste tree/ *Nochi*)/Neem/*Leucas* (common leucas/*Thumbai*)

The following procedure should be followed for fumigating the storage godown:

Take hot coal in a vessel with a wide mouth. Take any two types of green leaves of Neem/Chaste tree/Common leucas/Holy basil in equal quantities and put it on hot coal. At the time of fumigation, the windows and doors of the seed storage godown should be closed tightly to avoid the entry of fresh air. Keep the vessel with hot coal and leaves at the centre of the storage godown. There should not be any gunny bags or easily inflammable material up to 3 ft around the fumigation vessel. The fumigation should be done only during evening hours. The fumigation vessel should be kept in the room for 30 minutes to 1 hour depending upon the size of the room. The dead moths and insects should be cleared from the storage godown next day morning. Fumigation process should be done once a month during storage period.

SEED TREATEMENT

An insecticide combined with a fungicide may be applied as a protectant. The most commonly used insecticide is DDT. DDT also has the advantage of long duration.

FUNGICIDE

Mercurials

Organic mercurials eg. (Agrason)

Organo mercurials are recommended for the treatment of *small grains, flax, cotton and safflower*. Proper dosage is critical. Over treatment, however, may result in seed injury and under-treatment may fail to adequately control disease. In general, the seed treated with the more volatile organic mercury compounds cannot be stored for more than a few days without lowering the viability of the seed, especially if the moisture content is high. The rate of application of organo mercurials should be watched closely. It should never be applied at more than the recommended rates. If the seed is to be stored for a while after treatment with a volatile fungicide, the moisture content of the seed should be below thirteen per cent.

IN ORGANIC MERCURIALS (EG. MERCURIC CHLORIDE, MERCURUS CHLORIDE AND MERCURIC OXIDE)

These chemicals can be treated with seeds, roots, tubers, garden and vegetable crops to control disease causing organisms. Excessive precaution should be taken while treating the seeds with these chemicals. Mercuric chloride is injurious to most of the seeds.

NON-MERCURIALS

Organic Non-mercurials (eg.) Bavistin

This is the mostly and widely used fungicides. Generally they are less effective than organic materials. But they are less damaging to the seeds and less dangerous to persons handling the seed. Excessive dosage is not harmful to the seed. Seeds can be stored for longer periods of time without suffering from the injury by the treatment. Organic non mercurials are not detrimental to the viability of injured seed. These fungicides will act as seed disinfectants or seed protectants.

Inorganic Non-mercurials

Copper carbonate, copper sulphate, cuprous oxides constitute the major inorganic non-mercurial compounds which are used as fungicides. Copper carbonate and copper sulphate are used as fungicides. Copper carbonate and copper sulphate are used on wheat as bunt preventives. Cuprous oxide prevents seed decay and damping-off vegetables, but is injurious to seeds of lettuce, crucifer and onions.

INSECTICIDE TREATMENTS (EG. MALATHION OR CARBARYL (SEVIN) OR IMIDACLOPRID)

Insecticides use in seed dressing as protectant gets increased over time. These may be combined use of pesticides with the fungicides in the seed treating process. The uses include:

- Protection against storage insects,
- Protection against certain soil insects that attack the seed.

Insecticides used alone may tend to damage the embryo of the seed. However, when used in combination with a fungicide, they interact with each other and the damage is not as severe.

HALOGENATION PRODUCTS OR HALOGEN MIXTURE

It is a mixture of calcium oxychloride (CaoCl2), Calcium carbonate ($CaCO_3$) and arappu leaf powder at the ratio of 5:4:1. Seeds are treated @ 3-5 g per kg of seeds and stored. It is suggested that the halogen(s) stabilizes the unsaturated fatty acid components of the lipoprotein membranes of cells which would possible render them less susceptible to peroxidative or autooxidative damages during ageing. Halogen mixture seed dressing also protect the seeds from storage insect pests and pathogens that affect the seed quality directly or indirectly. Recently halopolymer (a mixture of halogens, herbal products and polymer) a seed protectant available in the market and can be treated before storing the seeds @ 20-25 ml (Concentration will vary according to the seed) per kg of seeds.

ACTIVATED CLAY SEED TREATMENT

If the seeds (particularly pulses) are stored for dual purpose (grain/ seeds), this treatment is recommended. Seeds are treated with activated clay at the rate of 1:100 (1part of activated clay and 100 part of seeds), packed and stored in suitable containers

STORAGE PESTS AND MANAGEMENT

There are heavy losses in the course of grain storage. Importance of the additional grain that can be made available for human consumption by pest free/pest controlled storage is intensely felt during unfavorable agricultural years. Surplus grains produced in the country only aggravate storage problems. More than 65 percent of the total grain produced is retained and stored by the farmers for food, feed and seed purposes till the next harvest. It is estimated that about 5-8% of grains are retained for seed, about 20% is hand-pounded and the rest is milled.

There are heavy losses in the course of grain storage. Importance of the additional grain that can be made available for human consumption by pest free/pest controlled storage is intensely felt during unfavorable agricultural years. Surplus grains produced in the country only aggravate storage problems. More than 65 percent of the total grain produced is retained and stored by the farmers for food, feed and seed purposes till the next harvest. It is estimated that about 5-8% of grains are retained for seed, about 20% is hand-pounded and the rest is milled. Source of infestation of stored product insects

- Field infestation
- Infestation by migration
- Infestation through conveyance
- Storage building or structures, birds, bird nests and ants, rodent burrows, etc.

MANAGEMENT OF INSECT PESTS OF SEEDS

Control of Insect pests

1. Preventive measures
2. Curative measures

Preventive measures

- Hygiene or sanitation
- Threshing floor/yard should be clean, free from insect infestation and away from the vicinity of villages/granaries.
- Clean the harvesting and the threshing machines before their use.
- Trucks, trolleys or bullock carts which are used for transportation seeds should be made free from insect infestation.
- Clean the storage structure/godowns before storage of newly harvested crop. All dirt, rubbish, sweepings and webbings should be removed from the stores and disposed/destroyed.
- All the cracks, crevices, holes existing in the floors, ceiling should be plastered with mud or cement permanently.
- All the rat burrows should be closed with a mixture of broken glass pieces and mud and then plastered with mud/cement.
- White wash the store rooms before storage of seeds
- Seeds should be kept in stores which are rat & moisture proof.
- Proper stacking of bags also helps in seed protection.
- Disinfestations of stores/receptacles

  Before the use, the receptacles/store rooms should be disinfested with approved residual insecticides preferably by spraying Malathion 50% EC3 ml/ L or dichlorovas 100%EC @ 1ml/lit.
- Legal method

  Entry of an insect which is not found in the particular area can be prevented by the imposition of Destructive Insect Pests Act, 1914.

Curative measures

1. Non-chemical control measures
2. Chemical control measures

Non-chemical control measures

Ecological control measures

3. Temperature
4. Moisture content of Seed
5. Availability of oxygen

STORAGE INSECT MANAGEMENT

Maintenance of store house hygiene

1. Cracks and crevices around corners have to be brushed to eliminate hiding pests. All debris should be removed. Provision of wire meshes to windows, ventilators, gutters, drains to prevent entry of rats, squirrels, birds, etc.
2. Reduce the moisture content of seed to prevent insect build up (usually below 10%). Previously used bags, bins, etc. should be dried in the sun repeatedly.
3. Elimination of conditions which favour storage pests. Uniformly graded seeds should be used, broken seeds should be removed before bagging since they favour pest build up. Stitching of all torn bags, filling bags up to the brim, no loose packing.
4. Surface treatment of storehouse before storage with malathion dust 4% @ 25 g/sq m or malathion 50% EC spray @ 10 ml/lit of water and 3 lit of solution per sq. metre.
5. Good dunnage by arranging wooden planks or bamboo poles or spreading thick polythene sheets on the floor. Treatment of dunnage materials with malathion as specified, arrange the bags in criscross pattern with a maximum of 15 bags and provide adequate space between the roof and the seed bags.

PROPHYLATIC TREATMENT OF SEEDS

Application of malathion 4 per cent dust 25 g/sq metre or malathion 50 per cent EC 10 ml per litre of water and 3 litres of spray solution for 100 sq.m. The chemicals have to be sprayed on the walls and floors and the treatment has to be repeated based on the extent of flying and crawling insects.

CHEMICALS

Two chemicals are widely used : Phosphine and Methyl Bromide. Others are dichlorvos, Carbondioxide, Ethylene oxide and HCN.

Phosphine: Available in a solid form (0.6 g pellets, 3 g tablets). The active ingredient is Aluminium phosphide mixed with Ammonium carbonate and Paraffin. After exposure to the atmosphere, the pellets decompose and release the active substance, hydrogen phosphide (PH_3), which has the same specific weight as air, and is thus evenly distributed in the fumigated material or chamber. Phosphine is also able to penetrate bags, carton boxes and other containers.

It must be borne in mind that fumigation particularly repeated fumigation, may seriously reduce the vigour and viability. This is particularly true for seeds with a higher moisture content of 14 per cent. Seeds with moisture content above 14 per cent should be dried, before fumigation.

Samples of seeds have to be drawn at fortnight intervals and the infestation can be classified as follows based on insects found per kg of sample.

When there is no pest Free

Upto 2 insects Mild

More than 2 insects Severe

The fumigant has to be chosen and the requirement worked out on the following guidelines:

Aluminium phosphide: Three tablets of 3 g each per ton of seed for cover fumigation (only selected blocks of bags)

Twenty one tablets of 3g each for 28 cubic metres, for shed fumigation (entire godown). Period of fumigation - 5 days. The major advantages of Phostoxin are that it lacks residues and does not affect flavor or germination and is easy to handle.

Methyl bromide: Above 5.6°C, methyl bromide is in the gas phase and is available in cylinders similar to those used for cooking gas. Since, it is odorless, other gases such as chloropicrin are sometimes added to facilitate detection of leaks. Because methyl bromide is 3.5 times heavier than air, care has to be taken that it is properly distributed within the goods to be fumigated (fan can be used). The recommended dosage is 20 g/m^3 for 24-48 hrs.

Special safety measures are required, since methyl bromide is absorbed through the skin. It tends to accumulate in commodities which are important whenever repeated fumigation is necessary.

OTHER MEASURES FOR PEST AND DISEASE CONTROL

Once the seed storage is completely free of insects, the most serious source of reinfestation is infested seed which is brought in seed may be brought from the field already infested, or it may be transferred from an infested storage. Such infestation is controlled by fumigation. Rather than fumigating the whole storage, it is better to have a fumigation room, or to fumigate the seed on a concrete floor under a tarpaulin before it enters the main storage room. The fumigation room should have its own door to the outside, and only after fumigation, should the seed be brought in to storage area.

FUMIGATION

Fumigation is effective only in gas-tight storage. Numerous effective fumigants are available. However, there is a small safety margin between the dose that is toxic to insects and a dose that will cause loss of germination or vigour of seed. Reasonably safe fumigants at temperatures below 30° C and seed moisture below 12% are the following (Parking, 1963).

Dosage	Exposure Period
Methyl Bromide 16 to 32 oz per 1000 ft3 (16 to 32 mg per cubic metre)	24 hours
Hydrogen cyanide 32 to 64 oz percent 1000 ft3 (32 to 64 mg per cubic metre)	24 hours
Hydrogen Phosphide 5 to 10 tablets per metric ton of seed (Phostoxin, Phosphine)	3 to 7 Days

It must be borne in mind that fumigation, particularly repeated fumigation, amy seriously reduce the vigour and even the germination capacity of seeds. This is particularly true of seeds with high moisture content. Seeds with moisture contents greater than 14 percent should be dried to below this value before fumigation. A high temperature also increases damage to seeds by fumigants. Hence, fumigation should be used only with entering seeds, and all other measures should be used to maintain insect control in the stored seed. Prophylactic biweekly or monthly fumigation of seed storages can lead to serious germination problems. It is far better to build an insect- proof storage, and make certain that seeds, bags or anything else placed in the storage are insect-free. Ofcourse, if a storage containing much seeds does become infested, then fumigation is required.

NATURAL PRODUCTS USED IN STORAGE

Pest Control

1. Neem products in pest control

- Take required amount of neem, pongamia and vitex leaves and shade dry it till it becomes papery. Seeds are filled up to ¾th of a storage bin and covered with a clean cloth. Mix the above leaves and spread a handfull on the surface of the seeds in the storage bag or bin. This method can also be followed in bigger storage containers.

  Neem oil can be mixed with the seeds at the rate of 2% by the weight of the seed. Using oil is more effective than the leaves.
- Seeds can be stored by mixing with Neem oil (2-3 ml / kg of seed). 50 kg gunny bags of any seeds need 150 ml of the oil for mixing.
- Neem seed powder can be mixed at the rate of 1% to the volume of the seed. This is practiced for the control of khapra beetles, rice weevils etc. which is found in storage.
- Mix 30 gms of ginger rhizome powder and 50 gms of neem kernel powder with 1 kg of any of the pulse variety such as cowpea, soyabean, redgram etc.

- The following practice is a traditional measure followed by several farmers for storage pest control. Spread the leaves of Neem and Pungam layer by layer over a cloth placed in a vessel for 1/4 feet. Then fill the vessel with seeds up to the surface level and cover it with a thick layer of sand to prevent pest attack.
- Seed coat of Mahua *(Madhuca latifolia)* @ 1-1.5 kg per kg of paddy seed is mixed before storage.

2. Other plant products in pest control

- Mix 50 grams of custard apple seed powder with 1 kg of any of the pulse variety like soyabean, cowpea, redgram, etc., to prevent the attack of the pulse beetle.
- Mix the seeds of Maize, Wheat etc., with dried fruits and leaves of *Vantulsi* (wild Tulsi - *Ocimum*) at the ratio of 1:100 to prevent from the weevils in storage.
- Store cereals and millets in bags or baskets made from the date palm fronds and after mixing it with neem leaves and ash. Plaster the top portion with cow dung to prevent the entry and spread of insects.
- Mix blackgram seeds with mustard oil @ 10-15 ml per kg of seeds and store it in earthen pots covered with dry cloth.

3. Wood ash in storage pest control

Wood ash is a safe and effective pest control material. Mix equal quantity of seed and wood ash to prevent the attack of beetles and other storage pests. *Lantana camara* leaf ash is very effective against pests attacking the sprouts of stored potato.

INSECT TRAPS FOR STORAGE GODOWN

Timely detection of storage pests plays a major role in the control measures. In order to detect the insects the following traps developed by the Tamil Nadu Agricultural University, Coimbatore can be used in the storage godowns.

1. TNAU insect probe trap
2. TNAU pit fall trap
3. TNAU 2 in 1 trap for pulse beetle
4. Indicator device
5. Automatic insect removal bin

1. TNAU insect probe trap

The insect trap should be kept in paddy or wheat bags vertically with the plastic cone downside. The round red cap should be placed at the level of the seed or grain. Insects will move towards air and enter into the main tube through the holes. Soon after its entry, it falls into the white detachable cone at the bottom, which can be unscrewed once a week to remove the insects. This trap can be placed on top of 6 inches of the seed or grain, where the insect activity is more during initial stage of storage. It can remove nearly 80% of the insects within 10-20 days.

2. TNAU pit fall trap

This trap is easy to handle and looks like a top. Top of the trap has minute 3 mm perforations and a cone shaped bottom. The inner side of the cone is coated with a sticky material to hold the trapped insects. This trap should be kept immersed in the storage structure and once the insects enters into it will get trapped in the sticky material.

3. TNAU 2 in 1 model trap

This trap contains the perforated tube, collecting tube, cone shaped pit fall trap, perforated lid and bottom tapering cone. It is suited for trapping the pulse beetles

4. Indicator device

It consists of a cone shaped perforated cup with a lid at the top. The cup is fixed with a container coated with a sticky material. Before storing pulse or cereals, 200 gms of the material should be taken in the cup. If it has any pest infestation, pests start emerging and slip into the trapping container. By observing the pest in the container, stored materials in the main storage can be sundried. 3mm perforated cups can be used for pulses and 2 mm cups for cereals.

5. TNAU Automatic insect removal bin

The storage bin has as outer container, inner perforated container, collection vessel and a lid. Seeds or grains can be stored in the inner container and the space between the inner and outer covering is well aerated. Insects enter the perforation and reach the aerated area. They fall into the collection vessel and can be removed. This type of bin can be used for storing paddy and pulses to get rid of storage pests like rice weevil, lesser grain borer, red flour beetle, saw toothed beetle etc. This type of bin is available in 2, 5, 25, 100 and 500 kg capacities.

RODENT CONTROL

Rats live in all our dwelling places. They eat food grains and seeds that are stored in the house and also in the storage godown. They shed droppings on the grain while they are eating it and can also spread diseases like plague, rat fever etc., in human beings which are quite dangerous. There are a variety of rats which cause damage to stored products. They are the house rat, house mouse, Norway rat, smaller bandicoot and larger bandicoot. A variety of physical, mechanical and cultural techniques can be followed for its control. Percentage of damage caused by rodents during storage is 2.50%.

PHYSICAL METHODS

Rat Proofing

The rat problem can be solved to a great extent if the entry of rats is prevented in houses, stores and godowns. This can be done by building rat proof godowns. The following should be kept in mind while constructing or selecting godowns.

- Godowns should be away from habitation.
- They should be constructed on higher plinth area.
- The godown should be a concrete structure.
- Trees or its branches should not be overhanging on the godowns' roof.
- Metal or wire mesh should be fitted on all windows, ventilators, gutters and drains.
- The manholes should be covered properly.
- The clearance between door and floors should not be more than ¼ inch. The door should also be provided with a 9 inch metal sheet lining at the bottom.
- The foundation of the storage place should be 3 feet above the ground level.
- Walls and floors should be plastered with smooth cement. Any rat hole which is observed must be immediately closed with cement and if the hole is big enough it should be filled with glass pieces.

  Automatic door closers should be provided to prevent the rat entry.
- Regular sanitation and inspection of godown is essential for effective rat control.
- Water stagnation close to the godown should be avoided.
- Hygiene and sanitation
- Timbers, bricks, papers, leaves or any rubbish material near the storage godown should be removed well before storage and cleaned.
- Empty storage containers should be cleaned then and there or removed from the storage godown immediately.

MECHANICAL TRAPS

In case of storage godown wooden cage or mice cage can be used for the control of rats. Bait is used in the trap to attract the rat to come into the trap. Bait may be any food like pieces of meat, dried fish, bread etc., that rats like to eat. Rats like the bait when it has sugar, molasses, or some sweet food, dry fish, coconut piece, onion etc. Check the trap or cage daily and make sure the bait is still there. Once the rat is caught into it, dip the cage into water to kill the trapped rat. After every usage, wash the trap thoroughly before next usage.

RODENT MANAGEMENT IN STORE HOUSES

Provide of wire mesh to windows, ventilators, drains and leave no gaps to doors. Use rodent baits with multi dose or anticoagulant rodenticides. The bait may be prepared as follows:

- Cereal flour 450 g
- Any edible oil 10 g
- Powdered jaggery 15 g
- Anticoagulant or rodenticide such as coumarin 25 g

Replace the consumed bait daily. If needed the single dose or acute poison bait may be prepared as follows:

- Food material 97 g
- Edible oil 1 g
- Zinc phosphide 2 g

Before providing the poisoned zinc phosphide bait, the plain or non-poisoned bait are to be provided for two or three days to make the rats accept the bait.

Indigenous methods of rat control

- Place unripe papaya fruit pieces in the corner of the storage godown. When rats eat these fruits, the mouth tissues get damaged due to the chemical substance in the papaya fruit.

  For one room, we can keep 2-3 pieces of the fruit.
- Take 2-3 kg of castor leaves and add 3 litres of water. Boil for half an hour and filter the extract. Take 2-3 kg of sorghum seeds and add it to the above extract. Boil it again for half an hour. Take these seeds in a vessel and keep it in the corner of the storage rooms.

  Rats feed on these and die.

CONTROL OF BIRDS AND MICROORGANISMS

Bird Control

About 0.85% of loss of grains at storage level is caused by birds. Birds cause appreciable damage in fields and also in stores. They are also responsible for spoilage, contamination with excreta, feathers and dead bodies in fields and godowns. They create a great nuisance and unhygienic condition in warehouses. Godowns can be made bird proof by equipping windows, ventilators and other entries with wire meshes. Strips of nylon or polythene can also be used for scaring birds near the godowns. Remove the nests of the house sparrow or pigeon found near the storage area.

Attack by Microorganisms and their Control

Various micro organisms affect stored grains such as fungi, bacteria, yeast, actinomycetes and protozoa. Out of all these microorganisms fungi is responsible for maximum damage/spoilage of seeds in storage. When a fungus is present, it causes off odour, kernel discolouration, loss of nutritive value and loss in viability. Fungi may also produce certain poisonous substances which are harmful and may be fatal to human beings, animals, poultry etc.

The environmental conditions that favours the development of fungi are, Moisture content above 12%. A temperature of 30-32°C. The degree to which the grain/seed has been previously infected with fungi. The amount of foreign matter such as dirt, dust, chaff etc., present in the stored product. Oxygen content in the storage godown and the condition of the seed stored.

Control Measures

Moisture content of the seed/grain should be reduced to a safe level. By doing this the chances of fungal growth is minimized. The safe level of moisture content for wheat and rice are 12% and 13% respectively. Reduction of moisture content can be done either by sun drying or with the help of grain dryers. Reduction of temperature to a range of 23°C – 30°C helps in the reduction of storage fungal growth. The best ways to avoid damage from microorganisms during storage are, to clean the food grains/seeds before storage. The seeds and food grains should be dried to an optimum level before storage. The food grains should be placed in receptacles where moisture increase is minimum during rainy season. The godowns should also beaurated on sunny days.

REFERENCES

Parimala, K., Subramanian, K., Mahalinga Kannan S. and Vijayalakshmi. K. 2013. Seed Storage Techniques - A Primer. Centre for Indian Knowledge Systems (CIKS), Chennai, 1-25.

Rajasri, M. and Kavitha, K. 2015. Storage Pests Attacking Stored Seeds and their Management. Rashtriya Krishi, 10(1): 1-5.

http://agritech.tnau.ac.in/seed_certification/seed%20storage_purpose.html

http://ecoursesonline.iasri.res.in/mod/page/view.php?id=17880

https://naldc.nal.usda.gov/download/CAT87208646/PDF

http://www.agriquest.info/seed_storage.php

http://www.fao.org/3/ad232e/AD232E07.html

http://agritech.tnau.ac.in/seed_certification/Seed%20Storage-sanitation.html

http://eagri.org/eagri50/GPBR112/pdf/lec30.pdf

https://hasanuzzaman.weebly.com/uploads/9/3/4/0/934025/seed_storage.pdf

http://agritech.tnau.ac.in/seed_certification/seed%20Storage_Storage%20factors.html

http://agritech.tnau.ac.in/seed_certification/seedtech_seed_seedstorage.html

http://agritech.tnau.ac.in/seed_certification/seed%20storage_Packing%20materialsI.html

http://eagri.org/eagri50/GPBR112/lec30.html

https://seednews.com.br/edicoes/artigo/1829-seed-storage-potential-edicao-julho-2009

Pages: 83-94

Seeds and Food: ***Processing and Storage Techniques***
Edited by: **Dr. Prasann Kumar and Dr. Pawan Kumar 'Bharti'**
ISBN: 978-93-88854-41-2
Edition: **2020**
Published by: **Discovery Publishing House Pvt. Ltd., New Delhi (India)**

4

Physiological Attributes of Sorghum

Prasann Kumar[1,2*], Shipa Rani Dey[1]

GRAPHICAL ABSTRACT

Keywords: Attributes, Crop, Physiology, Sorghum

INTRODUCTION

Sorghum is considered as the most significant crop in arid and semi-arid regions of the world. Globally it occupies around 45 million hactares

[1] Department of Agronomy, School of Agriculture, Lovely Professional University, Jalandhar - 144 411 (Punjab) (India)

[2] Divison of Research and Development, Lovely Professional University, Jalandhar - 144 411 (Punjab) (India)

with Africa and India accounting 80% of the global acerage. INTSORMIL (International Sorghum and Millets Research) program is an important driver for invest of its resource in physiological research of sorghum. The recent idea on the growth model of the sorghum development has been an ongoing attempt in several centers at the global levels.

Seed Germination and Seedling Establishment

We have observed that, there is a drastic mismatch between the germination percentages of the seed planted in the lab condition and field condition. It depends on the nature of germination, emergence and seedling establishments of the plants. Blum, 2013, reported that only 33% to 51% of sorghum seed planted in the field will transform into an established plant and others remain unable to attain the whole plant stature (Figure 4.1).

Fig. 4.1: Germination potential of sorghum seeds in Petri plates

Source: Photographed by Prasann Kumar

Dormancy

This is the resting period of the plants or plant parts. Seed dormancy is the delayed germination of the freshly harvested seeds. It is a very common phenomena frequently observed in the sorghum. Clark *et al*, in the year 1968, reported that seed pericarp and tests may contain the germination inhibitor and which lead to the dormancy in the sorghum and when this pericarp was removed from the seed surface then it is observed that germination rate will enhance. Dormancy in seed is associated with ABA because the hormone can be detected in both developing and mature seeds and is proved to be inhibited when applied exogenously. In general dormancy is defined in a functional sense. Seeds that do not germinate given optimal conditions of temperature, water and oxygen are considered dormant, whereas those that do germinate are considered non-dormant. Broadly, seed dormancy is divided into two basic types: primary dormancy, acquired during seed development and maturation whereas, secondary dormancy results from factors after the seed is shed. It is reported that in some seeds the secondary dormancy is caused by accumulation of ABA in the seed embryo (Figure 4.2).

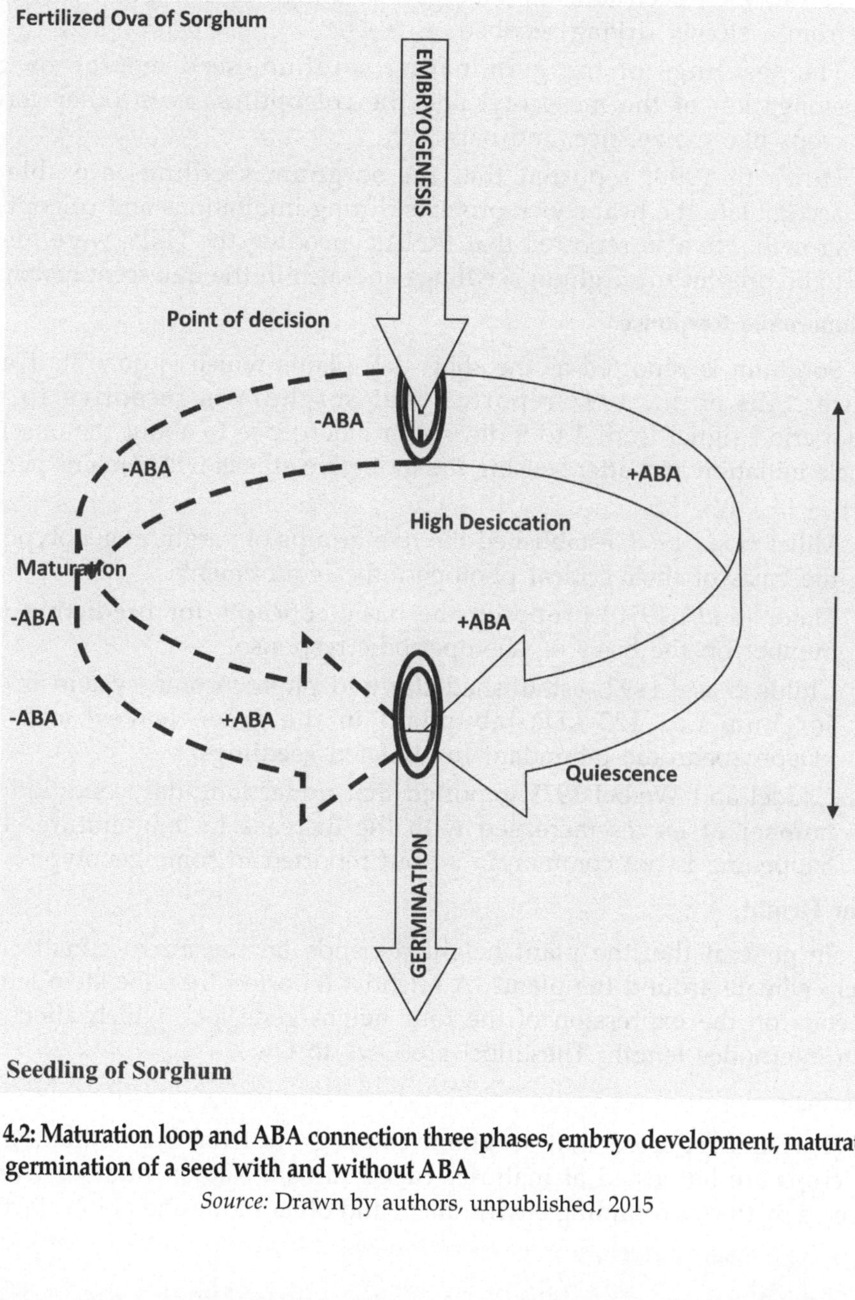

Fig. 4.2: Maturation loop and ABA connection three phases, embryo development, maturation and germination of a seed with and without ABA

Source: Drawn by authors, unpublished, 2015

- The optimal content of moisture in the sorghum seed is around 8% to12%.
- In general, the maximum rate of sorghum germination has been reported to be around 30ºC to 35ºC.
- It is observed that, sorghum is planted in wet soil and emergence is totally dependent on stored water in the soil. In this condition, the germinating seed and the emerged seedlings must capture moisture from a slowly drying seedbed.
- The seedlings of the germinating sorghum seed emerge by the elongation of the mesocotyl and the coleoptiles, as in other cereal crops like maize, rice, and oats.
- Howarth 1990, reported that the sorghum seedlings are able to accumulate the heat shock proteins during imbibitions and coleoptiles growth. He also reported that tRNAs encoding the HSPs were found to be present in sorghum seedlings and also in the quiescent embryos.

Photoperiodic Response

Sorghum is reported as the short day plants which is quantitative in nature. Ellis *et al.,* 1997 reported that sorghum is receptive to the photoperiod signal from 4 to 9 days after emergence to about the onset of panicle initiation and after sensing the inductive effects will remains persist about 4-14 days.

- Miller *et al.,* 1968, established the five groups of sorghum genotype on the basis of their critical photoperiodic requirements.
- Major *et al.,* 1990, proposed the basic concepts for predicting leaf number on the basis of photoperiodic response.
- Childs *et al.,* 1992, established the two phytochrome system in the sorghum i.e., 123 kDa [abundant in the green leaves] and 126 kDaphytochrome [abundant in etiolated seedlings].
- Caddel and Weibel 1971, reported that under long day condition the number of leaves increased with the increase in temperature. This happening is not common in all but reported in some genotypes.

Plant Height

In general the, the plant height depends on the micro climate and macro climate around the plants. A scientist reported that, the stem length depends on the expression of the four height gene loci, which affect the stem internodes length. These loci are Dw1 to Dw4.

Tillering

Farmers reported that sorghum can regrow from basal tillers after the crops are harvested at maturity called ratoon. Ratoon number will be affected by the surrounding environment and other biotic and abiotic factors.

Tillers initiation depends on the photoperiods and temperatures. Conditions of the soil also affect the tillering capacity of concern plants. GA3 application exogenously will inhibit the tiller initiation.

Leaf Structure and its Role in Sorghum

Sorghum is C4 plant hence Krantz anatomy will be observed in the cross section of the leaf. The general physiological features of the leaf are high photosynthesis rate, low photorespiration, high water use efficiency, light saturation at higher irradiance and the adaptation of the plant metabolism to warm climate.

- Krieg and Hutmacher (1986) observed that the relative amount of leaf internal to external CO_2 concentration in sorghum was 0.58 to 0.60 in field- grow plant under semiarid conditions.
- Downes (1970) found that photosynthesis still proceeds at a low rate at 15°C.
- The higher amount of wax is found at the surface of the leaves of the sorghum so it's called waxy bloom.
- Ebercon *et al.* (1977) reported that the deposition of the waxes on the leaf lamella is genetically controlled and responsible gene is the *Bm* gene.

Growth of Roots and its Function in sorghum

Crown roots of the sorghum are initiated from buds in the basal stem internodes. Their growth rate will vary according to environment and genetic factors (Figure 4.3).

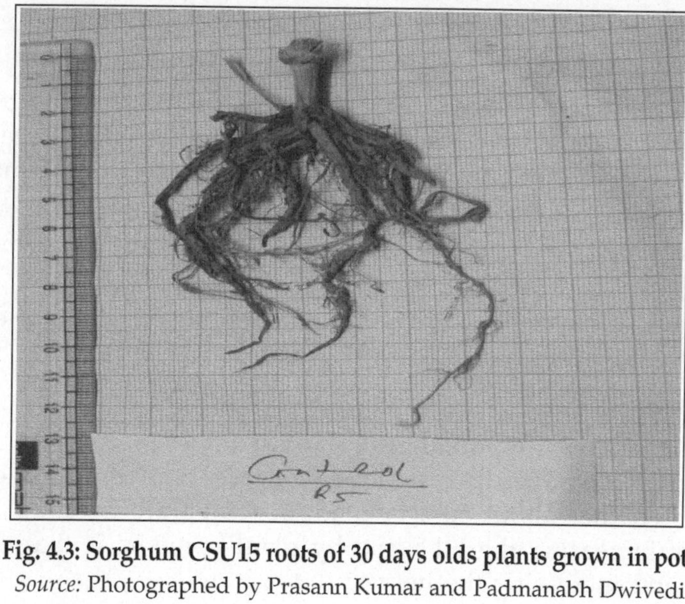

Fig. 4.3: Sorghum CSU15 roots of 30 days olds plants grown in pots

Source: Photographed by Prasann Kumar and Padmanabh Dwivedi

- Blum *et al.*, 1977, reported that root initiation rate is cyclical and it reaches the rate up to 1.5 roots per day.
- Wilson 1988, reported that the effect of the most common environmental factors, such as water, available nutrients, perception of light and ambient CO_2 concentration, root growth can be explained reasonably well by its relationship to shoot growth.

Canopy of the Sorghum

The productivity of the plants can be measured by the dry matter produced by the above ground part of the plant. Accumulation of the dry matter produced is the function of radiation intercepted by the canopy and its efficiency of conversion. Partitioning of assimilates into different economic plant parts will determine the total amount of the dry matter invested in that particular economic part. The final canopy architecture of the sorghum canopy can be measured by the leaf number per plant, leaf size, leaf senescence and density of the plant and their stratification in the field.

- Leaf Area Index will impart the maximum contribution in total solar interceptions.
- Jackson 1993, reported that the root may have a role in affecting shoot senescence. He suggests that soil conditions may be sensed by the shoot via. three major endogenous plant hormones, which are produced in the root, such as ABA, Ethylene and Cytokinins.
- A scientist reported that the maximum LAI of sorghum is normally around 4 to 6 m^2m^{-2} and it may reach up to 10 m^2m^{-2} in sorghum planted under higher density and higher fertile soil.

Biomass Accumulation

This is universally accepted that the growth curve of the plants followed the sigmoid curve. Similarly sorghum displays the typical sigmoid growth curve. Before the heading the Leaf Area Index will be maximized.

- Reduced rate of LAI after its achieving the heading is dependent of its genotypes used and surrounding stresses of the biotic and abiotic approaches.
- The stem dry weight of the sorghum continues to increase even after the heading and grain maturity (Vietor and Miller, 1990).

Harvest Index

Blum *et al.*, 1991, reported that Harvest Index in sorghum may vary about 6% in tall and mature African landraces and Prihar and Stewart 1991, reported that about 50% in modern temperate hybrids. The basic principle of increasing the HI using by plant breeders is that decreasing the height and increasing the harvest index.

Differentiation of Panicle and their Growth

Mature panicle of the sorghum can be identified by one feature like it consists of whole of primary branches arises from each internodes of the panicle rachis.

- Total number of grains in a panicle can be determined by three parameters such as number of branch whorls, number of primary branches per whorl, and the number of grains per primary branches. It reported that, the grains per branch are normally the highest in the basal whorls and it decreases acropetal (Blum, 1970).
- Temperature extremes are a reported cause of male sterility. In sorghum it is reported >42°C (Stephens and Quinby, 1933).
- A whole grain mass per panicle can be determined by the grain number and weight per grain.
- Wilson 1975, reported the negative association between grain number per panicle and weight per grain in sorghum.
- Within the grain the endosperm cell division is completed at about 10 to 12 days after anthesis.
- The exponential growth phase of the grain is after endosperm cell division and maximum accumulation of the starch will occurs in this phase.
- Eastein 1993, reported that the physiological maturity of the sorghum grain can be established by the dark placental region at the end of the grain (Figure 4.4).

Fig. 4.4: Mature panicle of sorghum of 120 days ready for harvest
Source: Photographed by Prasann Kumar and Padmanabh Dwivedi

The stalks of the sorghum are rich in juice, which can be processed into sugar, jiggery or distilled to produce ethanol for the biofuel production. It is estimated that, the yield of the biofuel per hectare per year is higher for sweet sorghum. In general, we want to share one thing that, two main approaches are currently used in biofuel production from ethanol/or alcohol: one is direct fermentation, which depends on the conversion of the plant materials into biofuel especially ethanol. In this approach, there are two ways are available for production of ethanol. First is, degradation of plant materials into sugars and finally sugars will be converted into alcohol. This is considered as the highly active part of the biofuel production. Second approach is indirect fermentation, i.e., through pyrolysis. One thing very interesting to say that, depending on the starting material converted to sugars, biofuel research could be divided into two different generations. The first generation biofuel use agricultural crops to produce simple sugars, which are subsequently converted to ethanol. The second generation biofuel use specific native, perennial growing plants that requires no cultivation, or entire prairie system flora for sugar and eventually ethanol production. The use of photosynthetic algae to produce biodiesel has been often been referred to as the third-generation biofuel. It is clear that, besides the sorghum, several others are also used for the production of biofuel.

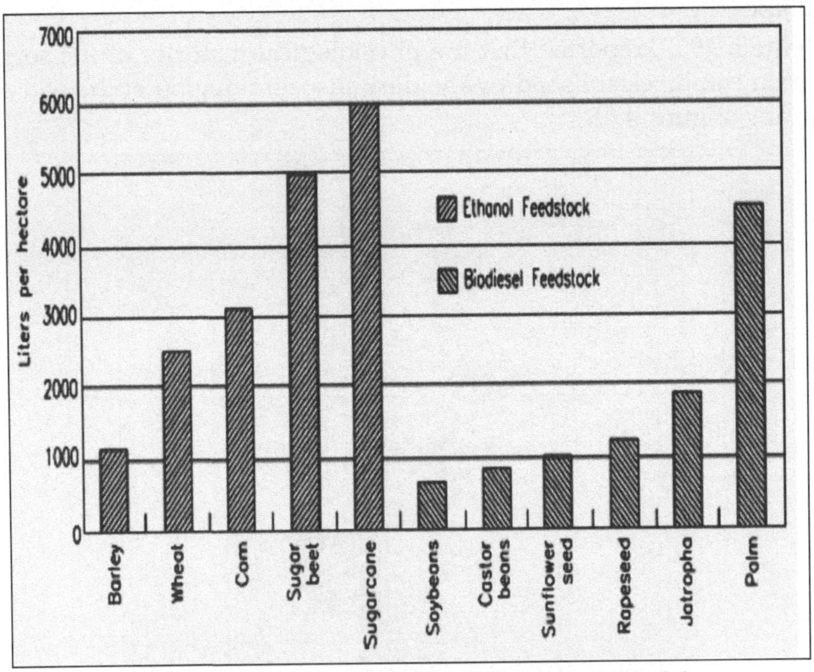

Fig. 4.5: Yield per hectare of the different raw materials use for the attainment of bio-ethanol and biodiesel

Source: Earth Trends. Global biofuel trands, 2007

Conversion of sorghum biomass feed stocks to liquid fuels such as ethanol requires a number of basic unit operations including pretreatment, enzyme production, hydrolysis, fermentation and ethanol recovery. Figure 4.5, gives the detailed account of steps necessary for the conversion of lignocelluloses biomass to ethanol and utilization of intermediates products. In general, the lignocellulosic biomass consists of three main structural units: cellulose, hemicelluloses and lignin. Scientist reported that the conversion of lignocellulosic biomass to alcohol is more difficult as compared to starch based feedstocks. Biomass to ethanol research emphases on reduced costs which requires improved cellulose and hemicelluloses conversion to sugar, combined xylose and glucose fermentation, lower pretreatment combined xylose and glucose fermentation, lower pretreatment energy requirement (Figure 4.6).

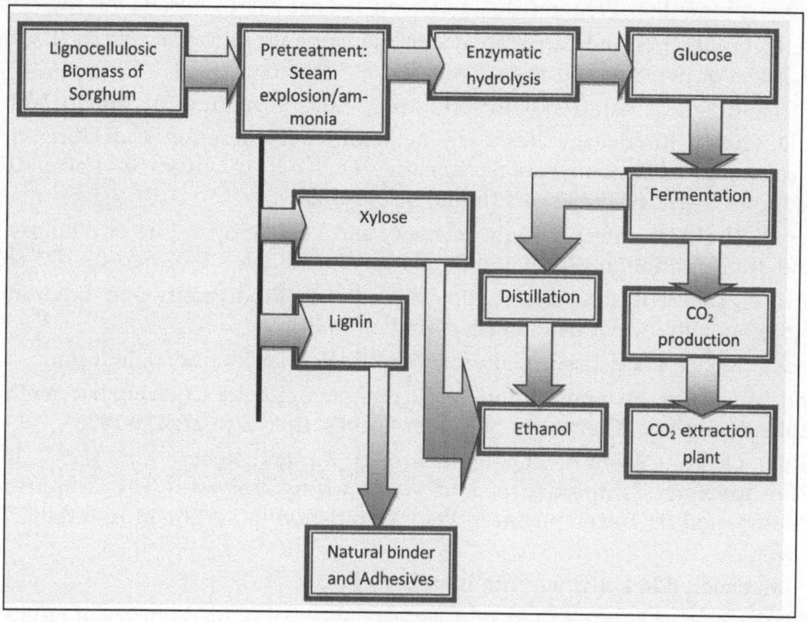

Fig. 4.6: Schematic diagram of conversion of lignocellulosic biomass to ethanol

Source: Naik *et al.*, 2010

CONCLUSION

The stalks of the sorghum are rich in juice, which can be processed into sugar, jiggery or distilled to produce ethanol for the biofuel production. It is estimated that, the yield of the biofuel per hectare per year is higher for sweet sorghum. In general, we want to share one thing that, two main approaches are currently used in biofuel production from ethanol/or alcohol: one is direct fermentation, which depends on the conversion of the plant materials into biofuel especially ethanol. In this approach, there are two ways are available for production of ethanol.

REFERENCES

Berstein, L., Bosch, P., Canziani, O., Chen, Z., Christ, R., Davidson, O., Hare, W., Huq, S., Karoly, D., Kattsov, V., Kundzewicz, Z., Liu, J., Lohmann, U., Manning, M., Mastsuno, T., Menne, B., Palutikof, J., Parry, M., Qin, D., Ravindranath, N., Reisinger, A., Ren, J., Riahi, K., Rosenzweig, C., Rusticucci, M., Scheider, S., Sokona, Y., Solomon, S., Stott, P., Souffer, R., Sugiyama, T., Swart, R., Tirpak, D., Vogel, C., Yohe, G. and Barker, T. (2007). Climate Change 2007: Synthesis Report. Inter-governmental panel on Climate change Secretariat, Geneva, Switzerland.

Blum, A. (2013). Sorghum Physiology. In Ed.Nguyen, H.T. and Blum, A. 2004. Physiology and Biotechnological Integration of Plant Physiology. CRC Press 2004.

Caddel, J.L. and D.E. Weibel (1971). Effect of Photoperiod and Temperature on the Development of Sorghum. Agrono. J., 63: 799-803.

Childs, K.L., M.M. Cordonnier-Pratt, L.H. Pratt and P.W. Morgan (1992). Genetic Regulation of Development in *Sorghumbicolour* VII Ma3R Flowering Mutant Lacks a Phytochrome that Predominates in Green Tissue. Plant Physiol., 99: 765-770.

Clark, L.E., Collier, J.W. and Langston, R. (1968). Dormancy in *Sorghumbicolor* (L.) Moench. II. Effect of pericarp and testa. Crop Sci., 8: 155-158.

Cuff, D.J. and Young, W.J. (1980). In: US Energy Atlas. Free Press/McMillan, New York.

Deka, D. (2004). Bio-energy Resource Availability, Production and Utilization. In: *Biodiversity and Environmental Biotechnology*, Dwivedi P, Dwivedi SK, Kalita MC (eds). Jodhpur: Scientific Publishers (India), pp. 462-480.

Downes, R.W. (1970). Effect of Light Intensity and Leaf Temperature on Photosynthesis and Transpiration in Wheat and Sorghum. Australlian J. Biol. Sci., 23: 775-882.

Dwivedi, P., Dwivedi, S.K. and Kalita, M.C. (2007). Biodiversity and Environmental Biotechnology. Scientific Publishers (India), Jodhpur.

Dwivedi, P. (2004). Plant Tissue Culture. Scientific Publishers (India), Jodhpur.

Ebercon, A., Blum, A. and Jordan, W.R. (1977). A Rapid Colorimetric method for Epicuticular Wax Content of Sorghum Leaves. *Crop Sci.,* 17: 179-180.

Ellis, R.H., Qi, A., Craufurd, P.Q., Summerfield, R.J. and Robert, E.H. (1997). Effect of Photoperiod, Temperature, and Asynchrony between Thermoperiod and Photoperiod on Development to Panicle Initiation in Sorghum. Ann. Bot., 79: 169-178.

Energy Statistics, (2012) (Nineteenth issue).

F.S.I. (1992). State of Forest Report 1991. Forest Survey of India, Ministry of Environment and Forest, Dehradun, India.

FAO, (2008). FAOSTATS [www. fao.org/metadata].

Fargione, J., Hill, J., Tilman, D., Polasky, S., Hawthorne, P. and Jason (2008). Land Cleaning and the Biofuel Carbon debt. *Sci.,* 319 (5867): 1235-1238.

Fitter, R. (1987). "Wildlife for Man". Excerpts. IUCN Special Report 18(1-3): 8-9.

Gahukar, R.T. (2011). Food Security in India: The Challenge of Food Production and Distribution. *J. Agric. Food Inf.,* 12(3-4): 270-286.

Gahukar, R.T. (2012). New Source of Feed Stocks for Biofuels Production: Indian Perspectives. *J. Petro. Technol. & Alternative Fuels,* 3(3): 24-28.

Hester, A. (2006). A Fresh Approach to US Energy Security and Alternative Fuels: The Western Hemisphere and the Ethanol Option. The Center for International Governance Innovation, Waterloo, Ontario, Canada. <http://www.cigionline.org/>

Howarth, C.J. (1990). Heat Shock Proteins in Sorghum and Pearl Millets-ethanol, Sodium Aresenite, Sodium Malonate and the Development of Thermotolerance. *J. Exp. Bot.*, 41: 877-883.

http://dolr.nic.in/wasteland.htm

Huber, G.W. and Corma, A. (2007). Synergies between Bio-and Oil Refineries for the Production of Fuels from Biomass. AngewChemInt Ed 46, 7184-201.

IEA (2007). World Energy Outlook. International Energy Agency, Paris.

IPCC (2007). Mitigation of Climate Change: Technical Summary. Inter Governmental Panel on Climate Change, Geneva.

Jackson, M.B. (1993). Are Plant Hormones involved in the Root to Shoot Communication? *Adv. Bot. Res.*, 19: 103-187.

James, W.E., Jha, S., Sumulong, L., Son, H.H., Hasan, R., Khan, M.E., Sugiyarto, G. and Zhai, F. (2008). Food Prices and Inflation in Developing Asia: Is Poverty Reduction Coming to an End? Asian Development bank, Manila, Philippines., http://www.adb.org/Documents/report/food-prices-inflation/food-prices-inflation. Pdf>

Ker, R.A. (1998). The Next Oil Crisis Looms Large- and Perhaps close. *Sci.*, 21: 1128-1131.

Koh, L.P. (2007). Potential Habitat and Biodiversity Losses from Intensified Biodiesel Feedstock Production. *Conserv. Biol.*, 21: 1373-1375.

Koh, L.P. and Ghazoul, J. (2008). Biofuels, Biodiversity and People: Understanding the Conflicts and finding Opportunities. *Biol. Conserv.*, 141: 2450-2460.

Krieg, D.R. and Hutmacher, R.B. (1986). Photosynthesis Rate Control in Sorghum: Stomatal and Nonstomatal Factors. *Crop Sci.*, 26: 112-117.

Kumar, P. and Dwivedi, P. (2011). Land Use Policy is the Key Driver for Biodiversity Management. *Intl. J. Agric. Environ. Biotech.*, 4(4): 291-297.

Major, D.J., Rood, S.B. and Miller, F.R. (1990). Temperature and Photoperiod Effects Mediated by the Sorghum Maturity Genes. *Crop Sci.*, 30: 305-310.

Miller, F.R., Barnes, D.K. and Cruzado, H. (1968). Effect of Tropical Photoperiods on the Growth of Sorghum when Grown in 12 Monthly Plantings. *Crop Sci.*, 8: 499-502.

Naik, S.N., Goud, V.V., Rout, P.K. and Dalai, A.K. (2010). Production of First and Second Generation Biofuels: A Comprehensive Review. *Ren. Sust. Ene. Rev.*, 14: 578-597.

Pacala, S. and Socolow, R. (2004). Stabilization Wedges: Solving the Climate Problem for the Next 50 Years with Current Technologies. *Sci.*, 305: 968-972.

Pate, R., Hightower, M., Cameron, C. and Einfeld, W. (2007). Overview of Energy – Water Interdependencies and the Emerging Energy Demand on Water Resources. Report SAND 2007-1349C.

Planning Commission, (2003). Report of the Committee on Development of Biofuel. Planning Commission, Government of India, New Delhi.

Prihar, S.S., and Stewart, B.A. (1991). Sorghum Harvest Index in Relation to Plant Size, Environment and Cultivar. *Agro. J.*, 83:603-608.

Raneses, A.R., Glaser, L.K., Price, J.M. and Duffield, J.A. (1998). Potential Biodiesel Markets and their Economic Effects on the Agricultural Sector of the United States. *Indu. Crops Prod.*, 9: 151-162.

Ravindranath, N.H. and Hall, D.O. (1995). Tree Plantation as Source of Fuelwood. In: *Biomass, Energy and Environment*. Oxford University Press, U.K., pp. 36-37.

Ravindranath, N.H., Lakshmi, C.S., Manuvie, R. and Balachandra, P. (2011). Biofuel Production and Implication for Land use, Food Production and Environment in India. *Energy Policy*, 39: 5737-5745.

Righelato, R. and Spracklen, D.V. (2007). Carbon Mitigation by Biofuels or by Saving and Restoring Forests? *Sci.*, 317 (5840): 902.

Righelato, R. and Spracklen, D.V. (2007). Carbon Mitigation by Biofuel or by Saving and Restoring Forests? Sci., 317: 902.

SBSTTA12 (2007). Recommendation XII/7- Biodiversity and Biofuel Production. Secretariat, CBD, Paris.

Sharma, D., Subramanian, B. and Arunachalam, A. (2010). Bioethanol Production from Lemnagibba L. *Curr. Sci.*, 98: 1162-1163.

Singh, B.P., Panigrahi, M.R. and Ray, H.S. (2000). Review of Biomass as a Source of Energy for India. *Energy Sour.*, 22(7): 649-58.

Stephens, J.C. and Quinby, J.R. (1933). Bulk Emasculation of Sorghum Flowers. *J. Ame. Soc. Agron.*, 25: 233-234.

TERI (2008). National Energy Map for India: Technology Vision 2030. Office of the Principle Scientific Adviser, Government of India, New Delhi.

UNEP-GRID

Vietor, D.M., Miller, F.R. and H.T. Cralle, H.T. (1990). Nonstructural Carbohydrates in Axillary Branches and Main Stem of Senescent and Nonsenescent Sorghum Types. *Crop Sci.*, 30: 97-100.

Von Braun, J. and Pachauri, R.K. (2006). The Promises and Challenges of Biofuels for the Poor in Developing Countries. IFPRI, Washington DC.

Wilson, J.B. (1986). A Review of Evidence on the Control of Shoot: Root, in Relation to Model. *Ann. Bot.*, 61: 433-449.

Wood, J. and Hall, D.O. (1994). Bioenergy for Development: Technical and Environmental Dimensions. *Environment and Energy Paper 13*, Food and Agricultural Organization of the United Nations, Rome.

World Energy Assessment, (2002). UNDP/UNDESA/World Energy Council.

Worldwatch Institute, (2006). Biofuels for Transportations: Global Potential and Implications for Sustainable Agriculture and Energy in the 21st Century. Worldwatch Institute, Washington DC, USA.<http://cgse.epfl.ch/webdav/site/cgse/shared/Biofuels/Biofuels/Biofuels fro transport- worldwatchlnstitute and the German Government pdf.

Youssef, N., Simpson, D.R., Duncan, K.E., Mcinerney, M.J., Folmsbee, M. and Fincher, T. (2007). In situ Biosurfactant Production by Bacillus Strains Injected into a Limestone Petroleum Reservoir. *Appl. Environ. Microbiol.*, 34: 1239-47.

Pages: 95-127

Seeds and Food: ***Processing and Storage Techniques***
Edited by: **Dr. Prasann Kumar and Dr. Pawan Kumar 'Bharti'**
ISBN: 978-93-88854-41-2
Edition: **2020**
Published by: **Discovery Publishing House Pvt. Ltd., New Delhi (India)**

5

Advances in Seed Preservation Techniques

R. Sridevi

INTRODUCTION

Seed is the basic unit in agriculture. Good quality seed will respond to other inputs. Seed has to be preserved with initial seed quality until it is planted. During preservation high seed germination, vigour and viability of the stored products have to be maintained. Longevity of stored seed is affected by a number of environmental factors. The three major factors are, seed moisture content, temperature and oxygen concentration in the storage environment. The effective preservation of seeds depends on their moisture content and the storage temperature.

The ability of seed to tolerate moisture loss allows the seed to maintain the viability in dry state. Storage starts in the mother plant itself when it attains physiological maturity. After harvesting the seeds are either stored in ware houses or in transit or in retail shops. During the old age days, the farmers were used farm saved seeds, in little quantity, but introduction of high yielding varieties and hybrids and modernization of agriculture necessitated the development of storage techniques to preserve the seeds.

To cope with the current and future demand of the increasing population for the food grains, it is emphasized to reduce the loss of seeds during and after harvest. Seeds are stored for varying periods to ensure proper and balanced public distribution throughout the year. Post harvest losses in India are estimated to be around 10 per cent, of which the losses during storage alone are estimated to be 6.58 per cent. But, with the advent of improved agricultural technology, the producer can afford to store the seeds for longer period with minimum loss.

Assistant Professor, Imayam Institute of Agriculture and Technology, Trichy, Namakkal - Thuraiyur Rd, Kannanur - 621 206, Tamil Nadu (India)

There are many factors that can narrow down the gap between potential and farm level yield. Among them, use of quality seed is the most important one (Ahmad, 2001). As quality seeds ensure better germination as well as better yield. But if the seed is inferior quality crop failure is unavoidable. To the farmers, for satisfaction crop production, a high quality seed is not only desirable but is also a satisfactory requirement in developed countries. Although seed quality is governed by genetic make-up, but commonly the quality of seeds is deteriorated during storage period. Seed storage and retention of seed viability is always an important consideration in agricultural practice. Poor storage condition gives rise to deterioration of seed quality and the resultant loss of viability. Poor storage conditions greatly affect seed vigour. Vigour of seed at the time of storage is important factors that affect storage life. The most important biotic and abiotic factors that affect seed quality are relative humidity, temperature insect and fungus. Due to high relative humidity seed sets equilibrium at high percentage of moisture. Higher temperature and higher moisture percentage increase respiration. Staying in this condition the seed lose germination. As a result the quality of the seed becomes bad and the seed is unusable for production.

Storability of seeds is mainly a genetically regulated character and is influenced by quality of the seed at the time of storage, pre-storage history of seed (environmental factors during pre and post-harvest stages), moisture content of seed or ambient relative humidity, temperature of storage environment, duration of storage and biotic agents (Khatun *et al*, 2009; Biabani *et al*, 2011). Damage of seed during storage is inevitable. These environmental conditions are very difficult to maintain during storage. The seed storage environment highly influences the period of seed survival. After planting of deteriorate seeds, seedling emergence may be poor and transmission of pathogens to the new crop may occur. Lower temperature and humidity result in delayed seed deteriorative process and there by leads to prolonged viability period (Mohammadi *et al*, 2011).

Assuming a good storage environment, the most practical way to further extend the storage life of seeds is to begin with seed of the highest possible vigour. Seed storage reduces vigour more than viability. The danger in long term storage is that damage can occur to the seed which is undetectable by germination tests under favourable conditions. This is dangerous for sowing purpose since the ability of the seed to resist stress is impaired. Factors affecting seed vigour include genetic background, the process of seed development, and handling during harvest and storage conditions and length (Bhaskaran *et al.*, 2005).

However, the sensitivity of seeds to accelerated ageing is tightly dependent on temperature and on their water content. At a constant temperature, loss of seed viability is faster with increasing moisture content, a key factor in seed longevity. At the cellular level, seed ageing is associated with various alterations including loss of membrane integrity, reduced energy metabolism, impairment of RNA and protein synthesis, and DNA degradation (Kibinza *et al.*, 2006). During storage, a number of physiological and physicochemical changes occur, termed aging. The rate at which the seed aging process takes place depends on the ability of seed to resist degradation changes and protection mechanisms, which are specific for each plant species.

Seed deterioration during storage is a gradual and inevitable process causing considerable losses. Seeds tend to lose viability and vigour during storage and information on storability of seed lots from harvest until the next planting season and also for carry over purposes is of immense importance in any seed production programme. Availability of good quality seed of parental lines is essential for any successful hybrid seed production. Seed mycoflora has been recognized as an important factor responsible for deterioration in quality of seeds during storage (Gupta and Aneja 2004). Hence, an understanding of how best these seeds can be stored at a relatively low cost with minimal deterioration in quality for periods extending over one, two or more seasons will be of great interest to the seed industry. Seed longevity depends upon a number of factors such as the genetic constitution, initial seed quality, storage environment, packaging material and pre-storage seed treatments. It has been ascertained that pre-storage treatments protect the seed from microbial infestation and also enhance the storage potential of seeds (Gupta 2003; Jakhar *et al.*, 2003).

Seed deterioration is inexorable and the best that can be done is to control its rate. Many factors contribute to the predisposition for seed deterioration. These include genetics where certain seeds are inherently longer lived than others. Seed structure can also influence seed deterioration. Simple differences in seed size can mean that smaller seeds with a greater surface area to volume ratio are more exposed to uptake of water that would make them prone to deterioration more than larger seeds.

During storage, seed moisture content and temperature are responsible for seed deterioration, many physiological and biochemical changes occur in seeds during seed ageing. Deteriorative changes enhance when seed exposure to external challenges increases and decrease the ability of the seed to survive. It is an undesirable attribute of agriculture. Annual losses due to deterioration can be as much as 25% of the harvested crop. It is one of the basic reasons for low productivity (Shelar *et al*, 2008). The process has been described as cumulative, irreversible, degenerative and inexorable process (Kapoor *et al*, 2011). Many physiological and biochemical changes occur in seeds during seed ageing. Some of the physiological changes have been observed during seed deterioration which is measures of seed vigor in many species during storage. The biochemical changes associated with seed deterioration is the increase in leakage of biomolecules, decrease in total soluble sugars and protein content where as amino acids and protease activity increases with seed deterioration but decrease in α- amylase activity has been reported in some species. As seed deterioration increases, seed performance progressively decreases. The physiology of seed deterioration is a distinguish consequence from seed development and germination. Losses in seed quality occur during field weathering, harvesting and storage. Several factors contribute to the susceptibility for seed deterioration. The basic causes are temperature, relative humidity, seed moisture content and by invasion of and damage to tissues by microorganisms and insects.

ADVANCED SEED PRESERVATION TECHNIQUES

Some of the advanced seed preservation techniques are:

- Modified atmosphere storage
- Controlled atmosphere storage
- Permafrost storage
- Ultradry storage
- Vacuum storage
- Cryopreservation

MODIFIED ATMOSPHERE STORAGE

Modified atmosphere is a common technical definition that describes the practice of modifying the composition of the internal atmosphere of a package in order to improve the shelf life. The modification process often tries to lower the amount of oxygen (O_2), moving it from 20% to 0%, In order to slow down the growth of aerobic organisms and the speed of oxidation reactions. The removed oxygen can be replaced with nitrogen (N_2), commonly acknowledged as an inert gas, or carbon dioxide (CO_2), which can lower the pH or inhibit the growth of bacteria.

Research to develop use of modified atmosphere with high levels of carbon dioxide (CO_2) as a possible substitute for chemical fumigants like methyl bromide and phosphine has gained emphasis because of the growing concerns about pesticide residues. Use of modified atmosphere with elevated levels of CO_2 has been considered as one of the safest methods to control storage pests. The use of this technique has been in practice in developed countries as early as in 1975. Nowadays consumers demand for more natural and high quality products. The supplying high quality products can be achieved by using an appropriate harvest technology and, most of all, the suitable technology of storage. A major cause of stored products degradation and deterioration are insect pest and microorganisms. Many studies have shown that modified atmosphere of elevated carbon dioxide and depleted oxygen is effective method against insect and microorganisms attacks seeds in storage.

Modified atmosphere (MA) reduces the respiration rate of seeds and activity of insects or microorganisms in seeds. The MA can be achieved in several ways: (i) by adding gaseous or solid CO_2, (ii) by adding a gas of low O_2 content or (iii) by allowing metabolic processes within an airtight storage to remove O_2, usually with associated release of CO_2 (Jayas *et al.* 2002). The effectiveness of modified atmosphere for controlling various stored products pests depends on the temperature and moisture content of the seeds, species and life storage of pests, gaseous composition and uniformity of gas distribution and exposure time of the MA treatment (Lukasiewicz *et al.* 1999).

There are many researches involving prediction of insects and microorganisms in storage seeds, e.g. Bera *et. al.* (2004) reported that complete control of *Rhyzopertha dominica* and *Corcyra cephalonica* in storage seeds was achieved with 20% concentration of CO_2. The 5 and 10% CO_2 concentration also reduced the insect population growth and seeds damage as compared to ambient storage. The researchers also have shown no adverse effect on germinability and vigour of seeds. Modified Atmosphere (MA) using carbon dioxide (CO2) is one of the methods which have been successfully used to preserve the seeds from deterioration by insect-pests and microbes (Jayas and Jeyamkondan, 2002). It also preserves grain quality and maintains high level of germination in the stored grain (Bera *et al.*, 2008). Low O2 and elevated CO2 atmospheres have been used for many years to control insect pests in grains (Bell, 2000) but its effect against fungi needs elucidation. MA storage has no toxicological risk and is environmentally clean. In chickpea all the modified atmospheric gaseous combinations viz., C2 [CO2 (80%) + N2 (20%) + O2 (0%)], C3 [CO2 (75%) + N2 (20%) + O2 (5%)], C4 [CO2 (70%) + N2 (20%) + O2 (10%)] and C5 [Vaccum packing] maintained seed viability above Indian Minimum Seed Certification Standards (IMSCS) for 14 months. Further, this technology can be used an alternative to chemicals which is safe, ecofriendly particularly beneficial in the absence of cold storage facility and in addition it can be used for maintaining quality of organically produced seeds and its storability (Shinde and Hunje, 2019).

PRINCIPLE

The principle behind modified atmosphere technologies is to reduce the rate of respiration, reduce microbial growth, and retard enzymatic spoilage by changing the gaseous environment surrounding the food product. This is achieved by reducing the concentration of oxygen (O_2), which is required in respiration, or by adding an inhibitory gas such as carbon dioxide (CO_2) or carbon monoxide (CO). The balance between O_2 and CO_2 is critical, and an optimal ratio is required for each specific product. Also, in MA storage the composition of the atmosphere surrounding the product is generally created and maintained by the interaction of the commodity's respiration with the permeation of respiratory gases through the packaging material. Modified atmosphere conditions can also be established and adjusted by pulling a slight vacuum and replacing the package atmosphere with a desirable gas mixture, which can be further, adjusted through the use of O_2, CO_2, or ethene (C_2H_4) absorbers.

METHODS FOR CREATING AND MAINTAINING MA

The reduction of O2 levels inside an enclosed space (storage room or polymeric film package) can be achieved biologically through respiration of the food product, or it can be obtained by replacing the atmosphere of the storage space with the desired gas mixture. In the first case, the reduction of O_2 to levels of 2 to 3% may require up to 25 days and depends on the characteristics of the commodity and the degree to which the storage room is airtight or the gas permeability characteristics of the packaging film. When a non-biological or active modification system is used, O_2 can be reduced to levels of 2 to 3% within hours. It has been shown, for some commodities, that a shorter O_2 reduction or pull-down period results in better post storage quality. Rapid O_2 pull-down or rapid CA requires the shortest possible time for crop harvest, room loading, product cooling, room closure, and O_2 reduction. Rapid O_2 reduction is obtained by either N_2 flushing or catalytic combustion. In addition, O_2 absorbers may be used, especially in MA storage. There are a wide variety of O_2 absorbers, e.g., dithionite, ascorbic acid, alkali containing glucose, H_2 gas in the presence of palladium catalyst, and iron-based products. Most commercially available O_2 absorbers utilize iron oxide (FeO), which becomes iron oxides (Fe_2O_3 and Fe_3O_4) and hydroxides ($Fe(OH)_2$ and $Fe(OH)_3$) after absorption of O_2. From the reaction mechanism of the O_2 absorber(s) and volume of the storage space, it is possible to determine the amount of FeO needed to lower the concentration of O_2 to approximate desired pre-chosen values. Modified atmosphere packages are dynamic systems where respiration and permeation occur simultaneously. In order to achieve and maintain a satisfactory atmosphere within a package, the rates of CO_2 production and O_2 consumption by the food product must be equal to diffusion rates of the respective gases through the package at a given temperature. Factors affecting respiration of produce in the package include mass and type of food product, temperature, O_2 and CO_2 partial pressures, ethylene levels, and light. Factors affecting gas permeability through the package include type, thickness, and surface area of the packaging film, as well as temperature, relative humidity, and gradient of CO_2 and O_2 in the sealed package.

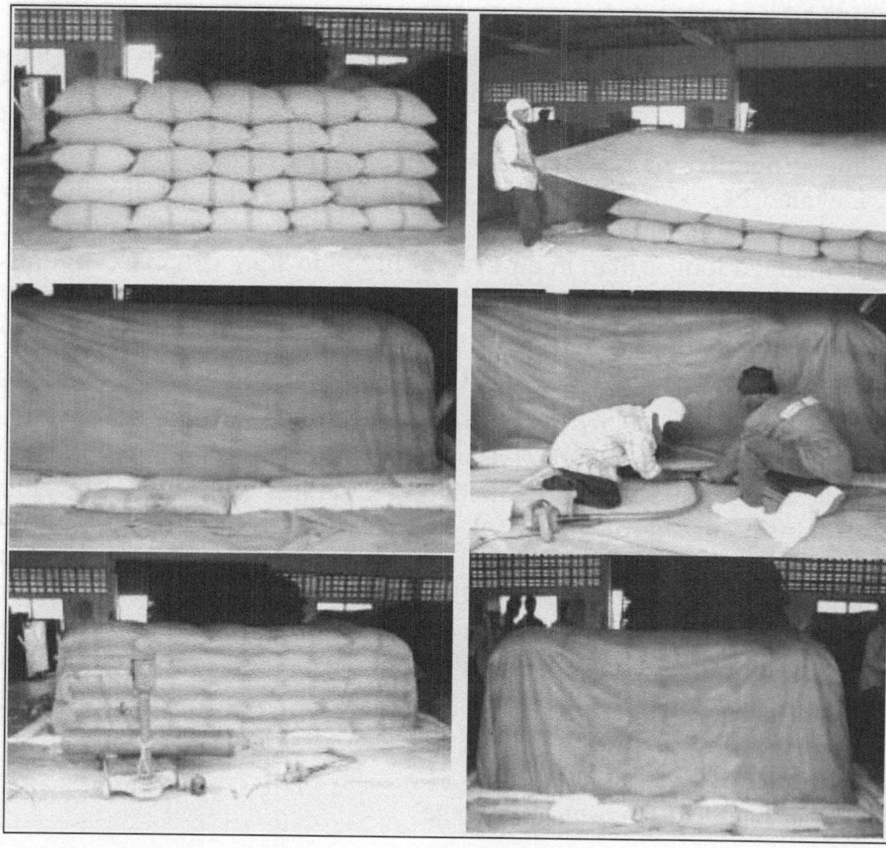

QUALITY CHANGES UNDER MA STORAGE

Seed Viability

Seeds can be stored for relatively long periods without a loss in viability, with a decreasing scale for longevity in oats, rice, barley, wheat, triticale, rye, sorghum and corn. The main factors that affect longevity are moisture and temperature with each 1% increase in seed moisture content (MC) halving the life of seed. This rule applies when seed moisture content is between 5 and 14%. Below 5% MC the speed of aging may increase because of auto-oxidation of seed lipids and above 14% MC storage fungi kill the seed. Also, for each 5°C increase in seed temperature, the life of seed is halved (from 0 to 50°C). The presence of O_2 decreases seed germination, even at low partial pressures in dry grain because of membrane damage caused by the production of free radicals and accumulating chromosome damage.

NUTRIENT CHANGES

A controlled atmosphere of 97 to 98% N_2, 1 to 2% CO_2, and 1% O_2 slows hydrolytic processes in the lipids of rice grain compared to grain stored in air. Pure N_2 atmospheres at 20°C stabilize protein and amino acids and the cooking properties of rice at 18.4 and 23.2% MC compared to storage in air. Elevated N_2, with negligible O_2, retain higher gluten quality in stored wheat than storage in air and the milling and baking properties of wheat are maintained longer than in air even at high moisture contents. An anoxic environment (N_2) slows the oxidative activity and better preserves the organoleptic properties of seeds.

FUNGI AND MYCOTOXINS PRODUCTION

Elevated CO_2 (20 to 60%) inhibits fungi and the production of mycotoxins by fungi in stored seeds including T-2 toxin, patulin, ochratoxins, penicillic acid, and aflatoxin. Reduction of O_2 is less effective in preventing mycotoxins than the elevation of CO_2. In dry grain, 20% CO_2 inhibits microflora; in wet grain 80% CO_2 is needed. Some species of Fusarium, Aspergillus, and Mucor are tolerant to high CO_2 levels. In wet grain, at 1 to 2% O_2 and 15 to 40% CO_2, typical microflora were the yeasts Hansenula and Candida (60 to 80% RH) followed by anaerobic fermentation caused by lactic acid bacteria and yeasts (>90% RH). Filamentous fungi gradually disappear during storage. Fungi do not grow at <1% O_2. Yeasts can survive at <0.5% O_2.

Benefits of modified atmosphere storage

- Reduces the activity of insects & microorganisms
- Reduces the respiration rate of seeds
- Maintains high level of germination
- Maintains the natural quality of stored products
- Extending the storage life of seeds

CONTROLLED ATMOSPHERE STORAGE

The use and manipulation of natural components of the atmosphere, e.g. oxygen, N, CO_2, to preserve the seeds is referred as controlled atmospheric storage. Oxygen, carbon dioxide, nitrogen concentrations, temperature and humidity is regulated in the atmosphere. Controlled atmosphere storage (CA) refers to the constant monitoring and adjustment of the CO_2 and O_2 levels within gas-tight stores or containers. CA is most effective when combined with temperature control. Controlled atmosphere storage (CAS) is one of the most important innovations in storage systems as the composition of gas in the storage affects their storage life. The CAS technology involves reduction of oxygen (O_2) and increasing carbon dioxide (CO_2) as compared to the ambient atmosphere. CAS implies continuous monitoring and precise adjustment of these gases within the storage container, to a predetermined level.

Controlled atmospheres can be thought of as a special case of fumigation, where the gases used are normal components of the atmosphere and biological systems. The gases most commonly used are nitrogen to displace oxygen, and carbon dioxide. There are only a few places around the world where controlled atmospheres are used routinely. The main problems with controlled atmospheres are long exposure times (typically 15 days or longer), the need for a high level of sealing, and the large volumes of gas required to establish or maintain concentration of >40% for carbon dioxide and 99% for nitrogen (<1% oxygen). Despite these limitations both types of controlled atmospheres are used where these constraints are not limiting, or where special requirements exist.

Use of controlled atmosphere is either in the form of hermetic storage or in the form of use of externally generated inert gas to displace the intergranular atmosphere of the stored grain. The use of hermetic storage which is very ancient in practice, involves sealing the grain in air-tight containers. Due to the respiration of the grain and due to the metabolic action of insects on their food, oxygen is consumed leaving CO2. The quantity of carbon dioxide found is dependent on the ratio of head space to grain volume and capacity of the structure. Ultimately, the level of oxygen falls raising the level of carbon dioxide and when the level falls to 2%, the insects die due to anoxia or asphyxiation. The death is due to lack of oxygen compounded by the toxic action of CO2. Use of nitrogen or carbondioxide to displace the intergranular air and to maintain the nitrogenous or carbondioxide enriched atmosphere is being experimented and the results revealed a good control of stored product insects. All stages of most of the common major pests are exterminated in this lethal-oxygen poor (less than 2%) atmosphere while the quality of the commodities stored remains much better than of those preserved by chemical methods normally operating in oxygen ambient.

CA UNDER NORMAL ATMOSPHERIC PRESSURE

Gas supply from pressurized cylinders – CA is a modified gas composition, usually produced artificially, and maintained unchanged by adding desired gases (CO, or nitrogen [N^2]), supplied from pressurized cylinders or otherwise. This supplementary introduction of gases is carried out when their concentration in the sealed container drops to below the desired level. The objective of CA treatment is to attain a composition of atmospheric gases rich in CO, and low in O, or a combination of these two gases within the storage enclosure or treatment chamber. These set concentrations are maintained for the time necessary to control the storage pests. A widely used source for production of such atmospheric gas compositions is tanker-delivered liquefied CO_2 or N_2 when the target CA gas composition is <1% O_2 or high CO_2 concentration. For large-scale application of N_2 or CO_2 vaporizers are essential. These vaporizers consist of a suitably designed receptacle with a heating medium (electricity, steam, diesel fuel, or propane), a super-heated coil with hot-water-jacket, and forced or natural draught.

Basic requirements

- Controlled atmosphere systems depend on either depletion of oxygen to asphyxiate Organisms or the addition of carbon dioxide to act directly and kill them.
- A storage structure capable of containing the gas;
- A source of suitable gas or a means of producing the required atmosphere O_2
- A method of maintaining the atmosphere for the required period of time.
- A method of aerating to remove the altered atmosphere after the treatment

Low oxygen atmospheres

- Oxygen deficient atmospheres are produced by flushing a storage with nitrogen
- Liquid nitrogen from tanks may be used As a gas source/
- Exothermic inert atmosphere generators that consume the oxygen to leave principally Nitrogen have been tested and show promilse for insect control.
- These generators burn propone or other hydrocarbon fuel to give an atmosphere of less than I percent oxygen with about 10 percent oxygen with about 10 percent Carbon dioxide and 89 percent nitrogen.

CO_2 atmospheres

- Oxygen can also be removed by the Metabolic activity of micro/ organisms and insects in hermetic storages, thus
- Producing an atmosphere where insects cannot service.
- Insects are generally killed more rapidly by carbon dioxide than they are by lack of oxygen.
- Banks (1979) suggested that an initial level exceeding 70 percent carbon dioxide and maintained above 35 percent for ten days is appropriates for complete insect control at temperatures above 20°C
- The carbon dioxide gas is applied to storage from a vessel of liquid carbon dioxide with appropriate vaporizers and pressure regulators to control flow rate.

Procedures for establishing controlled atmospheres

- Two phases
- Purge phase - The normal Atmosphere is replaced with the prescribed atmosphere
- Maintenance phase - Where the atmosphere is maintained for the desired period of time

Nitrogen atmosphere

Purge phase

- Liquid nitrogen supplied directly from a road tanker with a heat exchanging facility where it is vaporized and brought to ambient temperature.
- It is then passed through a flow meter (e.g) "Rotameter"
- Five cm (2in) I.D.PVC drainage piping can be used to carry the gas a flow of 3m/min(106fit$^{3/}$min) from 300 to 7000 tone capacity, this rate may be increased (e.g.to 8 m^3/min)
- In bins fitted with aeration ducts modified to introduce gas. When gas is introduced directly into the bin at the walls, an increased input rate may be less efficient at lowering the oxygen tension
- In cases where a low efficiency distribution system is used, pockets of air may remain which are not purged directly but in which the oxygen is removed through the slower diffusive and convective faces.
- In these instances a slower purge rate allows these processes to occur and Is not wasteful of gas.
- A vent of at least 50CM (10in)must be left open in the roof during the purge to prevent dangerous pressure build/up
- It is important that the heat exchanging facility is adequate to bring the gas close to ambient (within 2°C)
- Cooling of the grain near the introduction point may result in moisture migrating to the cold area on long storage
- At 3m/min (106 ft$^{3/}$min) 3 forced drought heat exchangers in parallal using 0.4 kW (0.5 h.p.) fans, with an atmospheric exchanger downstream in serious
- O_2 reduced to 1%
- The may be terminated, the top vent and introduction ports closed and maintenance input of gas commenced.
- The nitrogen purge based on the ratio of the seed volume.
- Barley has a higher porosity and will require more nitrogen than wheat
- In one trail with barley where the filling ratio was 0.80, a volume of 1.9m^3 N_2/tonne was consumed.
- At 3m/min the purging of a 2000 tonne bin of wheat takes about 12 hours

Maintenance phase

- After termination of purging, gas input rate is low to maintain the atmosphere
- Input rate was determine by bin capacity, gas tightness and weather
- At the correct rate, with grain temp exceeding ambient ones, the O_2 tension at the base of the bin will rise slightly during the day and fall to about 1% at night.
- If the grain temp is below ambient, if the atmosphere contains more than 3% CO_2, effects seen in headspace, not in base

HERMETIC STORAGE

Hermetic storage is a type of modified atmosphere (MA) that has now been applied for the protection of stored agricultural commodities including cocoa beans, coffee, rice, corn, pulses and seeds. It is also called "sealed storage" or "air-tight storage" or "sacrificial sealed storage" or "hermetic silo storage". This method takes advantage of sufficiently sealed structures that enable insects and other aerobic organisms in the commodity or the commodity itself to generate the MA by reducing the O_2 and increasing the CO_2 concentrations through respiratory metabolism.

One of the oldest forms of food preservation in the world, hermetic storage, provides an airtight, safe and pesticide-free means of storing dry food commodities. However, whilst the oldest form of hermetic grain storage discovered in North Africa and the Middle East involved underground sealed pits, modern methods use large, flexible, plastic envelopes - called Cocoons™ or SuperGrainbags™ - to create a sealed environment where any pests present die from lack of oxygen.

In hot, humid countries, insects, moulds, and rodents can cause storage losses of up to 25 per cent. Large metal or concrete silos commonly used in more temperate climates work poorly due to moisture and condensation problems, so storing grains for long periods of time can prove a challenge. However, with modern hermetic storage, constant moisture content can be maintained. In addition, the low oxygen atmosphere in the container prevents insect damage, development of aflatoxins (a particular problem in groundnuts and maize), and loss of flavour and aroma in crops such as coffee, cocoa, and basmati rice. It also preserves the potential for germination in seeds.

Hermetic storage is a practical technology and can be adapted for the protection of commodities in quantities as small as a conventional grain bag to bulk of many thousands of tonnes. Most importantly, it is user-friendly and environmentally benign, making the use of pesticides and fumigants unnecessary during storage, thus protecting farmers and consumers from the associated risks of chemicals or development of aflatoxins. Hermetic storage (HS) technology has emerged as a significant alternative to other methods of storage that protect commodities from insects and molds. This technology, also termed sealed storage, airtight storage, or assisted hermetic storage, is a form of bio-generated modified atmosphere (MA). HS is based on the principle of generation of an oxygen-depleted, carbon dioxide-enriched interstitial atmosphere caused by the respiration of the living organisms in the ecological system of a sealed storage. Among the advantages of hermetic storage, the generation of a MA in an environmentally safe and sustainable manner eliminating the need for chemical treatments, fumigants, and climate control.

The rapid growth in adoption of HS is due to the increasing demand for environmentally safe and sustainable technologies that are simple to use and are now supported by the greater availability of scientific information and field experience. Some HS units are characterized by their ease of installation, rodent protection, favorable costs, ease of relocation, and very modest requirements for infrastructure.

Hermetic storage has provided a successful storage method for protection of commodities without fumigants or need for refrigeration for insect control and quality preservation of stored products. Hermetic storage is achieved in specially constructed plastic structures for the preservation of cereal seeds and other commodities. Plastic structures suitable for long-term storage systems, as well as intermediate storage of seed have been developed and applied. These storage systems based on the hermetic principle were designed for storage at the farmer cooperative and small trader level with 10 - 1000 tonnes capacity for enclosing stacks termed Cocoons, small scale storage suitable for small portable containers of 60 kg to 2 tonnes called SuperGrainbag and quality preservation, insect control and prevention of condensation during shipment of commodities in shipping containers known as TranSafeliners.

Successful use of hermetic storage is based on the need to achieve the following goals:

- Low oxygen, high carbon dioxide atmosphere to prevent infestations (molds and insects), and oxidation

- Preventing entry of moisture
- Protection from rodents
- Preservation of Germination and Vigor in Stored Seeds
- Quality Preservation – Aroma and Flavor

Hermetic storage is sustainable; it is user-friendly and it is an environmentally benign technology that does not necessitate the use of chemical pesticides (Villers *et al.* 2001). The technology can be adapted to the protection of commodities in sizes ranging from that of conventional grain bag size to many thousands of tons.

PRINCIPLES OF HERMETIC SEED STORAGE

Hermetic storage is a technology that enables farmers to store their own seed for long periods without loss due to insects and without using any insecticides. The technology consists of enclosing seed in air-tight containers that prevent or minimize gas exchange. Insect aerobic respiration depletes O2 and increases CO2. Insect feeding ceases, and therefore insects begin dying (Murdock *et al.,* 2012). There is no need for insecticides. Additionally, hermetic storage can impede the growth of fungi as these organisms also need oxygen to proliferate (Quezada *et al.,* 2006). This technique can maintain seed quality for up to one year of storage.

Hermetic storage is based on the principle of generation of oxygen depleted, carbon dioxide-enriched interstitial atmosphere caused by the respiration of the living organisms in the ecological system of a sealed storage. A sufficiently low oxygen and elevated CO_2, atmosphere is created through a natural metabolic process based on insect respiration and, in cases where the commodity has sufficiently high moisture, the respiration of the microorganisms within a sealed storage system. Applications for which hermetic technology has been most widely accepted are long-term storage of cereal grains, primarily rice, corn, barley, wheat and a variety of seeds to preserve germination potential and vigor and quality preservation of high-value commodities such as cocoa and coffee.

Humidity and managing moisture can be challenge. Hermetic storage locks in and locks out moisture. Adequate drying of seed prior to storage is not a problem in the dry climate, but can be a major problem in the humid tropics, especially during the first season harvest. In the humid tropics, simple moisture meters can be used to quantify seed moisture prior to storage. Seed must be dry prior to storage, approximately 12-14% moisture. Drying seed is a real challenge in the humid tropics. High moisture contents in hermetically stored grain such as maize can lead to loss in germination and viability and thus dryness must be ensured (Weinberg *et al.,* 2007). Hermetic storage can also keep seed dry in the event of flooding.

The simplicity and profitability of hermetic storage are resulting in significant adoption, but it cannot be assumed that farmers are already employing this technology everywhere and correctly. It is therefore important to emphasize both necessary (drying, proper sealing, avoiding bag puncture risk) and unnecessary practices (insecticide supplements) in hermetic storage education.

Types of Hermetic Storage Systems

A hermetic storage system can be made from specially designed PVC containers such as:

- Cocoon™- commercially available
- the GrainSafe™
- the smaller 50kg IRRI Super bags - available to farmers and processors at low cost
- locally available containers - useful in rural settings, where local containers can be easily converted into hermetic storage systems

The size of hermetic storages can range from 3 liters to 2,000 tons. They can be used for paddy, brown rice, and other cereal crops such as maize and also coffee. Larger hermetic systems have also been used with milled rice.

PERMAFROST STORAGE

The world's seed collections are vulnerable to a wide range of threats - civil strife, war, natural catastrophes, and more routinely but no less damagingly, poor management, lack of adequate funding, and equipment failures. Unique varieties of our most important crops are lost whenever any such disaster strikes, and therefore securing duplicates of all collections in a global facility provides an insurance policy for the world's food supply.

The global seed vault on permafrost (a layer of soil that is permanently frozen in very cold regions of the world) is an answer to provide the best possible assurance of safety for the world's crop diversity, and in fact the idea for such a facility dates back to the 1980s. However, it was only with the coming into force of the International Treaty on Plant Genetic Resources, and an agreed international legal framework for conserving and accessing crop diversity, that the seed vault became a practical possibility.

It was designed as an impregnable deep-freezes to protect the world's most precious seeds from any global disaster and ensure humanity's food supply forever. But the Global Seed Vault, buried in a mountain deep inside the Arctic Circle, has been breached after global warming produced extraordinary temperatures over the winter, sending meltwater gushing into the entrance tunnel. The vault is on the Norwegian island of Spitsbergen and contains almost a million packets of seeds, each a variety of an important food crop. When it was opened in 2008, the deep permafrost through which the vault was sunk was expected to provide "failsafe" protection against "the challenge of natural or man-made disasters".

IN THE EVENT OF GLOBAL DISASTER, THE ULTIMATE CROP BACKUP SYSTEM

LOCATION

The Svalbard Global Seed Vault (Norwegian: *Svalbard globale frøhvelv*) is a secure seed bank located on the Norwegian island of Spitsbergen near the town of Longyearbyen in the remote Arctic Svalbard archipelago, about 1,300 kilometres from the North Pole. The facility preserves a wide variety of plant seeds in an underground cavern. The seeds are duplicate samples, or "spare" copies, of seeds held in genebanks worldwide. The seed vault will provide insurance against the loss of seeds in genebanks, as well as a refuge for seeds in the case of large scale regional or global crises. The seed vault is managed under terms spelled out in a tripartite agreement among the Norwegian government, the Crop Trust, and the Nordic Genetic Resource Center (NordGen).

HISTORY

The history of Svalbard Global Seed Vault starts as early as 1983.The first initiative for the creation of a safety deposit for seeds in permafrost was taken by the Nordic Genetic Resource Centre (NBG) as early as the early 80s. Svalbard, along with Greenland and the Jotunheim mountains, was assessed as a possible location at an early date. NBG visited Svalbard in 1983 and it was eventually decided to store seeds 300 metres inside a disused mine, mine 3, near Longyearbyen, where there was permafrost of minus 3-4 degrees.

NBG's positive experience of Svalbard led to the question of similar safety deposits being taken up by the International Board for Plant Genetic Resources (IBPGR) and the UN's Food and Agriculture Organisation and a meeting between the board and the Norwegian authorities was arranged.

In 1989 IBPGR started surveying the relevant alternative sites in Svalbard. Norway offered to take care of the actual construction of the vault, while FAO and IBPGR would take care of 3 the administrative operating costs through the creation of a fund based on capital from external donors.

After the FAO's International Treaty for Plant Genetic Resources for Food and Agriculture came into force in 2004, a group of Nordic and international experts under the direction of Noragric at the Norwegian University of Life Scientists (UMB) were appointed to carry out a preliminary study. In September 2004 the group put forward an unambiguously positive report, which concluded that suitable locations were to be found in Svalbard. In November 2004 the report was presented at FAO's Commission for Genetic Resources for Food and Agriculture.

The Norway government backed the initiative and in 2005 an interdepartmental steering group was set up for the project, consisting of the Ministry of Agriculture and Food (LMD), the Ministry of the Environment (MD), the Ministry of Foreign Affairs (UD), the Ministry of Justice (JD) and the Consumer and Administration Ministry (FAD). Statsbygg, as constructor, also participated on the steering group as an observer. The group is chaired by and has its secretariat in the LMD. Planning commenced in autumn 2005 and building commenced in May 2007. The facility was inaugurated on 26th February 2008.

MISSION

The Svalbard Global Seed Vault's mission is to provide a safety net against accidental loss of diversity in traditional genebanks. While the popular press has emphasized its possible utility in the event of a major regional or global catastrophe, it will certainly be more frequently accessed when genebanks lose samples due to mismanagement, accident, equipment failures, funding cuts and natural disasters. Such events occur with some regularity. In recent years, some national genebanks have also been destroyed by war and civil strife. There are some 1,400 crop diversity collections around the world, but many are in politically unstable or environmentally threatened nations.

THE PURPOSE

It was the recognition of the vulnerability of the world's genebanks that sparked the idea of establishing a global seed vault to serve as a backup storage facility. The purpose of the Vault is to store duplicates (backups) of seed samples from the world's crop collections. Permafrost and thick rock ensure that the seed samples will remain frozen even without power. The Vault is the ultimate insurance policy for the world's food supply, offering options for future generations to overcome the challenges of climate change and population growth. It will secure, for centuries, millions of seeds representing every important crop variety available in the world today. It is the final back up.

SEED STORAGE

The seeds are stored in four-ply sealed envelopes and then placed into plastic tote containers on metal shelving racks. The storage rooms are kept at –18 °C (–0 °F). The low temperature and limited access to oxygen will ensure low metabolic activity and delay seed aging. The permafrost surrounding the facility will help maintain the low temperature of the seeds if the electricity supply should fail.

Priority for storage will be given to samples of crops that are important for sustainable agriculture and food security. It receives samples from the international genebanks of the Consultative Group on International Agricultural Research (CGIAR), as well as certain national genebanks. The focus will be on safeguarding as much of the world's unique genetic material as possible and on avoiding duplication in seed vault. Among the types of seed samples held at Svalbard will be traditional varieties/landraces, modern varieties, and wild species related to crops.

The Seed Vault has the capacity to store 4.5 million varieties of crops. Each variety will contain on average 500 seeds, so a maximum of 2.5 billion seeds may be stored in the Vault. Currently, the Vault holds more than 980,000 samples, originating from almost every country in the world.

Ranging from unique varieties of major African and Asian food staples such as maize, rice, wheat, cowpea, and sorghum to European and South American varieties of eggplant, lettuce, barley, and potato. In fact, the Vault already holds the most diverse collection of food crop seeds in the world.

The focus of the Vault is to safeguard as much of the world's unique crop genetic material as possible, while also avoiding unnecessary duplication. It will take some years to assemble because some genebanks need to multiply stocks of seed first, and other seeds need regenerating before they can be shipped to Svalbard. A temperature of -18°C is required for optimal storage of the seeds, which are stored and sealed in custom made three-ply foil packages. The packages are sealed inside boxes and stored on shelves inside the vault. The low temperature and moisture levels inside the Vault ensure low metabolic activity, keeping the seeds viable for long periods of time.

FREE OF COST

The Svalbard Global Seed Vault will provide facilities free of cost for safety deposits under "black box conditions" on request from public or private holders of seeds of distinct genetic resources that are important to humanity. Priority will be given to the safety deposit of plant genetic resources of importance for food security and sustainable agriculture.

ACCESS TO SEEDS

Vault seed samples are copies of samples stored in the depositing genebanks. Researchers, plant breeders, and other groups wishing to access seed samples cannot do so through the seed vault; they must instead request samples from the depositing genebanks. The samples stored in the genebanks will, in most cases, be accessible in accordance with the terms and conditions of the International Treaty on Plant Genetic Resources for Food and Agriculture, approved by 118 countries or parties.

The seed vault functions like a safe deposit box in a bank. The bank owns the building and the depositor owns the contents of his or her box. The Government of Norway owns the facility and the depositing genebanks own the seeds they send. The deposit of samples in Svalbard does not constitute a legal transfer of genetic resources. In genebank terminology this is called a "black box" arrangement. Each depositor signs a Deposit Agreement with NordGen, acting on behalf of Norway. The Agreement makes clear that Norway does not claim ownership over the deposited samples and that ownership remains with the depositor, who has the sole right of access to those materials in the seed vault. No one has access to anyone else's seeds from the seed vault. The database of samples and depositors is maintained by NordGen.

The Syrian Civil War caused another seed bank, the International Center for Agricultural Research in the Dry Areas (ICARDA), to move its headquarters from Aleppo to Beirut. Due to difficulties by ICARDA in transferring its collection, in 2015 the Svalbard Vault authorized the first withdrawal of seeds in its history. A second, larger, withdrawal was made by ICARDA in September 2017. ICARDA also continued to deposit duplicate seed samples throughout this time, including returning varieties it had withdrawn and grown in 2015. As of March 2018 these are the only withdrawals from the Svalbard Vault so far.

BLACK BOX SYSTEM

The depositors who will deposit material will do so consistently with relevant national and international law. The Seed Vault will only agree to receive seeds that are shared under the Multilateral System or under Article 15 of the International Treaty or seeds that have originated in the country of the depositor. Each country or institution will still own and control access to the seeds they have deposited. The Black Box System entails that the depositor is the only one that can withdraw the seeds and open the boxes.

ULTRA DRY STORAGE

The concept of ultradry technique was 1st introduced as a measure to reduce or avoid the requirement of refrigeration in germplasm facilities Ultra dry is defined as water content less than 5% water content in equilibrium with 10% RH at 20°C.

Ultra-dry seed storage is a technique for decreasing the seed moisture content to less than 5% and stored at ambient temperatures, it can reduce the cost for constructing and maintaining the genebank and has brought worldwide attention because of its potential economic effect and promising application in germplasm conservation.

Ultra-dry storage, also called low moisture content storage, is a technique for decreasing seed moisture content to below 5-6 per centusing different methods and then stored hermetically at ambient, but preferably cooler temperatures. Some studies have confirmed that low moisture content storage can not only be used to maintain the quality of seeds, but also improve their storability (Wang *et al.*, 2005). It can greatly reduce the cost of constructing and maintaining the gene bank.

When dealing with ultra dry seeds, enormous savings of energy can be made by avoiding the use of too low temperatures during storage. Temperature may be the key factor when seeds are merely dried but it loses relative importance for ultra dried seeds. Ultra dry seeds may be sensitive to O_2 therefore; it is a factor that, at least tentatively, should be taken in to account.

Today facing with the great loss of plant biodiversity around the world, one way to protect is to store the plant seeds in gene bank. The effective preservation of seeds depends on their moisture content and the store temperature (Hsu *et al.*, 2000; Tsou and Mori, 2002), but in developing countries where the costs of cold storage are prohibitive. Low moisture content conservation (it also called ultra-dry seed storage) through longterm storage of seed is possible for a significant proportion of higher plants. Where feasible, long-term seed storage serves as a safe and relatively inexpensive method of plant genetic resources conservation.

A lot of studies have been confirmed that ultra-dry seed storage not only can be used to maintain the quality of seeds but also improve the storability of seeds (Wang *et al.*, 2003). Positive results of ultra-dry storage to improve storability have been reported (Zhu *et al.*, 2001; Huang *et al.*, 2002; Wang *et al.*, 2005; Li *et al.*, 2007).

According to Ellis (1998) maximum longevity is acquired when desiccation takes places at 10-12% RH at 20°C. Desiccation to 2-3.7% moisture content (10% RH and 20°C) did not improve seed viability of several species after 5 and 10 years storage when it was carried out at -20°C, although it improved at 20°C (Hong *et al.*, 2005). Optimal seed moisture for conservation depends on storage temperature (Vertucci and Roos, 1993), for example for pea optimal water content for storage at -20°C would be 0.12 g water/g dry weight, which could be acquired with equilibration at 57% RH at 25°C.

Medium to long-term seed conservation in gene banks as well as the delivery of high quality commercial seed lots under the humid tropical climates are practically impossible without cooling facilities, because seed deteriorates rapidly under the prevailing conditions of high temperature and relative humidity (RH) that causes high equilibrium seed moisture content (MC) (Daniel and Ajala, 2004). But investment in cooling facilities and energy is too cost intensive for economical operation of seed gene banks and for operating sustainable commercial seed industry in the humid tropics.

The problem is further exacerbated by epileptic power supplies in many of the humid tropical countries with developing economies and infant seed industries like Nigeria where these studies were conducted. Low-input storage techniques that can minimize operational costs and technological sophistication associated with cooling will benefit seed storage operations in the humid tropics if workable procedures are investigated and standardized. Thus, considerable research efforts are currently focused on dry storage for low-input seed conservation under ambient humid tropical conditions (Somado *et al.*, 2006; Daniel, 2007). But there is paucity of information on statistical evaluation of potential seed longevity in low input seed storage systems at ambient humid tropical conditions (FAO/IPGRI, 2004).

Dry and ultradry storage at high temperature conditions are recommended technologies for low-input seed storage for several seed types in these climates and specifically for maize. This is because it is cheaper to reduce storage atmospheric RH around the seed (and consequently the equilibrium seed MC) in closed containers than to reduce temperature with cooling facilities. The containerized silica gel storage method should achieve this objective. This study was designed to evaluate the potentials of desiccant aided dry-storage in closed containers (containerized-drystorage) for preservation of seed physiological quality as well as for seed longevity enhancement.

Different Ultra drying methods

- Dry room or drying chamber
- Desiccant - Silica gel/charcoal
- Saturated salts/Lithium Chloride solutions
- Air conditioned room/vehicle
- Incubator drier

DRY ROOM OR DRYING CHAMBER/CABINET

Drying rooms should be fitted with an airlock to minimize moisture entering from outside. A typical dry room, set at 10-15% RH at 10-25°C, will dry seeds of any species and at any mc in about 30 days.

DESICCANT

Seed drying procedures, drying time (~one month) depends on the initial moisture content of the seeds, the amount of seeds and the dryness of the desiccant.

TYPES OF DESICCANTS

The most commonly used desiccants are Silica gel, Activated charcoal, Bentonite and Beads (Zeolites).

Ultradrying with silica gel

- Ultra drying could be achieved following different ways, but perhaps the most practical one might consist of storing the seeds in balance with dehydrated silica gel.
- Leaving some gel afterwards with the stored seeds inside the tight container is most useful because the colored indicator would show any accidental entry of moisture.

Advantages of the use of silica gel

- It provides a practical method to desiccate the seed samples
- It reaches moisture levels of 2-3%, lower than those obtained by most
- It keeps these levels indefinitely in tight containers

- It warms over possible anomalies (i.e. moisture intake) in the container - when a colored indicator.
- It can be regenerated after its use through a new dehydration process with heat.
- It delays also ageing by absorbing toxic gases produced during the process

Saturated salts

Lithium Chloride: at 20°C produces a RH of about 12%

Calcium Chloride: at 25°C produces a RH of about 30%

Air-tight jar with lithium chloride solution, showing plastic mesh support to hold seeds above solution. Only plastic coated metal components should be used as salts may be very corrosive.

Coloured saturation indicators

- Sometimes a humidity indicator is included in the desiccant to show, by colour changes, the degree of water saturation of the desiccant.
- One commonly used indicator is cobalt chloride (CoCl2).
- Anhydrous cobalt chloride is blue.
- When it bonds with two water molecules, (CoCl2•2H2O), it turns purple.
- Further hydration results in the pink hexaaquacobalt chloride complex [Co (H2O)6]Cl2.

Advantages of Desiccant for ultra-drying of seeds

- Provides practical method
- Can dry seeds to a specific and low MC (2-3 %)
- Protected from molds, insects and rodents
- It warns over possible seed desiccation
- Can re-use desiccants
- Real cost saver
- Seed quality is preserved for several years
- It further delays ageing by absorbing toxic gasses -Ethylene
- Used in Humid regions
- Conservation of germ plasm for longer period
- Used for the post-harvest drying and processing industry
- No need for cold storage to maintain seed viability

Disadvantages of Ultra-drying seed storage

- Investment cost is very high
- Separation of desiccants from the seeds is difficult, again it requires labour to separate

- If the colour indicators are not used for ultra-drying may cause overheating and desiccation problem will occur so that the germination percentage of seed will be decreased.
- During regeneration of desiccants, may cause lung diseases if the precautionary measures are not followed.

VACUUM STORAGE

Vacuum packaging refers to packaging in containers which one all air has been removed before sealing. This is actually a form of "Modified Atmospheric" storage. Partial vacuum and such gas as CO_2, O_2 and N_2 on the longevity of various kinds of seed, result from these studies are variable and in some instances appear contradictory. The higher the O_2 content of storage environment the shorter the viability period of seeds. Seed storage condition plays an important role in seed production system. Good storage condition can reduce deterioration rate of seed. Tropical region has high relative humidity that affects on seed storage quality. Seed can be stored only in 3-4 month in uncontrolled atmospheric condition. Seed moisture content, Relative humidity and temperature during storage are responsible for the main effect on seed storage quality.

In high relative humidity, seed moisture content can be increased to equilibrium moisture content by absorbing moisture from the air. The high moisture content seed result high respiration rate, biochemical activities and degradation of storage. Preamjit (1975) found that seed storage at 20°C could maintain their 90 percent germination in 9 months storage while stored the seed at 30°C had only 5-10 percent germination. Effect of moisture content and temperature can regulate the storage ability of the seed. Soybean seed with 7% moisture content in sealed package maintained germination by more than 70 % in comparison to atmospheric storage (Nangju *et al.*, 1980). Seeds deteriorate during prolonged storage. The rate of deterioration for stored seeds depends on the storage conditions such as temperature, seed moisture and oxygen. As storage temperature and seed moisture increase, seeds deteriorate more rapidly. The oxygen tension in storage atmosphere also affects seed longevity, but the effects are variable, depending on crop species and storage conditions. Under aerobic condition, the loss of seed longevity has frequently been related to cellular injury resulting from reactive oxygen species (ROS) attack during storage.

Ellis and Roberts (1981) quantified the relationships and developed equations to estimate seed viability after storage in any environment. Many researchers have also invest igated the effect of air (oxygen), vacuum and other inert gases on seed survival, however, the reported results were variable and sometimes contradictory. Tao (1989) reviewed the literature and concluded that the benefit from vacuum storage is limited and variable; hence it should not be used for conservation by multi-crop genebanks.

Nevertheless, much of the confusion on the effect of various gases and vacuum in previous reports appears to have resulted from lack of appreciat ion of the role of seed moisture content (MC). Ibrahim and Roberts (1983), investigating seed viability in lettuce, found evidence for an interaction between MC and the partial pressure of oxygen at MCs below a critical value (15%), oxygen was found to be deleterious to seed survival, but above this MC the response changed and oxygen increased longevity. Ibrahim and Roberts (1983) also found that the lower the MC below 15%, the greater the relative beneficial effect of excluding oxygen. Eliminating oxygen from storage, therefore, is expected to improve the longevity of seeds, especially at the low MCs (5 ± 2%) used for long-term conservation.

ROLE OF VACUUM SEALING IN EXTENDING SEED LIFE

Vacuum sealing of seeds is an effective way to extend their viability, for two main reasons. First, maintaining seeds under a vacuum keeps humidity out of the storage container, which is very important in areas where humidity is high during at least part of the year (e.g. during rainy season). Secondly, vacuum sealing reduces oxygen levels. Partial or complete removal of oxygen has been found to extend the life of dry, orthodox seeds in storage (Groot *et al.* 2015; Ohlrogge and Kernan 1982). Vacuum reduces exposure of seeds to free radicals, forms of oxygen that damage cells. Reduced oxygen also helps control insect pests in stored seeds. In a 12-month research trial conducted at ECHO's seed bank in Thailand, Lawrence *et al.* (2017) found that the weevil population in vacuum-sealed cowpea seeds stayed low, while weevils rapidly multiplied in non-vacuum-sealed seeds. They concluded that vacuum sealing can be a low-cost way to control seed pests without using chemicals.

Vacuum-sealing is more practical for long versus short-term seed storage. Opening a container or bag of seeds lets air in, eliminating the vacuum. Thus, vacuum sealing could be cumbersome for seed containers that need to be opened frequently (e.g. in response to frequent requests for seeds). For short-term storage, storing seeds in airtight containers—with no vacuum—is better than storing them in paper envelopes or open containers subject to high humidity. [NOTE: Filling an airtight container full of seeds accomplishes the same things as vacuum; humidity is excluded, and oxygen is lowered as air spaces are occupied by seeds. Oxygen can be reduced even further by mixing sand or ash with the seeds. Vacuum is usually easier, though, than keeping multiple containers full of seeds.]

SUITABLE CONTAINERS

Plastic tubes or bags are used with food or commercial vacuum sealers. Plastic works best for smooth-coated seeds like beans; seeds that puncture the plastic cannot be stored in this way. Plastic bags can also be punctured by insects (Thompson 2016). Other good options for vacuum storage include jars, plastic containers, buckets, or pots. Mason jars are an excellent option, because they come in a range of sizes and are available in most places. Gaskets can often be made with strips of rubber to make a container airtight.

Regardless of the material you use, two main factors must be considered:

- Whether or not the container is airtight.
- How easily the container can be connected to a pump or other technology that is used to draw a vacuum.

Technologies for Vacuum-sealing

Air can be removed from a container of seeds in multiple ways. We present several options in the remaining sections of this Technical Note. None is a perfect solution for every context. Consider the following factors when selecting a method for vacuum sealing seeds:

- **Cost and availability of local materials**. Materials that can be found locally are easy to replace and cost less than materials that have to be purchased elsewhere.
- **Level of difficulty**. Aim for an approach that is easy to use and replicate, and that does not require complex modifications.
- **Usage level**. Consider how often you need to vacuum seal seeds, and in what quantity. A functioning seed bank would likely require that a vacuum be drawn on many batches of seeds throughout the year, so a seed bank would probably need a more robust technology than an individual farmer or gardener would need.

Hand operated Vacuum packing system for seed storage

- Vacuum packing system was developed to facilitate the storage of dry seeds.
- Systems providing sealed container with reduced O_2 content.
- It prevents rehydration of seeds, thus extent their viability
- The reduced O_2 content suffocates adult insects that are stored with the seeds
- And also extents the viability of the seeds by slowing down the seed respiration rate.

Advantages of vacuum packaging

- Extents shelf life aids in controlling oxidative rancidity prevent the growth of normal spoilage bacteria, aerobic organism such as *pseudomonas* is suspended and lactic-acid bacteria are favored. The latter can grow to high numbers without causing spoilage.

- Reduced moisture loss and freezer burn prevents movement of water out of the product in to the surrounding head space. Prevents loss of moisture at product surface and eliminates freezer burn.
- Requires minimal storage space package is drawn product taking up minimal space.
- Leakers are easily detected a small puncture in a vacuum pack is easy to detect by looking for loose packages.

CRYOPRESERVATION

The word cryopreservation is derived from the Greek word *kryos*, which means cold. *Cryopreservation* is a method of preserving biological tissue or cells at extremely low temperatures. Although there are many applications of cryopreservation, the most common uses of the process are to preserve sperm, embryos, eggs, and plant seeds. Cryopreservation occurs when tissue is frozen, generally in liquid nitrogen, until it reaches a temperature range of at least -148 degrees Fahrenheit (-100 degrees Celsius). At these temperatures, tissue is preserved in a state similar to that of suspended animation. The metabolic processes of biological tissue slow down dramatically in the extreme cold, which in turn slows down the natural decaying process.

The storage of seeds of many plant species in liquid nitrogen at –196°C is now well developed and applied to agricultural crops and for the purpose of rescue of rare and endangered plant species. First of all, it concerns the orthodox seeds with moisture content of 13-15% and lower. Cryopreservation, i.e., the storage of biological material at ultra- low temperature, usually that of liquid nitrogen (-196°C), is the only technique currently available to ensure the safe and cost efficient long-term conservation of these different types of germplasm. At this temperature, all cellular divisions and metabolic processes are stopped. The plant material can thus be stored without alteration or modification for a theoretically unlimited period of time. Moreover, cultures are stored in a small volume, protected from contamination, and require a very limited maintenance.

Cryopreservation is a methodology that enables the preservation of biological material (viable cells, tissues and organs) in a non-dividing state with almost zero metabolisms. This state is attained through the exposure of the material to ultra-low temperatures as low as -196°C in liquid nitrogen (LN) or in nitrogen's vapor phase at -150°C. At this temperature, molecule movements are drastically reduced, there is no liquid phase in the cells (Vasco, 2003), and all of the metabolic processes such as respiration and enzymatic activity are deactivated, which allows for the assurance of conservation of biological material over long periods because biological deterioration is arrested (Benson *et al.*, 1998). The cells, however, must maintain their structure intact, which will enable them to return to their normal activities after thawing. This technique has been shown to be efficient for the storage of various parts of the plants such as seeds, pollen, somatic and zygotic embryos, and plant parts such as roots, bulbs, tubers, buds, and apical meristems, among others (Bajaj, 1995). It also enables the acquisition of whole plants from cells isolated from plant organs and tissues through the use of tissue culture techniques, leading to the establishment of *in vitro* germplasm banks (Engelmann, 1991).

Seed banking at low temperatures and low moisture contents usually allows the preservation of plant material for long periods of time. However, loss of viability can occur with prolonged storage, depending on species. It has been claimed that biochemical processes are virtually stopped at ultra-low temperatures (liquid nitrogen, -196°C), reducing biological deterioration in seed storage. Cryopreservation could improve cotton seed longevity and, therefore, be an important tool for the genetic resources conservation of this crop. Stanwood & Bass (1978) reported the high germination percentage of *Gossypium hirsutum* L. seeds with moisture content lower than 13% after cryopreservation and rapid thawing.

For the long-term conservation of plant germplasm and cryopreservation, at ultralow temperature (liquid nitrogen, -196°C), is actually the valuable technique. Cryopreservation of biological tissues can be successful only if intra-cellular ice crystal formation is avoided. Crystal formation can be prevented through verification (Sakai, 2000). Two requirements must be met for a cell to vitrify; rapid freezing and a concentrated cellular solution (Panis and Lambardi, 2005). Sugars play a very important role in the acquisition of resistance to desiccation and to freezing in liquid nitrogen (Suzuki *et al.*, 2005, 2006).

A significant advantage of these new techniques is their operational simplicity, since they will be mainly applied in developing tropical countries where the largest part of genetic resources of problem species is located. For many vegetatively propagated species, cryopreservation techniques are sufficiently advanced to envisage their immediate utilization for large-scale experimentation in genebanks. Research is much less advanced for recalcitrant seed species. This is due to the large number of mainly wild species, with very different characteristics, which fall within this category, and to the comparatively limited level of research activities aiming at improving the conservation of these species.

However, there are various technical approaches to explore to improve the efficiency and increase the applicability of cryopreservation techniques to recalcitrant species. In addition, research is actively performed by various groups worldwide to improve the knowledge of biological mechanisms underlying seed recalcitrance. It is hoped that new findings on critical issues such as understanding and control of desiccation sensitivity will contribute significantly to the development of improved cryopreservation techniques for recalcitrant seed species.

A very positive development in the establishment of cryopreservation protocols is that an increasing number of researchers make systematic use of analytical tools (e.g., histo-cytology, differential scanning calorimetry) which provide a scientific basis to the success/failure of an experimental treatment. Such a rational and scientific approach should greatly facilitate the establishment of freezing protocols, especially for problem species. It is important to stress, however, that cryopreservation is not seen as a replacement for conventional ex-situ approaches (Withers and Engelmann, 1998). Cryopreservation offers genebank curators an additional tool to allow them to improve the conservation of germplasm collections placed under their responsibility. In conclusion, it can be realistically expected that in the coming years, cryopreservation will become more frequently employed for long-term conservation of plant genetic resources.

SEED STORAGE

Proper storage of seed is vital to conserving its vigor and vitality. Seeds can last from a few years to centuries, depending on the species and the storage conditions. In general, most seeds stored in cool, dry conditions will survive longer than seeds stored in a wet, warm environment. In many parts of the world, agricultural seeds are stored in bins that are open to the ambient conditions, often resulting in short storage life and poor seed quality in hot, humid regions, as well as losses due to insects and rodents. As the viability period for seeds decreases by half for every 1% increase in seed moisture content or 10°F (~5°C) increase in temperature, sealed bins and controlled environments are used to maintain seed viability for longer periods. A common rule of thumb is that the temperature (in Fahrenheit) plus the relative humidity in the air (in percent) should total less than 100 for satisfactory seed storage.

At seed banks that store seeds to preserve genetic diversity, seeds are dried to optimum moisture content, evaluated for quality and genetic purity and sealed in moisture-proof containers. For short-term storage, seeds are dried and placed in sealed containers at 5°C. They are stored at temperatures below freezing for long-term preservation (0°F or -20°C), including the use of cryopreservation, or freezing in or over liquid nitrogen at -180°C, for extremely long-term storage. But when it comes to seed storage, one size does not fit all. Some species have short-lived seeds that do not tolerate dehydration and are therefore difficult to store. Plants producing these *recalcitrant seeds* must be maintained as living populations, making them vulnerable to loss due to changes in land use or weather patterns. The vigor and viability of seeds stored even at low temperatures declines over time. The continued maintenance of specific seed lines requires that they periodically be removed from storage and used to produce a new crop of seeds. Seed storage facilities therefore need not only modern storage equipment but also the land, personnel and expertise to periodically grow the stored seeds under conditions that maintain their genetic diversity and purity in order to replenish the original seed stock. Thus, core seed repositories such as the U.S. National Center for Genetic Resources Preservation in Ft. Collins, Colorado, are complemented by a number of branch stations in different growing environments to store and replenish seed collections of diverse species. *Recalcitrant seeds* are seeds that do not survive drying and freezing and therefore cannot be stored for long periods of time. Some plants that produce recalcitrant seeds include avocado, mango, lychee and some horticultural trees.

Steps involved in cryopreservation

- Selection of materials
- Addition of cryoprotectant
- Freezing
- Storage in liquid nitrogen
- Thawing
- Washing, reculturing and regeneration

Selection of material

- Seeds
- Pollen
- Protoplast
- Somatic and zygotic embryos
- Apical and lateral buds

- Root, bulbs and tubers
- Cell suspensions
- Meristem/shoot tip cultures
- Calluses

ADDITION OF CRYOPROTECTANT

A cryoprotectant is a substance used to protect biological tissue from freezing damage (i.e. that due to ice formation).

TYPES OF CRYOPROTECTANTS

They are the permeating types such as Ethylene glycol, Glycerol, Dimethyl sulfoxide (DMSO), Propylene glycol and Acetamide or nonpermeating such as high molecular weight compounds like Saccharides (Sucrose, Trehalose, Glucose, and Galactose) and macromolecules (Ficoll, Polyvinyl pyrrolidone).

Freezing

Slow freezing

The selected plant material is taken in the cryo vials.

Two phases:

- **Phase I,** in which freezing is slow and the temperature is reduced at a set rate (1 to 10 °C/min) to values close to -40 °C using a equipment - programmable freezer (cryostat).
- **Phase II,** in which freezing is induced rapidly through direct immersion of the material in LN (-196 °C).

Vitrification

The term vitrification, which means 'turned into glass'

Vitrification is a process of ultra rapid cooling of a solution and transition of water directly from the liquid phase into an amorphous phase or glass, while avoiding the formation of crystalline ice

Thawing/Rewarming

- For the recovery after cryostorage, rapid rewarming is usually required to avoid recrystallisation
- Plunging the vials into water bath at 37-40 degree C for1-2 minutes with vigorous shaking (approximately 180 rpm).

Washing, Reculture/Regeneration

- The thawed culture is washed several times to remove cryoprotectant.
- The cells/tissue/shoot tips may be transferred to the required germination media after thawing for regeneration.
- Mediums – Murashige and skoog, agar medium

- Some special requirements like addition of GA3, activated charcoal, sucrose for regeneration.
- Cultured under diffused light.

Advantages of cryopreservation

- Long term conservation of germplasm.
- Requires less space and little maintenance.
- Conservation of vegetative propagated plants, recalcitrant seeds, rare germplasm or even species threatened with extinction and wild plant species.
- Storage of genetic material with specific characteristics and for genetic improvement programs.
- Storage of germplasm free of pathogens.
- Maintain their genetic stability and phenotypic characteristics.

REFERENCES

Ahmad, S. (2001): Environmental Effects on Seed Characteristics of Sunlower (*Helianthus annuus* L.), *Journal of Agronomy and Soil Science,* 187: 213.

Bera, A., Sinha S.N., Gaur A. and Srivastava C. (2007): Effect of Carbon dioxide Rich Atmosphere on Storage Insects and Fungi, *Indian Journal of Agricultural Science,* 77: 756-761.

Bhaskaran, N., Bharathi, A., Vanangamudi, K., Natesan, P., Natarajan, N., Jerlin, R. and Prabakar, K. (2005): Textbook on Principles of Seed Production and Quality Control, *Kalyani Publishers,* India.

Biabani, A., Boggs, L. C., Katozi, M. and Sabouri, H. (2011): Effects of Seed Deterioration and Inoculation with *Mesorhizobium cicerion* yield and Plant Performance of Chickpea, *Australian Journal of Crop Science,* 5(1): 66-70.

Gupta, A. (2003): Role of Seed Mycoflora in Deterioration of Soybean Seed during Storage under Ambient Conditions. In: Singh, D.P. (Ed.). Implications of Plant Diseases on Produce Quality, *Kalyani Publishers,* Ludhiana, India. pp. 85-96.

Gupta, A. and Aneja, K.R. (2004): Seed Deterioration in Soybean Varieties during Storage-Physiological Attributes, *Seed Research,* 32(1): 26-32.

Jakhar, S.S., Duhan, J.C. and Kharab, R.P.S. (2003): Effect of Fungicide Treatments and Containers on Pearlmillet Seed Storability, *Indian Phytopathology,* 56: 484-485.

Jayas, D.S. and Jeyamkondan S, (2002): PH-postharvest Technology: Modified Atmosphere Storage of Grains Meats Fruits and Vegetables, *Biosyst Eng,* 82: 235-251.

Kapoor, A. (2011): Physiology and Biochemical Changes during Seed Deterioration in Aged Seeds of Rice (*Oryza sativa* L.), *American Journal of Plant Physiology,* 6(1): 28-35.

Khatun, A., Kabir, G. and Bhuiyan, M.A.H. (2009): Effect of Harvesting Stages on the Seed Quality of Lentil (*Lens culinaris* L.) during Storage, *Bangladesh Journal of Agricultural. Research,* 34(4): 565-576.

Kibinza, S., Vinel, D., Come, D., Bailly, C. and Corbineau, F. (2006): Sunflower Seed Deterioration as related to Moisture Content during Ageing, Energy Metabolism and Active Oxygen Species Scavenging, *Physiologia Plantarum,* 128: 496-506.

Mohammadi, H., Soltani, A., Sadeghipour, H. R. and Zeinali, E. (2011): Effect of Seed Aging on Subsequent Seed Reserve Utilization and Seedling Growth in Soybean, *International Journal of Plant Production*, 5(1): 65-70.

Murdock, L.L., Margam, V., Baoua, I., Balfe, S. and Shade, R.E. (2012): Death by Desiccation: Effects of Hermetic Storage on Cowpea Bruchids, *Journal of Stored Products Research*, 49: 166-170.

Quezada, M.Y., Moreno, J., Vázquez, M.E., Mendoza, M., Mendex-Albores, A. and Moreno-Martínez, E. (2006): Hermetic Storage System Preventing the Proliferation of *Prostephanus truncatus* Horn and Storage Fungi in Maize with different Moisture Contents, *Postharvest Biology and Technology*, 39: 321-326.

Shakuntal A.N.M. and Basave Gowda. (2017): Ultra-dry Seed Storage: A Novel Technology for Enhancing Seed Longevity, *International Journal of Chemical Studies*, 5(5): 1851-1857.

Shelar, V.R., Shaikh, R.S. and Nikam, A.S. (2008): Soybean Seed Quality during Storage: A Review, *Agricultural Review*, 29(2): 125-131.

Shinde, P and Hunje, R. (2019): Seed Viability and Seed Health as Influenced by modified Atmospheric Gases Condition on Kabuli Chickpea (*Cicer arietinum* L.) Varieties, *Journal of Entomology and Zoology Studies*, 7(1): 713-719.

Wang, X.F., Jing, X.M. and Lin, J. (2005): Starch Mobilization in Ultradried Seed of Maize *Zea mays* L. during Germination, *Journal of Integrated Plant Biology*, 47: 443-451.

Weinburg, Z.G., Yan, Y., Chen, Y., Finkelman, S., Ashbell, G. and Navarro, S. (2007): The Effect of Moisture Level on High-moisture Maize (*Zea mays* L.) under Hermetic Storage Conditions – in vitro Studies, *Journal of Stored Products Research*, 44(2): 136-144.

http://ecoursesonline.iasri.res.in/mod/page/view.php?id=928

http://www.ivalsa.cnr.it/en/research/cryopreservation-preservation-in-liquid-nitrogen-196c-of-plant-germplasm.html

http://www.kew.org/msbp/scitech/publications/SCTSIP_digital_book/pdfs/Chapter_50.pdf

http://www.knowledgebank.irri.org/step-by-step-production/postharvest/storage/grain-storage-systems/hermetic-storage-systems

http://www.regjeringen.no/en/dep/lmd/campain/svalbard-global-seed-vault/front-page.html?id=462227

http://www.statsbygg.no/Aktuelt/Nyheter/7201/

https://en.wikipedia.org/wiki/Svalbard_Global_Seed_Vault

https://www.millermagazine.com/english/modified-and-controlled-atmospheres-for-the-protection-of-wheat-quality/.html

Pages: 128-141

Seeds and Food: ***Processing and Storage Techniques***
Edited by: **Dr. Prasann Kumar and Dr. Pawan Kumar 'Bharti'**
ISBN: 978-93-88854-41-2
Edition: **2020**
Published by: **Discovery Publishing House Pvt. Ltd., New Delhi (India)**

6

Hatchery Seed Production Technology and Grow-out Farming of Monosex Tilapia *Oreochromis Niloticus* in North 24 Parganas, West Bengal

Subrato Ghosh

ABSTRACT

Grow-out farming of monosex male Tilapia Oreochromis niloticus both in conventional earthen ponds and in advanced indoor tank-based culture systems has emerged as a profitable venture in freshwater fish farming business in India. Monosex culture is the management practice most widely used to prevent the production of low-valued small and stunted O. niloticus. The Bengal Hatchery located in North 24 Parganas district, WB has developed a successful technique for the commercial mass production of stockable-sized sex reversed Tilapia fry. A description is given here on the technique followed in typical modern egg incubation system in this hatchery and this communication is a genuine representation of the on-site conversation made by present author with proprietors of Bengal Hatchery on 9/6/2019. All the facts and figures are true and authentic. Additionally the state-of-the-art of grow-out farming practice of this hormonally-manipulated fish has been presented, which is being done at another reputed private hatchery namely Adhikari Hatchery and Fish Centre located in same district, where author visited on 15/6/2019.

INTRODUCTION

Oreochromis niloticus or the Nile Tilapia was once considered as a low value foodfish in India, but in recent times has gained wider consumer

Formerly Part-time Lecturer, Master of Fishery Science Department, Utkal University, Bhubaneswar, Odisha, (India)
Corresponding address: 122/1V, Monohar Pukur Road, P.O. Kalighat, Kolkata - 700 026, West Bengal, (India)

acceptance. Normally *O. niloticus* is a prolific breeder and its uncontrolled breeding and excessive recruitment in ponds is undesirable. It leads to stunted growth. The development of hormonal sex-reversal techniques led to rapid expansion of the exclusively male sex *O. niloticus* seed production industry and strengthened the enthusiasm of grow-out culture of *O. niloticus*. In its population, males grow faster than females and thus the farming of monosex populations of *O. niloticus* is preferred and has gained importance. Farming practices of the fish from extensive to super-intensive both for fresh and brackishwater are expanding day by day in Asia and many countries of the world (Hussain, 2004). Fry-stages 2-5 days old (sexually undifferentiated) are fed with powdered supplementary feed containing the sex reversal hormone 17á-methyltestosterone at its standard dosage; normally it is done till 28th day post-hatching to produce complete masculine all-male *O. niloticus* population. In males, metabolic energy gained from food is channelized towards growth. The monosex Tilapia attain 175-275gm and 400-500gm body weight at the end of three and six months of culture period respectively in village grow-out farm ponds in West Bengal conditions from an initial fry stage of 30-45 days. They are adaptable to semi-poor water conditions and are suitable for culture in wastewater-fed freshwater ecosystems (Sarbajna *et al.*, 2010).

DESCRIPTION OF BENGAL HATCHERY

The Bengal Monosex Tilapia Hatchery, located at Vill. Gobindapur-Jorapukur, P.O. and GP Taranipur under Swarupnagar CD Block in North 24 Parganas district, West Bengal (WB) has been producing high quality hatchery-reared monosex Tilapia fry commercially on a large scale since May 2016 and is presently a leading monosex Tilapia seed production unit in WB. Normally those are sold at a size 20-24mm (40-42 days old; 6000nos/kg) and also at comparatively smaller size (28-30 days old; 7500nos/kg). Professional fish breeders Sri Anisur Rahaman Par and Sri Lovelu Par are joint proprietors of this hatchery-cum-seed farm.

Adjoining the main fish hatchery premises, there are fourteen earthen freshwater ponds taken on lease covering a total area of 30 bigha (990 dec), four of which are larger and sum up to 18 bigha (590 dec). Most of these ponds are meant for *O. niloticus* broodstock maintenance and monosex Tilapia fry production; others used for producing fry/advanced fry of *Anabas testudineus, Heteropneustes fossilis, Mylopharyngodon piceus* and *Ompak pabda*. Within main hatchery, twenty-four rectangular cement cisterns each 7 feet × 5 feet × 3.5 feet in dimension have been constructed. Yolk sac absorbed *O. niloticus* fry are shifted into these cisterns from rectangular egg incubation-cum-hatching trays. Additionally there are five large cement cisterns each 9 feet × 8 feet × 3.5 feet in dimension (conditioning tanks), a large *O. niloticus* egg incubation-cum-hatching complex, comprising plastic jug-like containers and a battery of plastic egg incubation trays, in four series, each 14 inch × 8 inch × 3 inch in dimension, separately provided with water supply system.

Water from pond is sieved and plankton-free water is let into the twenty-four cisterns. Underground water has been found to contain high level of iron, so not used in hatchery. Early fry of *O. niloticus* are reared here for 4-5 days and acclimatized to hormone-mixed supplementary feed (locally termed 'medicinal feed'). On the 5th day, those are shifted to a series of rectangular blue-coloured nylon net containers or *hapa* 3.5-4.0mt × 1.5mt × 1mt in dimension, fitted in two ponds and covering almost the entire surface area. As observed on 9th June, 2019, there were altogether 120 *hapa* enclosures, each containing 20000-22000nos Tilapia fry reared on hormone-treated feed. Paddle-wheel aerators are operated during night hours in these two ponds in order to prevent depletion of dissolved oxygen and ensure 100% survivability of monosex Tilapia fry.

FRY TRANSPORT AND SALE

The 28-30 days old monosex Tilapia fry are harvested from *hapa* containers and shifted into the five conditioning tanks containing well-oxygenated water. Those are temporarily reared for 4-6 hours under sprinkler shower system before being packaged in polythene oxygen packets for transportation and sale. Their stomach is emptied and faecal matter released in conditioning tanks, which facilitates transportation. Those are sold @ Re 0.30-0.45/-/piece. Sale is maximum during pre-summer, monsoon and post-monsoon months, minimum during May-June. Monosex Tilapia fry are sold everyday from this hatchery during 4.5-5 months. Fry are harvested on 28th-30th day during peak period of demand and sale, otherwise on 40th-42nd day. During transportation, the 40-42 days old monosex Tilapia fry are packed @ 1500nos/oxygenated packet containing 4-5lits water, smaller stage is packed @ 2000nos/packet. Those are supplied to grow-out Tilapia farmers in different districts of WB, to Chennai, Mumbai, different districts of Odisha and Andhra Pradesh by air cargo.

SEED PRODUCTION TECHNOLOGY

In broodstock pond of this hatchery, male and female *O. niloticus* broodfishes 200-500gm in weight and 7-8 months in age are being maintained since February every year. Fishes are stocked at a higher density in comparison to normal. In every 33 dec water area, 2500nos and 1250nos of female and male fishes respectively are stocked at the beginning of spawning season. For every 3750nos broodfishes in 33 dec pond, 15-16kg floating pelleted feed (5mm dia pellets separately supplemented with Vitamin-Mineral) is used everyday. Alternatively, in large nylon net breeding hapa of 10-12mt in length and 6-8mt in breadth fitted in ponds,

100nos males and 200nos female fishes are kept in each. Sexual maturity in ponds is reached at 5-6 months of age. After completion of spawning and courtship, a 100gm female produces about 150nos eggs in a single spawn.

An unique feature in reproductive biology of *Oreochromis niloticus* is its mouthbrooding or mouth-incubating habit, a means of parental care exhibited by the fish. After the eggs are released (laid) and fertilized in pond environment (which is completed within 2-3 hours), the female matured broodfish immediately collects and carry/hold the eggs in mouth cavity until the larvae hatch out and develop into fry-stage (with complete absorption of yolk sac). During this period, the female does not eat and eggs cannot escape (Peria-Mendoza *et al.*, 2005; Singh *et al.*, 2018). At Bengal Hatchery, matured females after being harvested are checked for the presence of fertilized eggs in mouth cavity. Skillful workers inside pond collect the fish on hand, mouth is opened applying gentle force on jaws and eggs are collected in fine-meshed soft scoop net from mouth of females individually. Eggs resemble yellow mustard seeds and about 250-400nos collected from each female every time. Those are carefully transferred in small round plastic trays with water and further transferred to egg incubation-cum-hatching unit.

Inside mouth cavity of *O. niloticus*, fertilized eggs have been found to exist in different stages of development:- just fertilized and fully yellow, yellowish brown, reddish chocolate with advanced stages of embryonic development. According to Sri Par, these stages are easily observed and distinguished. Pigmented body, eyes and tail region of larvae are visible inside egg in its most advanced stage of development, which will hatch out shortly. Skillful workers segregate the eggs collected from different females into separate containers based on colour and other characteristics. Eggs lying in initial stage of development are first placed inside jug-like egg incubation jars and placed in rectangular egg incubation trays after 48 hours. Mass of fertilized eggs in jug moves up and down vertically along with water circulation. Freshwater is supplied into egg incubation-cum-hatching complex directly from overhead tank. Eggs in advanced stage of development are placed directly in rectangular trays having facilities of constant water movement.

Fertilized eggs in initial stage of development (resembling mustard seeds) hatch out in between 78-96 hours and the advanced stage (almost similar to coriander seeds, reddish-chocolate) hatch out in between 60-72 hours. After hatching, *O. niloticus* larvae with yolk sac are maintained for another 90-100 hours in rectangular trays until yolk sac is absorbed. Using innumerable tiny stone chips in a separate chamber, water used in egg incubation-cum-hatching trays can be made iron-free, can be recycled and reused. After complete yolk sac absorption, the fry (each weighs about 10mg) are transferred to the rectangular cement cisterns.

FEED FOR TILAPIA FRY IN HAPA

Commercially available floating pelleted feed meant for *O. niloticus* is pulverized in machine (also high protein CP powder feed) and fed to the tender stages, without hormone after 28th day. During 3rd-28th day of age, feed is provided routinewise successively at 8.00am, 11.00am, 1.00pm, 3.00pm, 5.00pm and 8.00pm in the *hapa* enclosures in pond, six times a day. For initial five days consecutively, 20gm hormone-mixed feed is applied in each *hapa* enclosure every time. From 6th-14th day, 35gm is applied and in the final stages, feed is applied @ 50-60gm/*hapa* every time. A professional 'fish doctor' engaged here prepare the hormone-mixed diet for growing *O. niloticus* early fry and monitor the operation of egg incubation-cum-hatching units.

During the period 2006-2016, hatchery-produced *O. niloticus* seeds had been procured at this hatchery from private hatcheries in Bangladesh and monosex Tilapia fry were produced here following routinewise treatment with hormonal feed. But since 2016, entire spawning/breeding and fry production activities are being conducted here. Sri Anisur Par and Lovelu Par are also having four own ponds of 36 bigha (1188 dec), 16 bigha (528 dec), 11 bigha (360 dec) and 7.5bigha (250 dec) in area where grow-out farming of *Anabas testudineus, Piaractus brachypomus* and Indian major carps is being practiced following proper semi-intensive methods. Induced breeding programme of *A. testudineus* and *H. fossilis* have been undertaken here since 2017. Ten permanent employees are working in this hatchery, which is equipped with advanced set-up and equipments. One of the employee, Sri Ajijul Islam explained the activities and principles of fry production of monosex Tilapia to author, in addition to Sri Par. In seed production process of *O. niloticus*, hormonal injection to broodfishes is not required. Committed aqua-entrepreneurs Sri A. R. Par and Sri L. Par have initiated monosex seed production of *O. niloticus* in hatchery, which will cater to the seed requirement for grow-out farming of the fish in WB and other states.

A female *O. niloticus* broodfish (250gm)

An adult monosex Tilapia

A bigger/advanced monosex Tilapia fry

A monosex Tilapia fry

Conditioning tanks in operation

Rectangular seed rearing tanks

Hapa enclosures for monosex Tilapia fry

Hormone-mixed feed applied to Tilapia fry

A closer view of feed application

Bengal Hatchery at North 24 Pgs, WB

Collecting eggs from mouth-brooding females

Jug-like egg incubation jars at hatchery

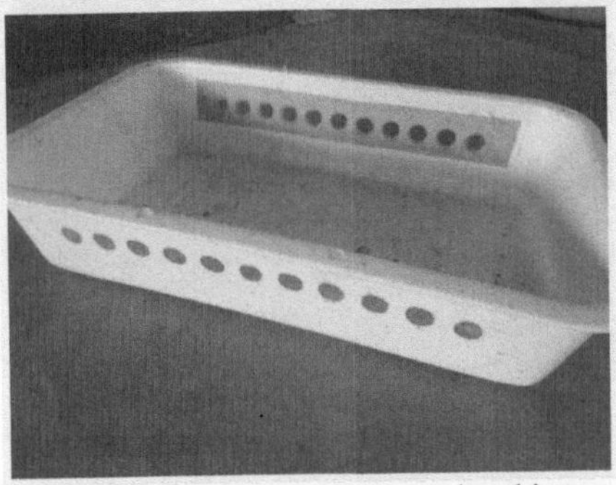

A rectangular egg-incubation-cum-hatching tray

O. niloticus broodstock pond at Bengal Hatchery

Monosex Tilapia fry at Bengal Hatchery

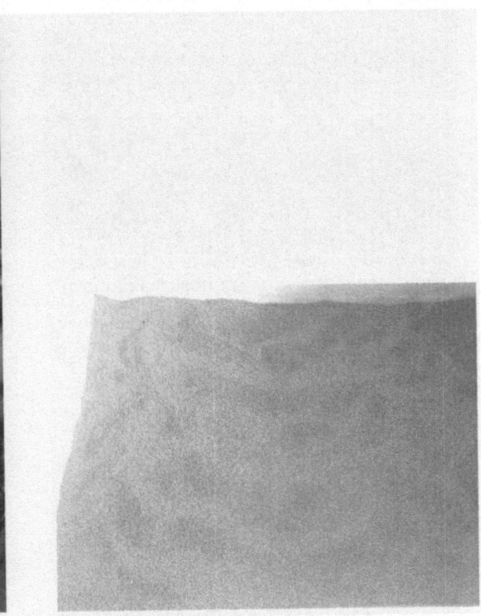

Broodfish diet supplemented with Vit.-Min.

ADHIKARI SCIENTIFIC HATCHERY AND FISH CENTRE

As the male Tilapia fish is well-adopted to supplementary feeding and due to its rapid growth, there is a huge profit in commercial Tilapia farming (Source: https://www.daily pioneer.com/2015/state-editions). Sri Madhusudan Adhikari, aged 56, proprietor of Adhikari Hatchery and Fish Centre is another stalwart in the subject of commercial large-scale production of fry and advanced fry of monosex male Tilapia. Sri Adhikari and Sri Nur Jaman Mondal, Manager of this farm entertained present author at his hatchery-cum-Tilapia farm on 15th June 2019. It is located at Vill. Lakshinathpur, P.O. Katakhali, GP Bajitpur under PS and CD Block Baduria, Dist. North 24 Parganas, WB. The hatchery complex and fish ponds are located at a serene environment beside Icchamati river and Katakhali bridge. Since 2006 and till 2010, Sri Adhikari used to bring hatchery-produced 6-8 days old yolk sac absorbed *O. niloticus* seeds at this hatchery from private hatcheries in Bangladesh, subsequently monosex Tilapia fry were produced here following routinewise 28-days treatment with hormonal feed. But since 2010, entire broodstock maintenance, spawning, egg collection, egg incubation-cum-hatching and monosex fry production activities of *O. niloticus* are being conducted in this hatchery, which was established in that year. Salt is added to water used in egg incubation-cum-hatching trays till yolk sac absorbed *O. niloticus* larvae are produced. Application for 21-28 days of feed treated with 17 alpha MT ensure consistently high (~99%) levels of male fish. Culture of monosex Tilapia has become very popular (De and Pandey, 2014). In 28-days of rearing, early yolk sac absorbed fry are stocked @ 30000-35000nos/hapa, which are of size 15 feet × 7 feet.

MAINTENANCE OF BROODFISHES

Including nursery, grow-out and broodstock earthen ponds meant for *O. niloticus*, there are twenty-eight in all covering 42 bigha (1386 dec) in area taken on lease, well-maintained and managed by his nine farm employees under his supervision. In a few ponds, broodstock of *H. fossilis* and indigenous magur *Clarius batrachus* are being maintained. Another 54 bigha water body is taken on lease that comprises four large fishponds. Sri Adhikari has one large pond 13.5 bigha (445 dec) of his own, where marketable sized Indian major carps are produced. In seven ponds out of twenty-eight, male and female broodfishes of *O. niloticus* are reared; grow-out culture of monosex Tilapia is practiced in 15 ponds. Altogether there are 30,000 and 10,000nos of female and male brooders respectively; female weighs 500gm on average and male 800gm, both one year in age.

From early January, fishes are maintained @ 3000 females and 1000 males/33 dec water body and *O. niloticus* monosex fry production activity is continued in this hatchery from mid-February till end of October/early November every year; 100gm of the androgen hormone 17-alpha MT (commercially prepared in Philippines) costs Rs 60000/-. In 33 dec pond, brooders are fed 25kg commercially-available floating pelleted fish feed (Rs 50/-/kg), once in 24 hours at 4.00pm. Feeding excessively or till satiation may lead to more fat deposition in abdomen in females, hindering proper production and development of impregnated ova. It will not spawn spontaneously. During peak summer, high pond water temperature prevents the occurrence of females with ripe oocytes, spawning activity of *O. niloticus* is hampered. With onset of monsoon, favourable condition prevails and mouth-brooding females can be found in broodstock ponds.

TRANSPORTATION AND SALE OF FRY FROM ADHIKARI HATCHERY

As observed on 15/6/2019 forenoon, the healthy 40-days old monosex Tilapia fry (3000nos/kg) were being collected from two conditioning tanks after maintaining them under continuous water sprinkler system; then graded according to uniform size and shifted to large nylon net hapa enclosures 25 feet x 12 feet in dimension (150000nos kept in each) fitted in adjacent pond for temporary storage. Those were fed and within next 12 hours will be transported in oxygen packed containers. From this hatchery, monosex Tilapia fry are supplied to fish farmers in different places at South 24 Parganas, Purba Medinipur, Coochbehar and other districts; Siliguri town in north Bengal; different places in Rajasthan, Jharkhand, Assam and Uttar Pradesh and at Andaman island. Those are also supplied to ongoing Fishery Project sites under Department of Fisheries, Government of WB at Salt Lake, Digha, Bakkhali and other places within the state.

Fry are sold mainly at two sizes; 8000nos/kg, 28-29 days old @ Re 0.30-0.35/-/piece and 5000nos/kg @ Re 0.40-0.45/-/piece. During transportation, the 2nd stage is packed in oxygenated containers @ 1500nos/packet with 3.5lits water. A part of the largest size 3000nos/kg is sold @ Re 0.50/-/piece and rest are raised to bigger-sized (somewhat stunted) monosex Tilapia fry in farm ponds of Adhikari Hatchery and Fish Centre. In 55-60 days of rearing from birth, *i.e.*, in 25-28 days period after 28th day when stocked @ 1,80,000nos/33 dec and fed daily three times at 9.00am, 1.00pm and 5.00pm, these attain 2.5-3.0 inch size (100-150nos/kg) and sold @ Rs 1.50/-/piece or Rs 220-250/-/kg {Note: When stocked in such high density, these attain only 8-10gm at the end of one month culture in pond and bigger monosex Tilapia fry are produced}. In the three conditioning tanks functioning in this hatchery, each of dimension 6 feet × 4 feet × 4 feet, 28-days old monosex Tilapia fry are stocked @ 200000nos/tank. Longer is the distance of transportation (18 hours), these fry will be maintained under water sprinkler system for longer duration prior to transportation (6-8 hours). Faecal matter evacuates out from fish body in the process.

IMPORTANT FEATURES IN MONOSEX TILAPIA FRY PRODUCTION

As explained by Sri Adhikari, about 250nos yolk-sac absorbed larvae are produced from eggs obtained from each mouth-brooding female *O. niloticus*, these weigh 60000nos/kg and hormone-mixed feed are fed to them from this stage for next 28 days. About 8-9kg eggs are obtained from 3000 brood females. In occasional conditions when the full 28-days course of hormonal feed is not completed, on 15th-20th day, it is sold locally to few farmers at a low rate who demand for the same. In conditions when hapa-reared *O. niloticus* fry accidentally escapes into pond in between 0 and 28th day and harvested in advanced fry stage, those cannot be considered as monosex Tilapia fry and provided to local fish farmers. But only monosex Tilapia fry after completion of full course of hormonal treatment are sold to professional fish farmers and customers mostly in distant region in good faith.

Sri Adhikari described four stages of *O. niloticus* egg development: pale or fully yellow as 1st stage; mouth slit/aperture developed inside reddish-coloured egg as 2nd stage; eyes and yolk sac fully developed and tail region coming out of egg as 3rd stage and yolk sac absorbed larvae as 4th stage. On 7th-8th day, yolk sac absorbed larvae are produced from 1st stage of fertilized eggs. After fertilized eggs are induced manually to be released from a mouth-brooding female *O. niloticus*, the same female will attain this condition again in next 40-42 days. Egg collection is done from females in all brooders' pond once in a week. Every time, 25-35% of females in a pond are collected for egg collection from mouth; another lot of 25-35% fishes are collected for egg collection next time and this process continues. In every season, 50,00,000-250,00,000nos monosex Tilapia fry are produced in this hatchery-cum-seed farm. Within one day, yolk sac absorbed *O. niloticus* fry are transferred from egg incubation-cum-hatching unit to hapa enclosures in pond. After initial 28 days period, the 28-days old monosex Tilapia fry are stocked @ 75000nos/hapa (25 feet x 12 feet) and maintained on commercially-available powdered feed (Rs 60/-/kg), till date of transportation and supply is scheduled. Rainfall in post-summer months favours the spawning of *O. niloticus* brooders. In growing monosex Tilapia under culture, previously applied hormone-mixed feed prevents the formation of female gonad, *i.e.*, ovary and makes them incapable of reproduction within next nine months (weight attained: 1300gm).

GROW-OUT FARMING OF MONOSEX TILAPIA

According to Sri Adhikari, in grow-out culture ponds of this farm, monosex Tilapia fry (5000-6000nos/kg stage) stocked @ 6000nos/33 dec (depth: 3.5-4.0 feet) and 8500-10000nos/33 dec in ponds with water depth greater than 3.5-4.0 feet has been raised to marketable size; it has been found to attain 100gm in 2.5-3.0 months, 200-300gm in 4 months, 1250gm in 7 months and 1500-1700gm in 10-11 months under culture. In order to produce fishes above 150gm body weight, stocking density has to be reduced or ponds larger in size are required. In grow-out ponds, monosex *O. niloticus* are fed commercially-available powdered (dust) feed for initial 18-20 days four times a day, subsequently the 0.6-0.8 dia feed (Growel Feed; Rs 100/-/kg resembling tiny mustard seeds) is used for next 15-20 days three times daily, further the 1.5mm dia floating pelleted feed is used (from 50gm size) and finally 3mm dia feed is used till time of harvest two times a day, 5.0-5.5kg/100kg fishes daily. Feeding to fishes is done at 9.00am, 1.00pm and 5.00pm daily. Sri Adhikari's method of monosex Tilapia culture is essentially semi-intensive.

From this farm, monosex Tilapia 100-300gm size are sold in local markets at Baduria, Swarupnagar and adjacent Blocks @ Rs 120-130/-/kg. Like farm-reared poultry birds, monosex Tilapia attain large size in short period of time if fed good quality feed routinewise and sufficiently. Provision of good quality supplementary feeding is essential, the fish converts feed to muscle (meat) efficiently. Liming is done in pond initially @ 33kg/33 dec water area before fry stocking and @ 4.5-6.0kg/33 dec water area once in a month. Fishes more than 3 months in age are fed 4mm dia feed. In rainy days, soaked mustard oil cake is used daily in evening @ 5kg/33 dec pond and in normal days, mustard oil cake is used once in a week in addition to pelleted feed. Normal production of marketable-sized monosex Tilapia obtained at this farm is 1000kg/33 dec in 3-4 months (considering 10% mortality). Low saline earthen ponds favour the growth of monosex Tilapia, Sri Adhikari mentioned.

In the nursery management method, monosex Tilapia fry (6000nos/kg) may be stocked in nursery ponds @ 66000-70000nos/33 dec and it attains 20-25gm in 30-45 days of rearing. In grow-out ponds of size 30-100 dec, these juveniles are stocked @ 6500nos/33 dec. After one month of culture, water replacement may be done @ 20-30% at every 21 days interval. Fishes (250-300gm) should be harvested on 90-120th day of stocking. In Bangladesh, production upto 15000kg/ha/year is obtained following improved management practices and production rate of 5000-6000kg/0.4ha/3-4 months has been reported (Source: www.swarnalatafisheries.com).

RED MONOSEX TILAPIA

In late 1960s, the first red Tilapia was produced in Taiwan by a cross between a genetic mutant strain reddish-orange female *Oreochromis mossambicus* and a normal male *O. niloticus*. Red Tilapia is considered as important to aquaculture in Asia (Welcomme and Vidthayanon, 1999). Sri Adhikari and Sri Mondal explained to author that the red variety of monosex Tilapia has good demand as an aquarium fish in its younger stages, can be consumed and its growth rate is faster than normal monosex Tilapia, attains about 150gm in two months. Fry stages are sold from this hatchery @ Rs 1.50-1.75/-/piece, at a price 3-4 times higher than normal monosex Tilapia fry. Altogether 3000 brood females of red *O. niloticus* are presently maintained in this hatchery, its fecundity is less in comparison to normal *O. niloticus*. About 2kg eggs may be obtained from 3000 brood females, high water temperature during peak summer hinders production of ripe oocytes in matured red Tilapia ovary. It may attain 1200-1400gm in adult stage in grow-out ponds. In the 2018-2019 breeding season, 30000nos of red monosex Tilapia fry have been produced at Adhikari Scientific Hatchery and supplied to Rajasthan and other places. Low breeding intensity in red Tilapia was also observed in Bangladesh (Kohinoor *et al.*, 1999).

The ability to produce all-male Tilapia fry has revolutionized the profile of this species *O. niloticus*, its production and consumption (Belton *et al.*, 2009). In addition to monosex Tilapia, fry of indigenous *C. batrachus* and Vietnam variety of *Anabas testudineus* are produced and sold from this hatchery. In grow-out culture at this farm, *C. batrachus* has attained 175-200gm in ten months and Vietnamese *A. testudineus* 200gm in five months. Sri Adhikari, a simple and soft-spoken person has immense expertise in the subject of fry/advanced fry production of economically-important fishes. He has provided much-needed employment to nine persons in his hatchery and could expand his farm to commendable dimension by dint of his honest efforts and self confidence.

Egg incubation trays in operation

Closer view of incubation trays with Tilapia eggs

Egg incubation jars in operation

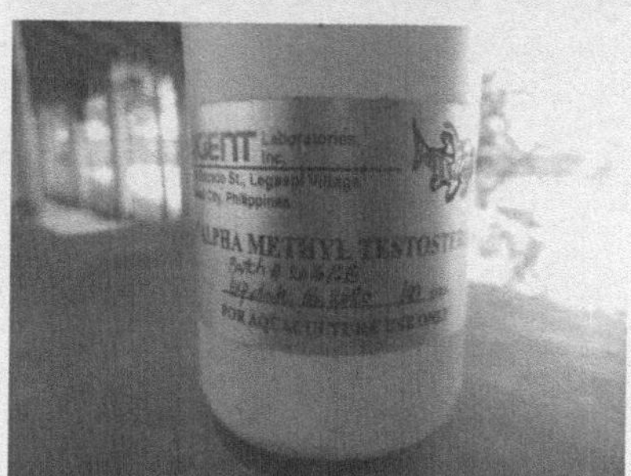

Hormone 17-alpha MT used in sex reversal

Tilapia hatchery when not in operation

Pipe fittings for egg incubation in jug-like jars

Haul of monosex Tilapia fry - 1

Haul of monosex Tilapia fry - 2

Monosex Tilapia fry in conditioning tanks

A view of Adhikari Scientific Hatchery

A stunted big-sized monosex Tilapia fry

Adult red Tilapia at Adhikari Hatchery

Sri N.J. Mondal, author and Sri M. Adhikari

Stocking of monosex Tilapia fry in pond

REFERENCES

Belton, B., Turongruang, D., Bhujel, R. and Little, D.C. (2209): The History, Status, and Future Prospects of Monosex Tilapia Culture in Thailand, *Aquaculture Asia*, XIV (2): 16-19.

De, H.K. and Pandey, D.K. (2014): Rural Aquaculture - now and then, *Economic Affairs*, Paper No. 157, 59(4): 497-504.

Hussain, M. G. (2004): Farming of Tilapia: Breeding Plans, Mass Seed Production and Aquaculture Techniques, *Bangladesh Fisheries Research Institute Publication*: pp. 149.

Kohinoor, A.H.M., Modak, P.C. and Hussain, M.G. (1999): Growth and Production Performance of Red Tilapia and Nile Tilapia (*Oreochromis niloticus* Lin.) under Low-input Culture System, *Bangladesh J. Fish. Res.*, 3(1): 11-17.

Peria-Mendoza, B., Gomez-Marquez, J.L. and Salgado-Ugarte, I. H. (2005): Reproductive Biology of *Oreochromis niloticus* at Emiliano Zapata dam, Mexico, *Revista de Biología Tropical*, 53 (3/4): 515-522.

Sarbajna, A., Gupta, S., Chakraborty, S.B. and Banerjee, S. (2010): Growth Performance of Sex-reversed Nile tilapia *Oreochromis niloticus* Cultured in Cages in a Waste-fed Freshwater Wetland, *World Aquaculture*: 8-10.

Singh, E., Saini, V.P. and Sharma, O.P. (2018): Orally Administered 17-α MT at different Doses on Sex Reversal of Red Tilapia (*Oreochromis niloticus*), *Int. Journal of Fisheries and Aquatic Studies*, 6(3): 301-305.

Welcomme, R.L. and Vidthayanon, C. (1999): Report on Impacts of Introductions and Stocking in Mekong Basin and Policies for Control. *Management of Reservoir Fisheries in Mekong Basin, Cambodia, Mekong River Commission*: pp. 62.

Pages: 142-148

Seeds and Food: ***Processing and Storage Techniques***
Edited by: **Dr. Prasann Kumar and Dr. Pawan Kumar 'Bharti'**
ISBN: 978-93-88854-41-2
Edition: **2020**
Published by: **Discovery Publishing House Pvt. Ltd., New Delhi (India)**

7

Methodology of Drying and Measurable Quality Attributes of Chilli
An Overview of Experiment

Prasann Kumar[1,2*], **Shipa Rani Dey**[1]

GRAPHICAL ABSTRACT

Keywords: Attributes, Chilli, Drying, Methodology

INTRODUCTION

Dried chilli is one of most widely used, as natural condiment, in food industry due to its color, flavour and pungency. The dried chilli products

[1] Department of Agronomy, School of Agriculture, Lovely Professional University, Jalandhar - 144 411 Punjab, (India)
[2] Divison of Research and Development, Lovely Professional University, Jalandhar - 144411 Punjab (India)

are now regularly used in several cuisines such as pizza, food mixture, salad dressings and instant soups. Several parameters like colour, hotness, ascorbic acid content, phenolic contents and capsaicin contents are studied in order to evaluate the quality of dried chilli. Being seasonal and perishable chili is usually short in supply during off seasons because of deterioration within a few days after plucking. Drying is not only traditional adopted method in preserving food and perishable vegetables but also reduces the storage volume as well as increases their shelf life. There are different drying methods adopted to optimize the compromise between efficiency and quality, such as sun drying, hot air drying (Laskaridou-Monnerville, 1999), microwave drying (Alibas, 2006; Soysal *et al.*, 2009) and freeze drying (Topuz *et al.*, 2011). Sun drying is traditionally adopted method for chilli drying which takes 7-20 days (depending on the weather) to reduce the moisture content desired level 10-15%. Dried chilli is prone to fungal growth and finally results in mycotoxins contamination. To prevent fungal growth several drying methods have been subjected during chilli processing. Presently hot air drying (HD) has become popular method due to relatively short drying time, uniform heating and more hygienic characteristics. The temperature ranges from 45 to 70°C in hot air drying reduces the processing time by 20 hrs (moisture content approximately 10%). High temperature also associated with loss of colour and nutritional value. In addition to that microwave vacuum drying (MVD) has been also shown similar effect as hot air drying (HD) but it reduces the drying time by 5-30 minutes. While freeze drying (FD) is found to be best method for maintaining colour quality of dried chilli. Moreover, quality varies with genotype as well as light intensity and growth temperature, age to fruit and fruit position on the plant apart from them processing technique also play key role in preserving quality and nutritive values of chilli. Therefore current study is conducted to assess the effects of drying methods on the colour (L*, a* and b*) nutritional attributes (ascorbic acid, β-carotene), capsaicin content, hotness, pH and total phenolic content of dried chilli.

MATERIAL AND METHODS

Raw Material

Good quality fresh fruits of five chilli (*Capsicum annuum*) varieties were purchased from the local areas of Vellore, Tamilnadu, India. These varieties under current study (PLR-1, CO_4, BIRD'S EYE, SAANAM S4, and PMK-1) are widely cultivated chilli varieties in Vellore region. Chilli were washed with water to remove the dust and finally rinsed with distilled water. The whole pods of chilli was blanched using hot water at 90°C for 3 min (Gupta *et al.*, 2002) and allowed to cool in cold water and then drained on perforated steel tray before drying. For efficient drying the chillies were cut into three parts viz. base, middle and tip. The reason behind this technique is to minimize damage in thin middle part as compared to tip and base for efficient drying. Then chilli was dried using four drying methods: hot air drying (HD), freeze drying (FD), sun drying (SD) and microwave vacuum drying (MVD). The entire dried sample was taken when the moisture content obtained was approximately 10-13% (Thai Industrial Standard Institutes: TISI 456-1983). The fresh chilli of each variety without drying was used as control. Experiment was performed with 3 replications.

Drying method

Sun Drying

100 g of chilli slices were spread uniformly as a thin layer on a net in a single layer and exposed to directly to sunlight (approximately 39°C) until there were no two consecutive changes in sample weight which took 10 days. The thermometer was placed on a empty tray besides a net of chilli (Balladin and Headley, 1999).

Hot Air Oven

100 g of capsicum of each variety distributed uniformly as a thin layer onto the stainless steel trays of size 0.3m×0.2m and subjected to dry in a hot air oven (Serwell Instruments Inc., Banglore India, 55 L volume) at 65°C until there was no two consecutive changes in sample weight which took 65 min for 23 hours (Balladin and Headley, 1999).

Microwave Oven

Domestic microwave oven of power rating 800W (Model MO- 9760A, Kitchen Appliances India Ltd., Kenstar, Aurangabad, India) with a hole on upper surface connected to polycarbonate vacuum decicator (Tarson Product Pvt. Ltd, Kolkata) through which the hose pipe was passed. One end of the hose pipe was connected to the lid of a polycarbonate vacuum desiccator (Tarsons Products Pvt. Ltd., Kolkata, India) kept inside the oven cavity, while the other, to a vacuum pump via a attached unit of vacuum gauge. Approximately 100 g of chilli was spread uniformly on perforated plate of desiccator kept inside the microwave oven and subjected to dry until there were no two consecutive changes in sample weight which took 65 min at 800W and 5KPa.

Freeze Drying

Freeze drying chilli was conducted at -50°C, 5KPa in a Lark freeze dryer until there were no two consecutive changes in sample weight which took 12 hrs. The final product was stored at room temperature in a desiccater and subjected to analysis within a week of collection.

Evaluation of Physical and Chemical Quality

Determination of Water Activity (a_w)

Water activity was determined using a water activity meter (Aqua lab) calibrated as a standard sample with known value (ranges 0.11-0.99).

Colour Measurements

All samples were cut lengthwise and spread out in single layer to evaluate the colours using Konica Minolta Chroma meter CR400. Instrumental colour data was expressed in the CIE system in the terms of L^* (lightness), a^* (redness and greenness) and b^*(yellowness and blueness).

Determination of pH

10 grams of each capsicum variety ground sample was diluted with 20 ml of distilled water. The pH was measured at room temperature 37°C with pH meter (Abon Portalble pH meter) which was calibrated with pH 4.0 and 7.

Determination of Ascorbic Acid

Ascorbic acid was quantitatively determined according to 2,6-dichlorophenolindophenol (DIP) dye method as described by (Deepa *et al.*, 2006) with some modifications. Samples (10 g) were homogenised with 10 ml of 2% metaphosphoric acid (w/v) using mortar and pestle. The extract was made up to a volume of 100 ml. 10ml were titrated against standard DIP dye, which was already standardised against standard ascorbic acid. Results were expressed in µg/gW ascorbic acid.

Determination of Total Phenolic Content

Total phenolic content was analyzed spectrophotometrically using the modified Folin–Ciocalteu colorimetric method as described by (Tavarini *et al.* 2008), with slight modifications. Each sample (1 g) was extracted with 10 mL methanol and then 125 µL of the methanolic extract were mixed with 375 µL of distiled (DI) water in a test tube followed by addition of 2.5 mL of 10% Folin–Ciocalteu reagent and allowed to stand for 6 min. Then 2 mL of 7.5% sodium carbonate solution were added. Each sample was incubated for 90 min at room temperature in darkness and the absorbance was measured at 760 nm using an UV/Vis spectrophotometer model (GE Healthcare Gene Quant 1300). Results are expressed as mg gallic acid/100gW.

Quantitative analysis of β carotene

Beta carotene was extracted from 0.25g chilli fresh as well dried fruit material using methanol and 10% diethyl ether in petroleum ether organic solvent and High performance liquid chromatography was employed to separate and quantify the β carotene as detailed previously (Fraser *et. al.*,

1994). The chromatographic separation of extracted carotenoids was performed on a reverse phase C18 column maintained at 25°C in an isocratic elution mode. The mobile phase comprising acetonitrile: methanol: isopropanol (85:10:5) was maintained at a flow rate of 1 mL/min. The carotenoids were monitored using UV detector set at a wavelength of 470 nm. Carotenoids were identified by their characteristic spectral properties, relative mobilities and co-chromatography with authentic standards. Amount of individual carotenoids were determined by integration of the peak areas.

Extraction for Capsaicin

The capsaicinoids were extracted from 0.2g of samples in 4 ml ethanol by being heated at 80°C for 4 h. Suspensions were periodically shaken every 30 min throughout the extraction process. The suspended material was allowed to cool and settle. The supernatant was filtered into a 2 ml glass vial by using a whatman's filter paper and then used for HPLC injection. The capsaicin content of the samples was quantified using HPLC using a Phenomenex C18 Column on a SHIMADZU HPLC (CMB-20A) equipped with a manual sampler, a gradient pump, and a UV/vis detector. Samples were eluted at a flow rate of 1.5 ml/min with a mobile phase of 40% acetonitrile and 60% deionized water at 30°C A UV/vis detector at a wavelength of 220 nm and 230nm were used to quantify samples at retention times of 2min for capsaicin when the injection volume of the samples was 20µl.

Scoville Heat Unit Conversion

In accordance to widely accepted Scovilled organoleptic test, the punginess of the analyzed samples was determined by converting the capsaicin content expressed in grams of capsaicin per gram of chilli. The conversion to Scoville heat unit was carried out by multiplying the capsaicin concentration in chilli weight by coefficient corresponding to the heat value for pure capsaicin that is 1.6×10^{7}.

CONCLUSION

The freeze drying (FD) method was observed most efficient drying method for retaining capsaicin content than other drying methods while MVD was found to be most efficient in minimizing the loss to nutritional attributes for almost each studied chilli varieties. The fresh samples have been exhibited high amount of β- carotene ascorbic acid and total phenolic content than dried samples of each studied varieties. Hunter colour parameters were also found varied in correlation with subjected drying methods as the genotype of chilli varieties varied. But the highest values for colour parameters were noticed in fresh samples than any dried sampled among the studied chilli varieties. Principal component analysis clearly suggest that MVD eas more suitable and drying method in preserving overall quality attributes as well as can be applicable for all chilli varieties.

The hotness of analyzed samples decreased as follow Bird eye, Saanam4, CO4, PLR1, PKM1 among the studied varieties and FD, MVD, HD and SD among the drying methods. The mean chilli consumption by people of Vellore city and the corresponding daily capsaicin intake were 13.41 g/person/day while the daily intake of capsaicin was 9.028mg/person/day

REFERENCES

1. Alibas, I., 2006. Characteristics of Chard Leaves during Microwave, Convective, and Combined Microwave-Convective Drying. Drying Technol. 24(11): 1425-35.
2. Balladin, D.A., Headley O., 1999. Evaluation of Solar Dried Thyme (Thymus Vulgaris Linné) Herbs. Renewable Energy 17(4): 523-31.
3. Bengtsson, A., Namutebi A., Alminger M.L., Svanberg U., 2008. Effects of Various Traditional Processing Methods on the All-Trans-β-Carotene Content of Orange-Fleshed Sweet Potato. Food Compo. Anal. J. 21(2): 134-43.
4. Carbonell, J.V., Piñaga F., Yusá, V., Peña J.L. 1986 The Dehydration of Paprika with Ambient and Heated Air and the Kinetics of Colour Degradation during Storage. Food Eng. J. 5(3): 179-93.
5. Chan, E.W.C., Lim, Y.Y., Wong, S.K., Lim, K.K., Tan, S.P., Lianto, F.S., Yong, M. Y., 2009. Effects of Different Drying methods on the Antioxidant Properties of Leaves and Tea of Ginger Species. Food chem. 113(1), 166-172.
6. Deepa, N., Kaur, C., Singh, B., Kapoor, H.C., 2006. Antioxidant Activity in some Red Sweet Pepper Cultivars. Food Compo. Anal. J. 19(6), 572-578.
7. Gupta, P., Ahmed, J., Shivhare, U.S., Raghavan, G.S.V., 2002. Drying Characteristics of Red Chilli. Drying technol. 20(10), 1975-1987.
8. Inyang, U.E., & Ike, C.I., 1998. Effect of Blanching, Dehydration method and Temperature on the Ascorbic Acid, Colour, Sliminiess and other Constituents of Okra Fruit. Int.J. Food Sci.Nutri. 49(2), 125-130.
9. Sweeney, J.P., Marsh, A.C., 1971. Effect of Processing on Provitamin A in Vegetables. Amer Diet Ass J.
10. Kizilaslan, A., 1993. A Research on Improving of Properties of Karidali Type Pepper Paste. Cukurova University.
11. Laskaridou-Monnerville, A., 1999. Determination of Capsaicin and Dihydrocapsaicin by Micellar Electrokinetic Capillary Chromatography and its Application to Various Species of Capsicum, Solanaceae. J. Chromatography A 838(1-2): 293-302.
12. Lin, T.M., Timothy D.D., Christine H.S., 1998. Characterization of Vacuum Microwave, Air and Freeze Dried Carrot Slices. Food Res. Int. 31(2): 111-17.
13. Minguez-Mosquera, M.I., Hornero-Mendez, D., 1994. Comparative Study of the Effect of Paprika Processing on the Carotenoids in Peppers (Capsicum annuum) of the Bola and Agridulce varieties. J. Agri. Food Chem. 42(7), 1555-1560.
14. Mangaraj, S., Singh, A., Samuel, D.V.K., Singhal O.P., 1994. Comparative Performance Evaluation of Different Drying Methods for Chillis. J.F. Sci. Technol. 38(3): 296-99.
15. Mueller-Harvey, I., 2001. Analysis of Hydrolysable Tannins. Animal Feed Sci.Technol. 91(1-2): 3-20.
16. Fraser, P.D., Truesdale, M.R., Bird, C.R., Schuch, W., Bramley, P.M., 1994. Plant Physiol. 105: 405-13.

17. Sanatombi, K, Sharma, G.J., 2008. Capsaicin Content and Pungency of Different Capsicum Spp. Cultivars. Notulae Botanicae Horti Agrobotanici Cluj-Napoca 36(2): 89-90.
18. Schweiggert, U., Schieber, A., Carle, R., 2006. Effects of Blanching and Storage on Capsaicinoid Stability and Peroxidase Activity of Hot Chili Peppers (Capsicum Frutescens L.). Innovative Food Sci. Emerg. Technol. 7(3): 217-24.
19. Siriamornpun, S., Kaisoon, O., Meeso, N., 2012. Changes in Colour, Antioxidant Activities and Carotenoids (lycopene, β-Carotene, Lutein) of Marigold Flower (Tagetes Erecta L.) Resulting from Different Drying Processes. J. Functional Foods 4(4): 757-66.
20. Soysal, Y., Ayhan, Z., EÞtürk, O., Arýkan, M.F., 2009. Intermittent Microwave-convective Drying of Red Pepper: Drying Kinetics, Physical (Colour and Texture) and Sensory Quality. Biosystems Eng. 103(4): 455-63.
21. Tavakolipour, H., Mokhtarian, M., 2015. Drying of Chilli Pepper in Various Conditions. Quality Assur. Safety Crops Foods: 1-8.
22. T Tavarini, S., Degl'Innocenti, E., Remorini, D., Massai, R., Guidi, L., 2008. Antioxidant Capacity, Ascorbic Acid, Total Phenols and Carotenoids Changes during Harvest and after Storage of Hayward Kiwifruit. Food Chem. 107(1), 282-288.
23. Topuz, A., Dincer, C., Özdemir, K.S., Feng, H., Kushad, M., 2011. Influence of different Drying methods on Carotenoids and Capsaicinoids of Paprika (Cv., Jalapeno). Food chem. 129(3), 860-865.
24. Topuz, A., Ozdemir, F., 2004. Influences of Gamma Irradiation and Storage on the Capsaicinoids of Sun-Dried and Dehydrated Paprika. Food Chem. 86(4): 509-15.
25. Tapuz, A., Ozdemir, F., 2007. Assessment of Carotenoids, Capsaicinoids and Ascorbic Acid Composition of Some Selected Pepper Cultivars (Capsicum Annuum L.) Grown in Turkey. J.Food Compo. Anal. 20(7): 596-602.
26. Vega-Gálvez, A., Lemus-Mondaca, R., Bilbao-Sáinz, C., Fito, P., Andrés, A., 2008. Effect of Air Drying Temperature on the Quality of Rehydrated Dried Red Bell Pepper (var. Lamuyo). J. Food Eng. 85(1), 42-50.
27. Yaldiz, G., Ozguven, M., Sekeroglu, N., 2010. Variation in Capsaicin Contents of Different Capsicum Species and Lines by Varying Drying Parameters. Ind. Crops Prod. 32(3): 434-38.

Pages: 149-167

Seeds and Food: ***Processing and Storage Techniques***

Edited by: **Dr. Prasann Kumar and Dr. Pawan Kumar 'Bharti'**

ISBN: 978-93-88854-41-2

Edition: **2020**

Published by: **Discovery Publishing House Pvt. Ltd., New Delhi (India)**

8

Seed Production of *Notopterus Chitala* and other Fishes and Fish Farming in Advanced Recirculatory Aquaculture System in North Bengal

Subrato Ghosh

ABSTRACT

Success stories of two leading, committed and progressive fish seed producers of north Bengal have been presented in this article, who are elderly and experienced enough and their success has motivated other fish farmers. Author has visited their fish hatchery sites in Jalpaiguri and Coochbehar districts, had intimate conversation with them and gained much knowledge. One of them has gained proficiency in captive breeding of the threatened fish Notopterus chitala which is indeed praiseworthy. All facts and figures presented here are fully trustworthy and genuine; this article is prepared based upon authentic information gathered and own on-site observations. Additionally some thoughts of fishery experts on doubling inland fish production in West Bengal and efforts of a progressive fish farmer have been discussed, who has installed and introduced the most modern version of Recirculatory Aquaculture System and is the first of its kind to be constructed in non-Government sector in north-east India.

ODLA FISH SEED HATCHERY AND SRI LAKSMIKANTA BARMAN

It is a well-established fact that inland aquaculture expansion, both fish seed production and grow-out fish culture has the potential to create new job opportunities, high income generation and improve food security among rural households. Fish, fisheries and aquaculture have been playing

Formerly Part-time Lecturer, Master of Fishery Science Department, Utkal University, Bhubaneswar, Odisha, (India)

Corresponding and postal address: 122/1V, Monohar Pukur Road, P.O. Kalighat, Kolkata - 26, Pin: 700 026, (West Bengal)

an important role in addressing nutritional and livelihood security of poor in developing countries (Gupta, 2008). In last 7-8 years, author had intimate on-site conversation with quite a few progressive and elderly fish farmers and fishery entrepreneurs in different districts of West Bengal, their success stories have been documented, narrated and published in both English and Bengali versions under author's initiative. They are modest, hardworking, active with strong passion, show keen interest in fish farming; provide extension services, recommend right doses of fertilizers, manure, fish seeds, lime, $KMnO_4$, etc. for fish ponds so that other farmers can grow their crop profitably and sustainably; take efforts in promoting best management practices in pond aquaculture. During the culture process, they often develop new ideas to improve their culture practices, fish production and to conserve indigenous inland fish resource. Accomplishments of progressive fish farmers indicate the possibility of obtaining high production levels from per unit water area in a year. From a publication (Sawant and Bandyopadhyay, 2003), we have been informed about a 70-year old fish farmer from Tripura, who has contributed commendable to fisheries development through his own unique efforts.

Sri Laksmikanta Barman, aged 66 is undoubtedly such a kind of fish farmer. By dint of perseverance, hard work, good farm planning and management, he has successfully established his activities like fish seed production in hatchery and marketable-sized fish production. Sri Barman is the most reputed and successful progressive fish seed producer-cum-grow out fish farmer in Coochbehar and neighbouring districts in north Bengal. He was pleased to entertain author at his farm site on 18/5/2019 and provided details of his management practices. Sri Barman is proprietor of Odla Fish Seed Hatchery, which is located at Vill. Bhogramguri under Gopalpur Gram Panchayat, Mathabhanga-I Block, PS Mathabhanga, Dist. Coochbehar, WB.

DIFFERENT COMPONENTS OF HATCHERY

Presently the total area of this conventional carp hatchery (excluding nursery ponds) is 1.5 bigha, *i.e.*, 50 dec. There are five circular egg incubation-cum-hatching pools (cement construction) of 11-12 feet outside diameter for each; one circular egg incubation-cum-hatching pool (tin construction); one large circular breeding pool of 22 feet diameter; two small breeding pools 10-12 feet diameter for each; four 8mm thick steel-bodied cylindro-conical type egg incubation-cum-hatching units for carps (each having 2 feet diameter, 3.6 feet and 1.5 feet height of upper and lower portions respectively); two large rectangular cemented water holding tanks, each measuring 50 feet × 35 feet; four small squarish rectangular cemented tanks (72-75 hour old carp spawn are harvested from egg incubation pools and stocked here before sale); one earthen broodstock pond 7-8 dec in area. About 25 *bati* (spawn measuring cup, 100ml capacity) may be produced from each cylindro-conical egg hatching unit in one operation, Sri Barman explained. Interestingly there is no overhead tank in this fish hatchery complex. Flowing water of adjacent Sutunga river is drawn up into rectangular tanks, aerated and used in breeding pools and egg hatching pools. Sutunga river passes the town of Mathabhanga before it flows into Jaldhaka river.

As observed on 18/5/2019, the hatchery was in full-fledged state of operation; different stages like just hatched-out larvae of *Labeo bata, Puntius javanicus*; 60-hour old larvae of *Labeo rohita, Cirrhinus mrigala* and *L. bata*; 72-hour old IMC spawn ready for harvest; 10-hour old fertilized eggs of *L. rohita* and other major carps were being maintained in moving water column in hatching pools. Author observed the harvest of IMC brooders from pond, selection of matured males and females of separate species, their transfer into rectangular cement tank for temporary storage; those will be used for scheduled induced breeding in evening hours.

FISH SEED PRODUCTION

During the carp breeding season, 130 *bati* of healthy carp spawn are produced everyday at Odla Fish Seed Hatchery. The rate varies accordingly: Rs 600/-/bati during March-April; Rs 500/-/bati during April-May and Rs 400/-/bati during May-June. In addition to daily sale of 72-76 hour old carp spawn in oxygenated containers to customers in nearby and distant regions from this site, Sri Barman rear spawn of major carps and *P. javanicus* in bigger nurseries for 30-32 days, till it becomes advanced fry (1.5-2.0 inch). In three months period/season of spawn production, 450-480 *bati* carp spawn are reared till advanced fry and subsequently to bigger fingerlings stage at this farm. In nursery ponds 100-160 dec in area, major carp spawn are stocked @ 13-15 bati/33 decimal (1 *bati* holds 35000nos major carp spawn; 80000nos for *P. javanicus*).

Sri Barman sell the advanced carp fry to retailers @ Rs 220/-/kg during May-June and Rs 150/-/kg during August. A part of such major carp fry are reared to bigger fingerlings' stage here at Sri Barman's fish farm for stocking in the grow-out ponds. As feed for growing carp spawn, he uses liquefied ground nut oil cake @ 2.0-2.5kg/33 dec everyday. From Odla Fish Seed Hatchery, spawn and fry stages of major carps are supplied to fish farmers in different districts of north Bengal. Sri Barman explained that if 25-26 *bati* major carp spawn is stocked in 100 dec pond area, it will lead to production of 700-720kg advanced/bigger fry in next 25-28 days under proper management practices. Carp spawn are transported from this hatchery in large oxygen-packed polythene containers, each carrying 20 *bati* spawn and 42-45lit water.

GROW-OUT FISH FARMING

Sri Barman is having five grow-out carp culture ponds in his possession (own property), total area 54 bigha, *i.e.*, 7.2ha and another eight ponds (total 5.6ha) have been taken on lease, which is 10-12km away from his home. Fishes are harvested from ponds almost everyday. Selected matured ones are sent to hatchery complex for breeding purpose, the adults and sub-adults are sold in wholesale markets at Dhupguri, Jalpaiguri, Moynaguri and Mathabhanga towns. Major carp fingerlings (150-200gm; 6-7 inches) are stocked in ponds @ 1200nos/33 dec and harvested at the end of next 90-100 days. *L. rohita* and *C. mrigala* reach 800-900gm (sold @ Rs 180-190/-/kg), *Catla catla* 1500-1800gm (sold @ Rs 250-270/-/kg). Thus at an interval of 90-100 days, marketable-sized fishes are harvested and sold continuously for 5-6 days every time.

Sri Barman stated that molasses @ 4kg/33 dec, mustard oil cake @ 7kg/33 dec and yeast @ 150gm/33 dec should be mixed in polythene-lined earthen pit (6feet × 4feet × 1feet) constructed on embankment and water added to it. After leaving the watery mixture undisturbed for 5 hours, the supernatant fluid should be applied in grow-out fish ponds. It leads to enhancement of zooplankton population sufficiently. In grow-out fish ponds, commercially-available pelleted fish feed is seldom used in this farm; Sri Barman mainly uses farm-made formulated feed comprising maize dust 40kg, pulverized paddy grains 20kg, rice bran 20kg, mustard oil cake 10kg, fish meal 5kg, soyabean dust 5kg and Vitamin-Mineral mixture @ 1kg/quintal feed. Feed is applied as dough balls @ 3.5-4.0kg/100kg fish everyday.

Sri Barman did experiments on growth of Amur carp in 2015; the 1.5 inch stage supplied by air from WB Government farm in Kalyani to Siliguri and later to his farm reached 2500-2700gm in one year. Sri Barman is producing seeds of *Heteropneustes fossilis* since 2016. Brooders 2+ years in age are maintained and used, 6-7nos weighing 1kg. He explained that injected matured females release eggs only after rubbing their abdominal region against nylon net kept beneath inside breeding chamber (water depth: 4-5 inches). *H. fossilis* larvae when stocked in 8-10 dec nursery pond @ 40,00,000nos/33 dec attain 16-18mm individually at the end of 25 days.

STEADY PROGRESS IN AQUACULTURE

During 1985-1986, Sri Barman received teachings and inspiration from Sri Banaspati Biswas, the then Fishery Extension Officer, Mathabhanga-I Block and after realizing the benefits, he shifted into fish farming profession from jute and tobacco farming, which he started initially. Sri Barman has been into fish seed production and grow-out farming since 32 years of age. He begun fish farming in 1.72ha parental water body and established the Chinese hatchery in 2002-2003. Presently 18 permanent labours in all work in his fish hatchery and farm; these people have been provided employment on full time basis.

In July 1986, he received one month District-level training on freshwater fish culture at Office of the Asst. Director of Fisheries, Coochbehar. In the following year, he received three-months State-level training at Freshwater Fisheries Research and Training Centre (Government of WB), Kalyani town. Sri Barman has recently earned one prestigious award, the 'Krishak Samman' Award from Hon'ble Chief Minister of West Bengal on 14th March 2017 for his significant contribution in development of fish culture in the state. In May 2015, he received felicitation as 'Fish enthusiast' at district level in Boroli Fish Festival and on 10th July 2017, he was felicitated by Sri S. Roy, MP, Dum Dum constituency at Bonhooghly FCS farm complex, North 24 Pgs. Initially this hatchery had its Registration in Department of Fisheries, Government of WB in 1990 and again obtained seed certification and accreditation from the Department on 3/4/2014. He gives suggestions on proper methods and scientific culture of freshwater fishes to his new customers who procure fish spawn and advanced fry from this hatchery and to his neighbouring farmers. As a social worker, he has trained around 50 underprivileged farmers in Coochbehar district and motivated them to start fish farming on a small scale.

Sri Barman is maintaining a stock of 120nos formalin-preserved warmwater and coldwater finfish specimens in glass jars displayed over shelves at his home, many of which are not found in southern West Bengal and quite a few are rarely found presently in north Bengal. Sri Barman expressed sincere gratitude to Sri Aloknath Praharaj, Former Asst. Director of Fisheries, Coochbehar who has helped him to grow and prosper in fish farming vocation. Hon'ble District Magistrate, Coochbehar; SDO, Mathabhanga Sub-Division and MP, Coochbehar constituency have visited Sri Barman's fish farm more than once. Sri Laksmikanta Barman has been given the recognition 'Pride of Coochbehar'. He appreciates WB Fisheries Department for providing him technical knowhow in the field of fish culture and fish seed production. Sri Barman is a dedicated fish farmer, who tries to find ways to enhance fish production from his ponds and is a role model to hundreds of aqua-entrepreneurs.

Sri Barman inspecting growth of IMC hatchlings

Sri L. Barman at his hatchery site

Cylindro-conical egg incubation units

Tin-bodied circular egg incubation pool

Mixture of molasses, yeast and mustard oil cake

A grow-out fish culture pond of Sri Barman

Sri Barman (left), author and others in pond

Author discussing with Sri Barman

Carp spawn transportation from Odla FSH

'Krishak Samman' awarded to Sri Barman

ULUPI MATSYA UNNAYAN PRAKALPA

Sri Malin Chandra Sen, aged 62, is proprietor of Ulupi Matsya Unnayan Prakalpa, which is one of the two fish hatcheries-cum-fish seed production units running successfully in Jalpaiguri district of north Bengal. It was established in June 1982 and located at Vill. Baikur Gourgram, Padmabati-2 Gram Panchayat under PS and Block Moynaguri, P.O. Helapakri, Dist. Jalpaiguri. This hatchery obtained accreditation and seed certification from Department of Fisheries, Government of West Bengal on 17/6/2015. Fry and advanced fry of Indian major carps, exotic carps, *Notopterus chitala*, *Clarias batrachus*, *Labeo calbasu* and *Labeo bata* are produced here. Sri Sen is the most successful progressive fish seed producer in Jalpaiguri district. Author made a visit to Helapakri town on 12th May 2019 and obtained authentic information from Sri Sen about his efforts and achievements.

Since May 2018, progressive and experienced fish breeder Sri Sen started induced breeding and seed production of *C. batrachus*. Male and female 150-300gm size is used, Wova-FH (Rs 480/-/vial) is used as inducing agent. In the 2018 season, Sri Sen produced 10000 fry of *C. batrachus* (2.0-2.5 inch size) from his 14 dec earthen nursery pond. Only 650-700 pieces were stocked in grow-out pond for further propagation, rest were sold in fry stage. In next five months of culture, those attained 4.5-5.0 inch size (60-75gm), he harvested 50-52kg marketable-sized *C. batrachus* and those were sold locally @ Rs 350/-/kg. During 1980-1981, Sri Sen participated in 15-days Block-level training on freshwater fish culture and fondly remembered the help and inspiration received from Sri Atul Biswas, the then Dy. Director of Fisheries, Northern Zone and Sri Subhas Ghosh, the then Fishery Extension Officer, Moynaguri Block. He was immensely benefited by the rich course content of 15-days programme. He received hands-on training on fish breeding and hatchery management of carps from Sri Pabitra Narayan Neogi, reputed fish seed producer at Dinhata Block of adjacent Coochbehar district.

EXPERIENCE ON *N. CHITALA* SEED PRODUCTION

Sri Sen has been practicing seed production and grow-out farming of *N. chitala* since 1982 and has good deal of experience. In that year, he procured 25-30nos of fry stages obtained from river Teesta (Rs 1.50/-/piece) and stocked in his pond for raising upto broodstock. Now he is maintaining 35-40 numbers of *N. chitala* broodstock (males and females, 4.5-5.0kg size; 4-5 years in age). Larger ones are sold and not preferred for captive breeding. Sri Sen has experienced that if 1.5-2.0 inch stage is stocked in grow-out pond @ 500nos/33dec, it will attain 1000-1250gm body weight in 4-5 months of culture and sold in local market @ Rs 350-400/-/kg. He has kept provision for entry of small fishes like *Esomus danricus*, *Amblypharyngodon mola* and *Puntius* sp into pond naturally during rainy season upon which growing *N. chitala* will prey. Fry stages of the less economically-important carp *Cyprinus carpio var communis* obtained *via* induced breeding are fed to *N. chitala* during winter months.

Presently Sri Sen has three grow-out fish ponds in his possession, total area 230 dec (0.92ha). Total pond area (including nurseries) is 1.14ha. According to Sri Sen, it takes 8-9 days for fertilized eggs of *N. chitala* to hatch out. From every female, 8000-9000nos fertilized eggs are obtained. *N. chitala* seeds 18-20mm size are sold @ Rs 2.00/-/nos and 25-40mm size (7-days old) @ Rs 5.00/-/nos from Ulupi Matsya Unnayan Prakalpa. About 40000 seeds (fry) of *N. chitala* are produced here in every season (April-May to July-August). Properly maintained broodstock do not require hormonal injection and old large wooden drawers are placed inside pond over bottom soil for egg attachment. Water depth maintained at 4.5 feet. About 20000nos newly hatched-out *N. chitala* larvae are maintained within a wooden compartment 6ft x 8ft, having 6-7 inches water depth. Within next 6-7 days, their yolk sac is absorbed and two boiled egg yolks are used as feed daily for every 10000 seeds thereafter.

Sri Sen stated that tender stages of *N. chitala*, 12-18mm size (riverine or captive-bred) should be reared in 10 decimal earthen pond @ 1000nos/dec for next 20-22 days, till it becomes 2.0-2.5 inch in size. Ponds should have proper nylon net fencing all around. Riverine seeds under culture attain 2000-2250gm at the end of 1 year. In rectangular cement cistern measuring 8ft x 6ft, 15000nos seeds (12mm stage) can be stocked and reared for next 15 days. Those attain 1 inch. In this initial stage, zooplankton is their ideal food which can be sufficiently produced in nursery pond by adding 1kg wheat flour, 0.25kg molasses and 5kg cow dung for every 1 dec area, Sri Sen explained. If the 15-days old stage, 15000 in number is stocked in every 20 dec pond, it will reach 3.5-4.0 inch in next 25 days, which may be sold to grow-out fish farmers @ Rs 15-18/-/piece. Spawn of carps of less economic value (*Aristichthys nobilis, Labeo bata, Hypophthalmichthys molitrix*) are fed to them. If raw cow dung is mixed with sugarcane molasses and left undisturbed for 10-12 hours in a small rectangular cement tank, the supernatant formed may be successfully applied in nursery fish pond for production of zooplankton. Larger ones of *N. chitala* 4.0-5.0 inch are sold @ Rs 20-24/-/piece. In transportation containers (18-20lit) meant for *N. chitala* fingerlings, spawn of big head carp may be introduced. Fingerlings may be produced in large *hapa*-type net enclosures fitted in pond. It also prefers early stages of *Glossogobius giuris* and freshwater prawn like *Macrobrachium lammarei*.

During breeding season, mating of *N. chitala* occurs in pond normally during night hours of full moon and new moon periods, female fish lays eggs. Just prior to these days, feeble water current has to be created in pond using shallow pump machine, which will trigger mating and egg release of the fish. Egg attachers wooden frame or large wooden drawers are lifted 2-3 days after these days to ensure about production of fertilized eggs. Entire wooden structure is carefully brought out from pond and transferred quickly into nursery pond (5-6 dec). Pond water must be clean enough, otherwise fungal attack will be evident upon eggs. The 2.0-2.5 inch stage attains 6-7 inches in next 45 days of culture, which if stocked in beels and wetlands during July-August will attain 3000gm in 1 year.

SEED PRODUCTION OF MAJOR CARPS

About 3000 *bati* (spawn measuring cup; 100ml) healthy spawn of major carps are produced here every season. Those are sold to fish farmers at a rate ranging between Rs 750/- (at the beginning of season) to Rs 300/- per bati. Bundh breeding system is followed here, there is no separate overhead tank neither circular breeding pool. The Bangla bundh has been constructed at a higher elevation in comparison to location of egg incubation-cum-hatching pool (Chinese model) and an earthen pond (from where oxygenated water is drawn into bundh). Paddle-wheel aerator is operated in this pond water prior to use. Every year, Sri Sen procures 6-8kg larger fingerlings of major carps from Naihati market, South 24 Parganas district and Ramsagar village, Bankura district and are propagated upto broodstock stage. Carp brooders are fed commercially-prepared floating-type pelleted supplementary feed, Wova-FH used for carp breeding.

A mini circular hatchery meant for seed production of *Ompak pabda* and *Mystus vittatus* is presently under construction at Ulupi Matsya Unnayan Prakalpa. Sri Sen has been felicitated as a progressive fish farmer of Jalpaiguri district on 10th July, 2005 by Dy. Director of Fisheries, Northern Zone and again felicitated at district level in 2018. In July 2015, seed production activity of *N. chitala* at this fish hatchery has been recorded live and telecast by DD Bangla (Doordarshan Kolkata), a television channel.

Author discussing with Sri Malin Ch. Sen

Adhesive fertilized eggs of *Notopterus chitala*

Structure of fish breeding unit 'Bangla bundh'

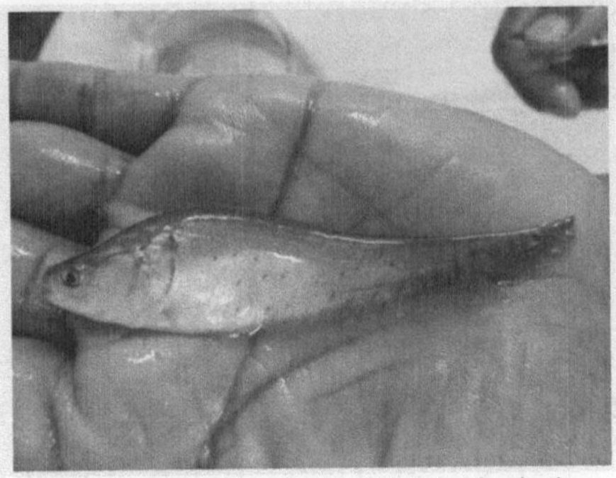

Notopterus chitala fry (3.5 inch size)

FISH FARMING IN RAS FACILITY

Aquaculture technologies currently receiving considerable R & D attention such as super intensive raceways, recirculatory systems and aquaponics are likely to make a significant contribution to future fish supply (Felix and Menaga, 2016). Fish farming in advanced-type Recirculatory Aquaculture System (RAS) facility has recently started at Jalpaiguri district, WB. In an effort to modernize fish culture practices, Sri Dibakar Sarkar at Vill. Amguri in north Bengal has installed and introduced the most modern version of RAS and is the first of its kind to be set up in non-Government sector in entire north-east India. Recently author had a glimpse of the entire structure and had intimate conversation with Sri Sarkar at his RAS site on 11/5/2019. Vill. Amguri-Kanyabari, P.O. Amguri, Block and PS Moynaguri, Dist. Jalpaiguri - it is at this place in north Bengal where the most advanced type of RAS has been installed. Since June 2018, progressive fish farmer and aqua-entrepreneur Sri Dibakar Sarkar and his father Sri Dilip Sarkar at the afore-mentioned address have installed the RAS facility in 3600sq.feet area (90ft x 40ft) beside their house and are propagating economically-important high-valued freshwater fishes like *Mystus vittatus*, *Mystus cavasius*, *Ompak pabda*, *Heteropneustes fossilis* and *Puntius javanicus* upto marketable size in a commercial scale successfully in their own endeavour in this indoor environment-friendly fish farming system.

Sri Sarkar explained that in such a kind of fish farming system, an imported technology and fully under control, used water is treated and purified by dual means of mechanical and biological filter systems, the latter depends on functioning of beneficial bacteria. Water inside fish tanks is incessantly purified, recycled and reused. In the circular tanks in RAS, fry-staged fishes can be stocked at a higher density in comparison to earthen pond system. Problems like slow growth and even fish mortality arise in conventional fish farming practices when physico-chemical parameters of pond water turns improper, bottom soil becomes unhygienic;

but such situations can be avoided in RAS. Presently certain issues like insufficient availability of quality water for fish culture in many rural areas, low water depth in ponds, shrunken pond water resource, deteriorating pond water and soil quality, water discharged from fish pond getting mixed with natural open freshwater resources and related environmental issues, spread of infectious/pathogenic microorganisms - all these factors have seriously impeded the steady development and prosperity of freshwater aquaculture in India. According to Sri Sarkar, RAS is a fruitful and viable alternative where such hindrances can be overcome, utilization of water for fish culture will not lead to its exhaust, more amount of fishes can be produced in less space, less requirement of labour for necessary monitoring and incidences of fish poaching will not occur.

DOOARS AQUACULTURE FARM

Sri Dibakar Sarkar (aged 30) and Dilip Sarkar are joint proprietors of Dooars Aquaculture Farm, where this RAS has been set up. After completing BSc in Zoology (Hons.) from Ananda Chanda College, Dist. Jalpaiguri, Sri Dibakar Sarkar got involved in commercial fish farming practices. For one decade he has been farming *Anabas testudineus* and indigenous *Clarias batrachus* in 22-25 dec earthen ponds and also monosex Tilapia, *P. javanicus, A. testudineus, H. fossilis* in 20nos of outdoor rectangular cement tanks, each 28ft × 10ft in area and 30000lit capacity. One outdoor polythene-lined monosex Tilapia pond (900sq.feet) and RAS have been constructed recently. They have spent Rs 48,00,000/- in establishment of this RAS system and fish farming can be continued (*i.e.,* sustainability of the system) for next 46-50 years uninterruptedly and efficiently without any major problem. It is the Israel model of RAS; a blend of experience, applied science and theoretical knowledge has led to innovation of this fish farming technology. Team of fishery scientists and technical experts from Israel and Bangladesh have visited this site and monitored the entire installation process of RAS. Resource-rich progressive fish farmers can also avail China or Canada model of RAS and the cost will be more or less similar to this model, Sri Sarkar stated. Entire area is covered with corrugated galvanized iron roofing (with ventilation facilities) at sufficient height from floor, transparent sheets used at few places.

MODE OF FUNCTIONING OF RAS

This RAS comprise eight circular fish culture tanks, each 10000lit capacity, diameter 4mt, total height 1.2mt and water depth 1mt. Body of tanks made up of zinc-aluminium alloy sheets, commercially termed Jaylon sheet. Each tank has translucent polythene sheet covering on inner wall and base, taking shape of a single huge container; fishes are maintained within it. Used water passes through centrally-located outlet and enters into drum filter, it has filter screen of 80-100micron mesh size. Suspended and settle-able particulate organic waste matter is captured and separated. Further the water passes through pipeline and enters into biofilter system, main objective is to eliminate toxic ammoniacal nitrogen and dissolved ammonia.

Sri Sarkar stated that it is the single pass biofiltration (SPB) model, 12 feet in height. Water is forcefully sprayed into biofilter system through nozzle, thus water gets enriched with dissolved oxygen and concentration of free/dissolved carbon dioxide is declined to its minimum. Subsequently adequate concentration of beneficial nitrifying bacteria (*Nitrosomonas* sp, *Nitrobacter* sp) significantly oxidizes the ammonia in water first into nitrite and next into nitrate. Sri Sarkar routinewise adds commercially-available biological media (resembling tapioca pearls) over biofilter bed to facilitate proper growth of beneficial bacteria. Water is now fit to be recycled back to circular fish culture tanks, harmful waste product and feed residues have already been detoxified in this process (Ghosh, 1983). Concentration of BOD, ammonia and nitrite is reduced to nil, that of nitrate remains within safe limit. An overhead tank 15000lit capacity has been set up outside RAS premises. Underground water drawn up *via* borewell is first treated and made iron-free, subsequently is supplied to overhead tank. From here, new freshwater is supplied into eight culture tanks in RAS as and when required.

Initially when fish culture begun in this RAS, it took three months to have sufficient growth of nitrifying bacteria in biofilter of RAS. Here bacteria is not recharged directly from outside. In this system, 50000lit of water is purified and recycled every hour and depending on the capacity of pumps, water in the entire RAS (eight tanks) is recycled and reused once in two hours, Sri Sarkar explained. Water is renewed/exchanged incessantly, considerable volume of water is saved. He has taken special measures for continuous power supply (electricity generation) in RAS. Fishes are nurtured in an ideal environment, it grows fast and fed quality supplementary feed. Like greenhouse agri-farming, this RAS is a notable technology-based development and holds great potential.

GROWTH OF FISHES

Sri Sarkar produces and harvests 60kg fishes (*O. pabda, M. vittatus, M. cavasius*) from every cubic mt volume of water (1000lit) in 135-150 days period. Fry-staged *O. pabda* is procured from a hatchery located in Hili Block of Dakshin Dinajpur district (1.5 inch size; 2000-2500nos/kg) and stocked in RAS @ 8000-8500nos/circular tank. In next five months, it reaches marketable size of 50-60gm and sold in local market in Jalpaiguri district @ Rs 500-600/-/kg. Young ones of *M. cavasius* (4000-4500nos/kg) reach 25-40gm size at the end of 150 days and sold @ Rs 450-500/-/kg. Growing fishes are fed floating-type supplementary pelleted feed (Rs 65-75/-/kg, 30-40% protein content) everyday. No kind of medicine neither any chemical additive are used for promoting fish growth or water treatment. Healthy fishes 600kg in amount is harvested from each culture tank at the end of each culture duration. *O. pabda* has to be fed 4-5 times a day; it shows cannibalistic nature in conditions of insufficient feed. Only dried feed should be applied in RAS, Sri Sarkar stated. Fry-staged *H. fossilis* are stocked @ 6000-7000nos/circular tank. In one month, it reaches 2.5-3.0 inches and harvested at the end of 120 days. Air bubble diffuser type aerators, 2-3nos may be used in each culture tank. In conditions of low water column in tanks and power cut, farming of *H. fossilis* do not pose a problem as these fishes have accessory respiratory organ. In comparison to fishes grown in ponds, fishes reared in RAS show a highly economical FCR.

Sri Sarkar received training on seed production and farming of monosex Tilapia at RGCA, Vijaywada Centre, Andhra Pradesh where 125 families of the fish are separately maintained. He had procured monosex Tilapia seeds (5gm size; Rs 2.50/-/piece) and stocked experimentally both in large outdoor cemented chambers and in RAS. Those reached to 200gm size in 60-75 days period when reared in RAS tanks and same size was found to be attained in 110-120 days when reared in outdoor rectangular chambers. Pipeline control valves of this RAS have been manufactured in Italy, the drum filter component in Germany and finally all equipments/ machineries are assembled at Israel. Fry stages of cultivable fishes are reared for 12-14 days in outdoor rectangular tanks before being transferred into RAS facility. A combination of commercially-available probiotic *Bacillus* sp (Rs 8000/-/kg) and molasses is used in each outdoor tank. Beneficial bacteria utilize molasses as carbon source and converts ammonia into protein efficiently. Ratio of carbon and nitrogen is maintained at 14:1 in each such tank.

POTENTIAL AND PROSPECT OF RAS

Initial investment in RAS can be lessened if rapid sand filter is used (indigenous technology) as an alternative to expensive but highly-efficient drum filter. In this way, settleable solid waste can be removed from used water of fish holding/culture tanks. About 350kg white sand will be required with particle size 2mm. In an indigenous biofilter model of 2000lit capacity (cement structure), dead oyster shells or freshwater mussel shells can be used, which provides a substratum for growth of nitrifying bacteria in the form of biofilm. Oyster shells with sufficient surface area are used for attachment of bacteria and for maximizing contact with passing water for removal of ammonia. It will cost Rs 65000/- and Rs 20000/- to set up such a rapid sand filter and biofilter tank respectively (Courtesy: Scientists of ICAR-CMFRI Visakhapatnam Regional Centre).

Sri Sarkar has also set up white cylindro-conical monosex Tilapia egg incubation-cum-hatching chambers, 60000 fertilized eggs can be kept in each. He further stated that since April 2013, a progressive fish farmer in Hyderabad has been farming *Pangasianodon hypophthalmus* in 40000lit circular tanks in modern RAS (cement tanks with coat of epoxy paint, 6mt diameter) facility. Fingerlings @ 3500nos/tank are stocked and harvested at 1kg size at the end of 180 days. This farmer is able to produce 100kg fish from every 1000lit volume of water. RAS can be installed under carbonated tin shed. As strict biosecurity measure and to prevent entry of pathogenic microorganism in RAS premises of Dooars Aquaculture Farm, shoes are not allowed inside and one has to wear white apron coat and disposable face masks after washing hands with $KMnO_4$ solution. Outsiders are not allowed inside RAS facility during an ongoing fish culture operation.

If indigenous components are innovated and used in RAS, it will become more acceptable to fish farmers in West Bengal in days to come, Sri Sarkar opined. Further research is necessary in this regard. Primary school teacher-cum-fish farmer Sri Dibakar Sarkar and his father, with support of two permanent labours have introduced this newer 'indoor fish farming' technology and advanced model of RAS in WB which holds great prospect. Fishes farmed here are considered as new candidate species in freshwater aquaculture. Aquaculture diversification, both in terms of system and species, has taken place here. Their pioneering endeavour is indeed praiseworthy, their indoor fish farm based on RAS will turn out to be a profitable venture and more fish farmers in different districts of WB and neighbouring states are expected to adopt this modern technology in near future. Author is truly grateful to Sri Dibakar Sarkar for providing much information on this new system.

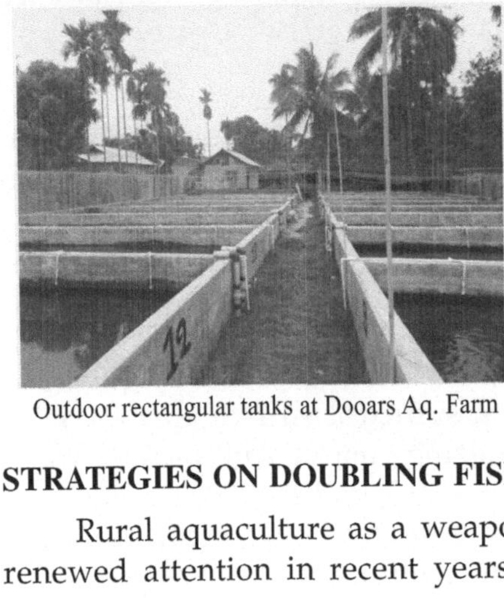

Outdoor rectangular tanks at Dooars Aq. Farm

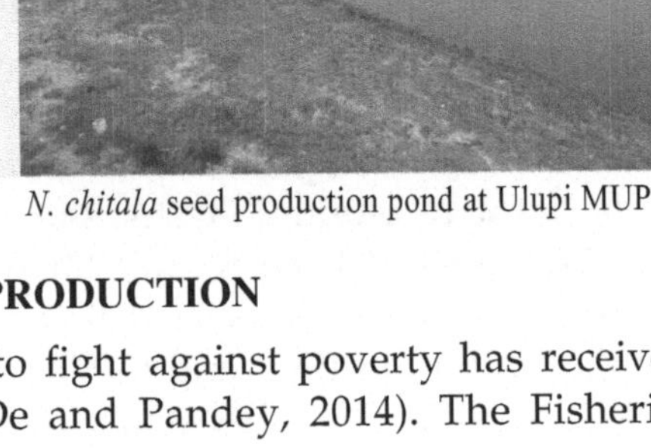

N. chitala seed production pond at Ulupi MUP

STRATEGIES ON DOUBLING FISH PRODUCTION

Rural aquaculture as a weapon to fight against poverty has received renewed attention in recent years (De and Pandey, 2014). The Fisheries

Department of the then Government of Bengal was first set up in 1911. It was revived in 1942 as it was felt necessary to cope up with the growing needs for increase in production of fish by exploiting all the available impounded water resources. A Technical Seminar entitled 'Technology intervention for doubling fish production - role of Good Management Practices and quality inputs: Vision 2020' was organized by Department of Fisheries, Government of West Bengal as a part of Bengal Fish Fest 2019 at ICAR-CIFE Kolkata Centre on 12/1/2019. It was a very good discussion session. Director of Fisheries, GoWB stated that fisheries and aquaculture sectors in WB are playing a potential role in upliftment of economic condition of rural people; fishery is a major economic activity in WB. She emphasized on better and sustainable fish supply in markets and highlighted major interventions of Directorate of Fisheries in improving fish production. Addressing the farmers, Hon'ble Principal Secretary, Department of Fisheries, WB mentioned it is a platform for knowledge sharing and experience sharing, we have to consider and document newer interventions, experimentations and technology development by fish farmers. They should speak about new Schemes that can be formulated and taken up by the Department for improving fish production. Commissioner of Fisheries, WB mentioned that 'Knowing helps in doing' and 'Doing is more important than knowing'; knowledge of experts must supplement the work of fish farmers on field. Farmers should transmit take-away message from this Seminar to colleagues and should reach to farthest points of villages. In 2017-2018, 17.42 lakh tonnes of inland fishes was produced in WB from 4,00,000ha water area, but production in Andhra Pradesh exceeds that of WB from 1,50,000ha impounded water area. We have to find out avenues of keeping pace with AP in terms of quantity of fish production.

Dr M.A. Hassan, Principal Scientist, ICAR-CIFRI, Barrackpore spoke on 'Good Management Practices (GMP) in Aquaculture'. He focused on certain aspects, like outcome of research conducted in laboratories is carried to fish farmers by WB State Government; knowledge-based farming as new initiative; WB blessed with good geographical location, quality water, fertile soil, productivity, sufficient sunlight for fish culture and considerable fish biodiversity; optimization, reuse and recycle of resources for optimum benefit; improving efficiency of pond water and fish feed; fish culture systems in WB; small irrigation tanks and canals as new sectors for fish production which needs technological intervention; modern technologies like RAS, cage and pen culture where more orientation and training are required (factors affecting growth and well-being of fish are taken care in RAS and ammonia controlled); use of balanced fish feed and proper feeding management; extensive (stocking @ 1-4 pieces/sq.mt), semi-intensive (5-10 pieces/sq.mt) and intensive types of finfish farming; doubling fish production and production of more aquatic products with significantly increasing the usage of basic natural property of water and soil resource; developing sustainable aquaculture system for production of food and export commodities that will not damage environment.

Dr Hassan defined GMP as production of healthy aquatic organisms using efficient and cost-effective methods to improve human capacity, spoke on fish as nutrition/health capsule; building fish culture systems providing an equitable cost-benefit ratio to support economic and social sustainability that will protect livelihood of aquaculturists and dependent communities; carrying capacity of pond water and soil and targeting optimum production; entrepreneurial approach required among fish farmers; fish seed, feed, fish health, social and environmental challenges in aquaculture; cluster approach and co-operative formation in fish farming; bird repeller as a biosecurity measure in ponds; sunlight as key input in natural pond productivity; making use of natural productivity (less intervention gives 2000kg/ha production); provision for water from culture ponds let out to sedimentation area where fine particles of waste settle down, subsequently to treatment pond and water recycled back to culture units; conversion of undrainable ponds into drainable ones.

Dr Hassan appreciated good work done by WB Government by constructing water harvesting structures under Jal Bharo Jal Dharo programme. He stated that depth and volume of water should be increased in fish ponds; pond waste management, silt removal and use of mechanical aerators; means of reduction of anaerobic condition in pond bottom; procurement of quality fish seeds from certified hatcheries; stocking fry stage with known genealogy for production of yearlings in facilities with water replenishment; replacement of brooders in hatcheries from that in rivers (high quality broodfishes found in river Son in Bihar); requirement of 25-40% soyabean protein in fish feed; concern for animal protein - 1.5kg trash fish is required to produce fish meal, from which 1kg farmed shrimp is produced; economic efficiency of feed is bad if FCR is high; irreparable damage of environment should be stopped. Dug-out fish ponds in AP are newer in existence (16-20 years old) in comparison to that in WB, those have proper gravity towards outlet and are modern aquaculture farms. Ponds in WB are small and undrainable, mostly dug out long back and need mud removal on regular basis. Dr Hassan cautioned that rodenticide Aluminium phosphide (Celphos) must not be used to harvest fishes - it saves manpower but is deleterious in long run. Recently shrimp consignment from WB was rejected by Japanese Government due to presence of Furazolidone antibiotic.

Dr T.K. Ghoshal, Principal Scientist, ICAR-CIBA, Kakdwip Research Centre spoke on 'Technological interventions in brackishwater (BW) aquaculture'. BW aquaculture is a sunrise and rapidly transforming sector; 60,000ha used for BW culture in WB out of 2,12,000ha and 30,000ha for scientific culture; achievements of developed and transforming BW fish farmers in Uttar Chandanpiri village, South 24 Pgs; domestic consumption of shrimps should be increased as ups and downs exist in export; requirement of high saline water as constraint for establishment of BW hatchery (for shrimp and finfishes) in WB; application of shrimp toilet technology; risk increases in BW aquaculture in conditions of high investment, more production and high return; reduction in input dependency and emphasis on pond management in shrimp culture; injection vaccine against viral diseases will be fruitless in shrimp as it is primitive organism with weak immune system; import of *L. vannamei* broodstock to India from Mexico; ICAR-CIBA produced SPF *L. vannamei* by selective breeding and now it gains 25-30gm in four months, high density stocking is possible; research progress in producing indigenous variety of *Penaeus indicus*; cage culture of *Lates calcarifer* and weaning to artificial diet from early stage; crores of investment in establishing *L. calcarifer* hatchery in private sector.

Being exotic species, farmers are not familiar of diseases in *L. vannamei* and 3.73 lakh tonnes of it produced in India in 2014-2015. Dr Ghoshal spoke about less protein requirement in feed of mullets as being non-carnivorous; widespread domestication and culture of milkfish in Indonesia and ICAR-CIBA's success in its breeding and grow-out culture; promotion of *Scatophagus argus* and *Etroplus suratensis* as ornamental fishes in WB; organic farming of *Penaeus monodon* for premium price at 6nos/sq.mt stocking and 1300kg/ha production (32.7gm av.); decline of *P. monodon* production in BW bheri due to WSD; possibility of developing branded product 'Sundarban tiger shrimp'; research initiatives to produce SPF *P. indicus*, its growth normally reduces after 20gm; *L. vannamei* culture is high input-oriented; its export price dropped in 2017 in USA as production was heavy and exceeded demand; necessity of crab *Scylla serrata* seed production; fattening boxes of female *S. serrata* in ponds kept completely submerged during daytime in summer by allowing air into PVC pipes (floating platform); stocking *L. vannamei* @ 50-60nos/sq.mt and 8-10tonnes/ha production - huge profit obtainable but not recommended for poor/marginal farmers; *L. vannamei* must not escape into natural water bodies from farm ponds; importance of strict biosecurity measures, effluent treatment pond in *L. vannamei* farms and knowledge sharing in BW sector. Dr Ghoshal opined that small PCR labs can be set up at district or sub-division level in WB for shrimp seed testing, where lesser-employed trained youths can be engaged with expertise and technological support of ICAR-CIBA.

Dr G.H. Pailan, Principal Scientist, ICAR-CIFE Kolkata Centre spoke on 'Role of quality feed, seed and fertilizer for doubling production'. We should aim at optimization of fish production rather than maximization; slow development of sustainable aquaculture occurs in conditions like improper pond preparation, lack of natural fish food organisms, non-compliance of recommended quality seed and limited approach to integrated fish farming; role of environment in augmenting fish production; criteria of checking physico-chemical parameters and good water quality; method of water sample collection for testing; farmer-friendly water testing kit developed by ICAR-CIFE for different parameters; proper fertilization schedule based on nutrient requirement of ponds; fish seed as important criterion for fish quality enhancement and better crop; supply of broodstock to hatchery owners as praiseworthy initiative of GoWB; parameters to assess improved breeding performance; genetic interventions on improved seed quality and considerations for broodstock upgradation; desirable broodstock nutrients for breeding performance.

Some expert farmers should only develop broodfish in WB and supply to hatcheries like that in China for good quality fry and fingerling production; preparation of fish feed using different protein source (plant and animal ingredients) with balanced amino acid composition; Tryptophan and Methionine required in brood fish diet and supplemented externally; soyabean meal is ineffective as lipid source for cultivable BW fishes as being devoid of EPA and DHA; Vitamin-C and E cause proper egg maturation and improve fecundity in broodfishes and crushed shrimp head portion as carotenoids in its diet; importance of phosphorous as macro-mineral, squid meal and cuttlefish meal in broodfish diet; egg production in broodfishes impeded in conditions of malnutrition, oxygen depletion and stress; early maturation and breeding of major carps made possible in Assam during March-April by simulating environmental conditions; formulation of supplementary fish feed with balanced protein and energy sources; prerequisite information for feed formulation; blood meal as feed ingredient should be avoided as its digestibility is less. All dignitaries gave thorough and thoughtful explanation on the subject of the Seminar; such strategies will definitely pave the way for a prosperous future of inland aquaculture in West Bengal. Fish farmers like Sri L. Barman, Sri M. C. Sen and Sri D. Sarkar have evolved innovations in aquaculture sector and it may be termed as 'farmer-led innovations'. In words of Sri L. Barman, it is 'Gramyo Bigyan' or village science.

Dr M.A. Hassan making presentation

Dr G.H. Pailan making presentation

REFERENCES

De, H.K. and Pandey, D.K. (2014): Rural Aquaculture - now and then, *Economic Affairs*, Paper No. 157, 59(4): 497-504.

Felix, S. and Menaga, M. (2016): Recent Advances in Aquaculture System Diversification, In. P. Jayasankar *et al* Eds. *Souv. National Seminar on Aquaculture Diversification - the way forward for Blue Revolution. ICAR-CIFA, Bhubaneswar, Odisha Publication*: 79-84.

Ghosh, D. (1983): Wastewater Treatment and Reuse (In Bengali), *West Bengal State Book Board Publication,* Kolkata, pp: 96.

Gupta, M.V. (2008): Challenges to be Addressed for Aquaculture to Meet the Growing Global Demand, In. *Souv. Brainstorming Meet on Aquaculture 2025 - Challenges and Opportunities, ICAR-CIFA, Bhubaneswar, Odisha Publication*: 1-13.

Sawant, B.T. and Bandyopadhyay, P. (2003): Saga of a Progressive Fish Farmer, *Kurukshetra,* 51 (3): 46-48.

Pages: 168-179

Seeds and Food: ***Processing and Storage Techniques***
Edited by: **Dr. Prasann Kumar and Dr. Pawan Kumar 'Bharti'**
ISBN: 978-93-88854-41-2
Edition: **2020**
Published by: **Discovery Publishing House Pvt. Ltd., New Delhi (India)**

9

Food and Crop Storage Technology

Prasann Kumar[1*2], Shipa Rani Dey[1]

GRAPHICAL ABSTRACT

Keywords: Crop, Food, Storage, Technology

INTRODUCTION

Storage is the art of keeping the quality of agricultural materials and preventing them from deterioration for specific period of time, beyond their normal shelf life.

[1] Department of Agronomy, School of Agriculture, Lovely Professional University, Jalandhar - 144 411 Punjab (India)
[2] Divison of Research and Development, Lovely Professional University, Jalandhar - 144 411 Punjab, (India)

The reasons for storage include:

- Perishable nature of agric. & bio-materials
- Provision of food materials all year round
- Pilling/provision for large scale processing
- Preservation of viability for multiplication
- Prevention of original varieties from extinction (Germ Bank)
- Preservation of nutritional quality
- Weapon for national stability
- Price control and regulation
- Optimization of farmers' gain/financial empowerment of farmers
- Opportunity for export market, etc.

STORAGE TYPES: CLASSIFICATIONS

Classification of storage types can be based on the following factors:

- Duration of Storage
- Size or Scale of Storage
- Principle of Storage

Storage systems are classified in terms of duration of storage as:

- Short Term Storage
- Medium Term Storage
- Long Term Storage
- Stored products in short term storage mostly do not last beyond 6 months
- Highly perishable products (such as egg, meat, fish and dairy products) are naturally stored for short term
- High loss of quality is associated with highly perishable crops in this storage except controlled systems are used
- Medium term storage involves keeping the quality of stored products without appreciable deteriorations for up to 12 months
- The quality of such stored products may not be guaranteed after 18 months
- Long term storage can guarantee the quality of stored products beyond 5 years
- Germ banks and some storage systems are known to preserve viability and proximate characteristics of stored materials for decades

Storage systems are classified in terms of size or scale of storage as:

- Small Scale Storage
- Medium Scale Storage
- Large Scale Storage

- Small scale storage systems have capacity for up to 1 ton, but not beyond
- They are mostly used at domestic and peasant levels
- They are associated with peasant farmers with small farm holdings
- Medium scale storage can accommodate up to a hundred tons of stored products
- Most of such storage systems are in the capacity range of 2-50 tons, with very few having capacity beyond 50 tons
- Some are used in breweries for temporary storage of spent grains
- Large scale storage can accommodated stored material in 100s and1000s of tons
- It is used either for temporary or permanent storage of very large quantity of various products
- It has a very high initial cost but eventually reduces overall unit cost of production

Storage systems can be classified in terms of principle of operation. These include:

- Physical Storage
- Chemical Storage
- Biological Storage
- Physical storage utilizes physical principles to achieve storage and preservation the quality of stored products
- The physical environment (in terms of moisture content, temperature and relative humidity) within the storage system is mostly controlled or manipulated to retard the activities of agents of deterioration or prevent deterioration. E.g. cold storage or controlled environment
- Chemical storage utilizes chemicals to stop or retard the activities of agents of deterioration
- The use of chemicals such as wax, actellic, or phosphosene dust or tablet to prevent respiration or insect infestation in stored produce are examples
- Some chemicals are however poisonous and their uses must be highly monitored, e.g. phosphosene
- Biological storage utilizes biological agents, especially micro organism, to stop or retard the activities of agents of deterioration or enhance the shelf life of stored products
- This is a very good area of the application of bio-technology in agriculture

The major physical, chemical & biological factors affecting the storage of bio-materials include:

- Micro organisms
- Insects, mite and pests
- Rodents
- Environmental factors

Major microorganism associated with storage include:

- Fungi
- Bacterial
- Yeast

The activities of microorganism result in:

- Color degradation
- Off flavor
- Moisture upgrading, wet spot & moldiness
- Loss of viability, etc
- Insects, mites and pests attack both the stored material and wooden components of the storage structure
- Weevils are the commonest insects in grains. They attack seeds and bore through them, and lay eggs in the seeds and storage structures
- They reduce seed weight, quality, nutritional value and viability
- Rodents are mammals that parasite on stored materials and attack storage structures
- They eat germs of grains and waste the remaining parts
- They are vectors. They also contaminate stored materials with their faeces, urine and carcasses

The environmental factors that mostly associated with stored products include:

- Temperature
- Relative humidity
- Equilibrium moisture content

Broadly, storage structures are classified as:

- Traditional Structures: Small sized and short term with high level of infestation. They are mostly made of unrefined local materials
- Modern Structures: Mostly large capacity and long term with better regulation of the storage environment. They are made of improved and refined materials
- These are devices used mostly for short term and small scale storage
- Occasionally they include some medium term and medium scale storage devices
- They require low level of scientific knowledge to construct, operate and maintain. They are mostly made of unrefined local material

Traditional storage structures include:

- Rhombus
- Crib
- Barn
- Shelf
- Pit/Underground Storage
- Plastic Containers
- Guard
- Polythene bag
- Earthen pot

Rhombus & Traditional Crib:

- These are used for grain storage, mostly materials in cob. Rhombus is mostly used in Northern Nigeria while the traditional crib is used in South Western and Eastern Nigeria
- Rhombus is cylindrical in shape while crib has rectangular shape. They are made of palm font leaf, clay, tree stem and bamboo
- Major disadvantages are moisture build as a result of rain, and microorganism infestation
- Sometimes coal or wood heat is introduced at the lower base to ensure drying

Barn, Shelf & Pit:

- These are mostly used for root and tuber crops. Barn and shelf could be suitable for onion & carrot. Barn, shelf and pit are recommended for cassava, yam and cocoyam
- These storage structures are affected by environmental conditions

Plastic Containers, Guard, Polythene bag &earthen pot:

- These structures are used at household and peasant levels for the storage of grain. Earthen pots are equally used for storage of fruits such as orange
- Though small scale and short term in nature, they are very effective if used under air tight conditions
- Items stored in these systems are locally preserved with wood or bone ash or powdered pepper

Modern storage structures include:

- Improved crib
- Ware house
- Silo

- Controlled atmosphere storage system
- Refrigeration
- Cold storage
- Evaporative coolant system (ECS)
- Hermetic storage
- Nitrogen storage

Improved Crib:

- This structure is an improvement over the traditional crib in terms of design, capacity, construction material and performance. It has upgraded the traditional crib to medium scale storage. Each unit can accommodate 10-20 tons
- Ware house is used for medium but mostly large scale storage for bagged or pilled/bulk products such as grains, flour, etc.
- Wooden pallets are used for staking. Material handling and ventilation equipment's are essential
- Prevention of roof leakage and water infiltration through the floor are most essential. Water proof materials are used for flooring & proper drainage important
- Silo is a cylindrically shaped structure used for bulk storage of shelled grains in large scale and for long term
- Moisture migration and condensation are major problems of silo. Hence, the need for accessories such as material handling and drying equipment's
- Design, operation and maintenance of silo require high level of skill & technicalities

Silo can be classified on the basis of:

- Aeration method/system
- Material of construction
- Level of technology sophistication
- Structural stability

Based on the aeration method, silo can be classified as:

- Mechanical ventilated silo
- Controlled atmosphere silo
- Hermetic silo
- Gas (nitrogen, oxygen, etc) silo

Based on the material of construction, silo can be classified as:

- Metal (aluminum, steel, etc.) silo
- Concrete silo

- Wooden silo
- Mud silo
- composite silo

Based on the level of technology, silo can be classified as:

- Conventional silo
- Instrumentalised silo
- Computerized/automated silo

Based on structural stability, silo can be classified as:

- Deep silo
- Shallow silo
- Controlled atmosphere storage system is a general classification that include all forms of storage structures that have devices for controlling and monitoring the environmental factors (temperature, relative humidity and moisture)
- Silo, ware house, refrigeration and cold storage could incorporate controlled atmosphere systems
- Refrigeration is a typical CA system that can operate below atmospheric temperature. The evaporator unit of a refrigerator could depress temperature a little below zero degrees through the aid of R12 gas
- A refrigerator is made up of components such as condenser, evaporator, compressor, throttle pipes, fan, thermostat, etc
- It is used for the storage of highly perishable crop and food materials
- Cold storage is a CA system that can further depress temperature below that of the refrigerator with the aid of R22 gas and maintain temperature below freezing point for a long time
- It has similar components like the refrigerator but more bulky, expensive and could store for relatively longer time

The unique advantages of cold storage include:

- Retardation of respiration and other metabolic activities
- Controls ripening, retards aging, softening, texture and color change. Preserves color & texture
- Retards moisture loss & wilting
- Retards microbial activities & spoilage
- Retards sprouting & undesirable growth, etc

The following information are essential in the use of cold storage:

- Temperature fluctuations affect temperature sensitive crops. Therefore, keep temperature and storage condition steady and constant

- Pre cool fruits to remove field heat before products are transferred into cold store
- Avoid storing incompatible products
- Ensure adequate ventilation within cold store and use appropriate relative humidity
- Evaporative coolant system (ECS) is another CA storage. It slightly depresses temperature below and increases the relative humidity above atmospheric conditions by natural means. It is appropriate for the storage of fruits & vegetables
- ECS utilizes the principle of evaporation occurring at the surface of a wet material to produce cooling inside. Wetted padded materials are normally used as medium of evaporation
- Hermetic storage structure prevents air absorption into the stored products in order to disallow metabolic activities of any form by the product, micro organism or insect
- Consequently, hot spot, wet spot and moisture build in storage systems are prevented
- Gas (nitrogen, oxygen, etc) storage structure provides devices that allows essential gas such as nitrogen or oxygen to be introduced and preserved in the system in order to prevent ripening or/and metabolic activities.
- Some silo and cold storage structures are provided with such facilities

Essential design considerations and parameters for modern storage structures include:

- Location & orientation
- Systems capacity
- System efficiency
- Handling methods & equipments
- Structural stability & requirements

Agric./bio-material have the following characteristics/ nature in relation to storage:

- Living organism
- Moisture rich
- Ripening process
- Bio degradable
- Hygroscopic: Shrinkage and swelling occur

Drying is essential during storage because of the following reasons:

- Metabolic activities of agricultural materials

- Variations in the ambient conditions
- Activities of microorganisms and insects
- Direct admission of water into storage systems through leaking roof, wall or floor
- Moisture build in storage structures due to condensation and wet spot, etc

A dryer is therefore required to supply heated air for drying during storage. A dryer has the following basic components:

- Heat source to supply heat
- Fan to move the heat
- Duct to channel the heated air
- Insulator to ensure minimal heat loss
- Control systems to regulate air parameters such as temperature, relative humidity, flow rate, enthalpy, entropy, etc

Classification of dryers is based on the following:

- Principle of operation (Natural, mechanical, solar)
- Mode of air & product movement (Co current, counter current, cross flow)
- Level of technology (conventional, semi-automated, fully automated)
- Source of heat supply (Solar, electrical, fossil fuel, bio-fuel, etc)

The knowledge of the properties of air and the interactions between these properties are essential in the drying of agricultural materials

Essential properties of air include:

- Vapor pressure
- Relative humidity
- Humidity ratio
- Dry bulb temperature
- Wet bulb temperature
- Enthalpy
- Entropy
- Specific volume

The psychometric chart relates all the essential air properties in a single chart and it is used for determining air properties at different drying conditions, at specified air pressure

Heated air is used for drying while cool air is used for refrigeration. During heating or cooling either of the following processes could occur:

- Sensible heating or cooling

- Heating with humidifying
- Cooling with dehumidifying

Two major types of drying rates associated with the drying of agricultural materials include:

- Constant drying rate: Rate of moisture removal is constant. This is mostly the case at the beginning of drying for very wet products such as fruits and vegetables
- Falling drying rate: Rate of moisture removal is not constant but decreasing because all free surface water and water of saturation are removed

Solar dryings are especially recommended for the tropical regions because of the high intensity and duration of solar radiation.

Solar dryer essentially consists of the following:

- Collector (flat plate or concentrator type)
- Air duct
- Solar storage (mostly optional), black stones are used locally
- Drying chamber

Material handling equipment are essential accessories for large scale storage structures

Material movement into and within storage structures for large scale structures is effective using material handling facilities such as:

- Folk lift
- Screw conveyor
- Belt conveyor
- Bucket elevator
- Pneumatic conveyor
- This shows the relationship and interaction between physical parameters (namely temperature, relative humidity and equilibrium moisture content) that affect the storage of agricultural/ bio-materials
- Essential aspects of moisture isotherm of importance include:
- Isotherm Equation (Henderson Eqn)
- Isotherm Curve: Sorption, Desorption & Hysterisis
- Local Isotherms and Storage Stability
- Dairy products, meat and fish are highly perishable materials because of their very high level of moisture and high microorganism activities associated with them
- Refrigeration and cold storage are mostly recommended for the storage of this category of material

- Fruits and vegetables are in the category of perishable agricultural materials
- They are also very rich in moisture content and can easily be bruised and wilt quickly
- They are the riches natural source of minerals vitamins, and anti-oxidants
- They cannot tolerate heat and high temperatures. ECS & refrigeration are recommended for their storage
- Root and tuber are tropical crops. They are very rich source of carbohydrate
- Care must be taken during harvest to avoid bruise in order to ensure effective storage
- Pit storage is recommended for cassava which must be harvested with its stem
- Shelf, barn and pit storage are recommended for yam and cocoyam
- This is a national plan supported by policies to provide large scale storage for agricultural and food material to ensure national food sufficiency, stability and price control especially at critical periods (war, famine, disaster, draught, flood, etc.)
- The use of large scale and long term storage structures such as silo, warehouse and cold storage are inevitable for such national plans

CONCLUSION

Strategic Food Reserve policies must be all embracing and consider the following factors:

- Socio economic factors
- Technical factors
- Capacity building
- Legal implications, etc.

REFERENCES

Adewumi, B.A and A.F Akerele. 2003. Evaluation of the storage qualities of onions in domestic environment. Proceeding of the Nigeria Society of Bio Technology, 25: 103-106.

Adewumi, B.A., J.C Igbeka and A.A Satimehin. 1990. Evaluation of Crib Storage Structures in South Western Nigeria. Paper Presentation at the Annual Conference of the Nigerian Society of Agricultural Engineers, Makurdi,.

Adewumi, B.A and O.S.V Oduwole. 1995. Problems Affecting the Utilization of Silo Storage in Nigeria" NSE Technical Transactions 3 (2): 27-32.

Adesida, M.A. 1889. Economics of Grain Storage in the Warehouses in Nigeria. Post Harvest News, 3:2-5, 2001.

Agboola, S.D. 1983. Information Booklet. Publication of the Nigerian Stored Products Research Institute (NSPRI), Lagos Nigeria.

Ajibola, O.O. 1994. Desorption Isotherms for Plantain at Several Temperatures. Journal of Food Science 51: 69-71.

Ajisegiri, A.S. 1989. Sorption phenomena and Storage Stability. Ph.D Thesis (unpublished), University of Ibadan, Ibadan.

Ajisegiri, A.S. 1990. Improving Local Rhombus for Grain Storage. Paper presentation at the Conference of the Nigeria Society of Agricultural Engineers, Makurdi.

Babarinsa, F.A. 2001. Grain Storage in silos without Insecticides. Post Harvest News 3:1-5.

Brummer, H. 1989. Grain Cooling in Steel silo. World Farming 8:30-35, 1983.

Cruz, J.P. and A. Diop. Agricultural Engineering in Development: Warehouse Technique.

Pages: 180-189

Seeds and Food: ***Processing and Storage Techniques***
Edited by: **Dr. Prasann Kumar and Dr. Pawan Kumar 'Bharti'**
ISBN: 978-93-88854-41-2
Edition: **2020**
Published by: **Discovery Publishing House Pvt. Ltd., New Delhi (India)**

10

Packages and Practices of Sorghum

Prasann Kumar[1,2*], Shipa Rani Dey[1]

GRAPHICAL ABSTRACT

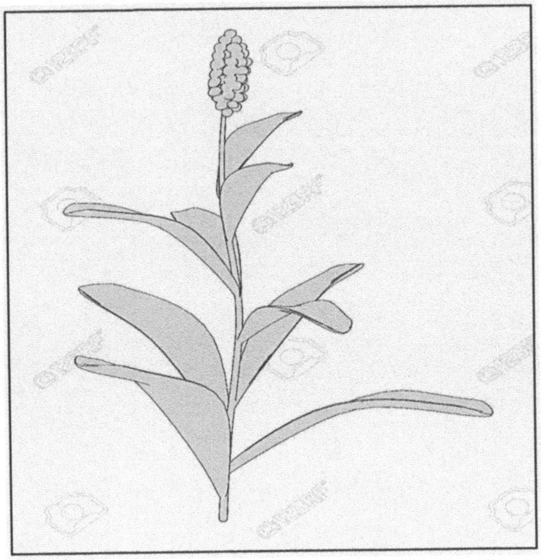

Keywords: Agriculture, Crop, Package, Sorghum

INTRODUCTION

- One of the major food grains of the world.
- Millions of the people in Africa and Asia depend on sorghum as the staple food.

[1] Department of Agronomy, School of Agriculture, Lovely Professional University, Jalandhar - 144 411 Punjab, (India)

[2] Divison of Research and Development, Lovely Professional University, Jalandhar- 144 411 Punjab, (India)

- It serves as an important source of cattle feed and fodder.
- It has capacity to withstand drought.
- It contains about 70 per cent carbohydrates, 10-12 per cent of protein and 3 per cent fat.

ORIGIN AND HISTORY

- Sorghum originated in north-eastern Africa, with domestication having taken place there around 5,000-8,000 years ago.
- The largest diversity of cultivated and wild sorghum is also found in this part of Africa.
- The secondary center of origin of sorghum is the Indian Subcontinent, with evidence for early cereal cultivation dating back about 4,500 years

AREA AND DISTRIBUTION

Leading countries of sorghum

- United States, Mexico, Nigeria, Sudan, India
- Madhya Pradesh stands first in productivity (14.95 q/ha), followed by Tamil Nadu (13.79 q/ha), Andhra Pradesh (13.58 q/ha), Gujarat (12.47 q/ha), Karnataka (11.43 q/ha) and Maharashtra (6.08 q/ha)

Nutrient composition of sorghum

Protein (g)	Fat (g)	Ash (g)	Crude fibre (g)	Carbohy-drate (g)	Energy (keal)	Ca (mg)	Fe (mg)	Thiamin (mg)	Riboflavin (mg)	Niacin (mg)
10.4	3.1	1.6	2.0	70.7	329	25	5.4	0.38	0.15	4.3

Fig. 10.1: Nutrient composition of sorghum

Source: based on review of literature

Taxonomic position:

Kingdom	Plantae
Division	Magnoliophyta
Class	Liliopsida
Subclass	Commelinidae
Order	Cyperales
Family	Poaceae (Grass)
Genus	*Sorghum*
Species	*bicolor*

Fig. 10.2: Taxonomic position

Source: based on review of literature

Classification of sorghum

Bicolor:

- Grain elongates, glumes clasping the grain which may be completely covered or ¼ exposed

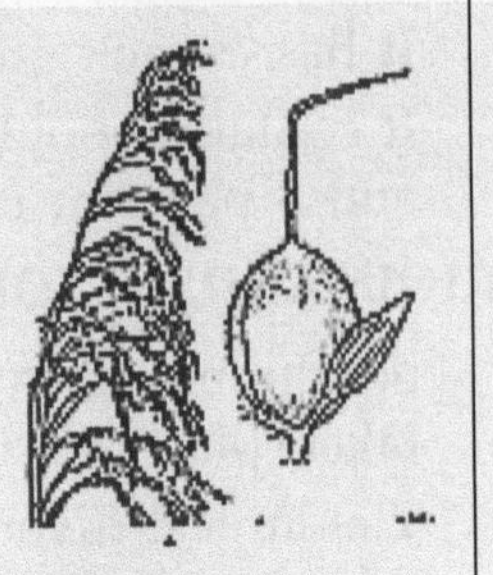

Guinea:

- Grains flattened dorso-ventrally

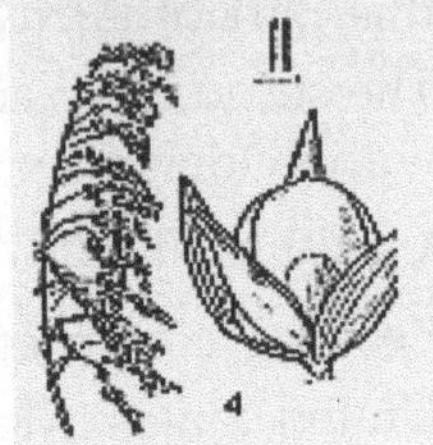

Fig. 10.3: Classification of sorghum

Source: based on review of literature

Caudatum:

➤ Grains asymmetrical glumes ½ length of the grain

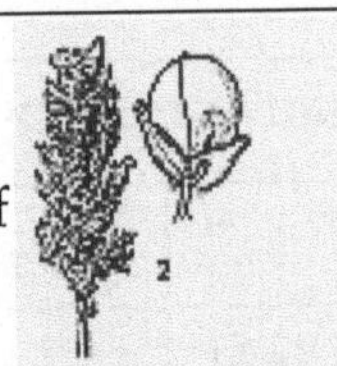

Kaffir:

➤ Grains symmetrical, glumes clasping in varying length

Durra:

➤ Grains rounded obovate, wedge shaped at the base and broadset slightly above the middle, glumes very wide

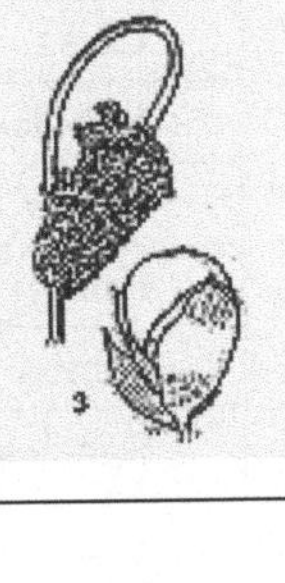

Fig. 10.4: Continuation of figure 10.3

Source: based on review of literature

BOTANICAL DESCRIPTION OF SORGHUM

Root system:

- Fibrous root system
- Seminal root which develops from the radicle with its lateral roots may persist throughout life of the plant.
- Seminal root lasts till the end of crop growth period.
- Fibrous roots developing from the lower nodes of the stem below ground level are the effective and active roots of the plant.

Stem:

- Erect, solid, 50 to 180 cm in height, pithy or juicy with green thickened nodes.
- Internodes are short at the base and longer above.
- Color of stem may be green of with purple wash.

Leaves:

- Simple, alternate, glabrous, long, midrib prominent;
- Ligule is short, membranous and fringed, present at the junction of leaf sheath and leaf blade.
- Below the leaf surface, waxy coating will be there which prevents evaporation of water.

Inflorescence:

Compact panicle or semi compact or loose panicle

Grain:

Caryopsis

Fig. 10.5: Inflorescence

Source: based on review of literature

SORGHUM POISONING

- Aerial shoot of sorghum contain cynogenic glycoside dhurrin, which by enzyme action hydrolizes to give hydrocyanic acid.
- As little as 0.5g HCN is sufficient to kill a cow.
- It gets reduced after flowering.
- The poison is destroyed when the fodder is made into hay.

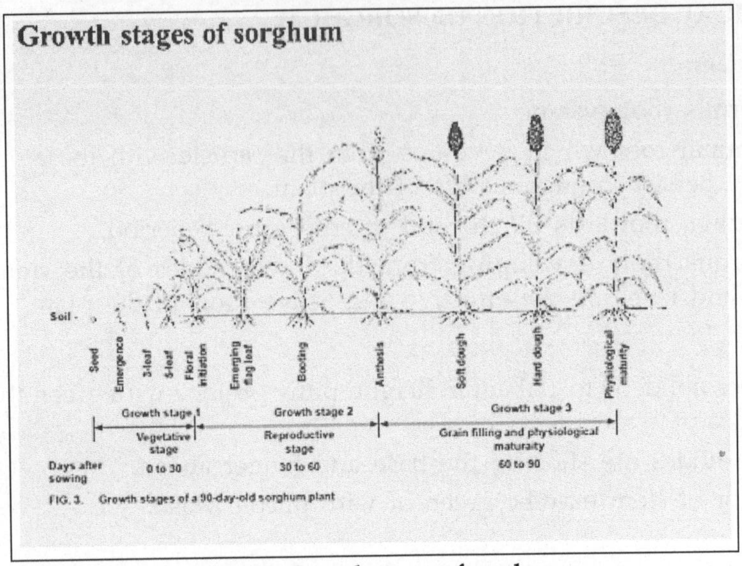

Fig. 10.6: Growth stages of sorghum

Source: based on review of literature

Climatic requirements:

- Sorghum is a warm-weather crop, which requires high temperatures for good germination and growth.
- The best time to plant is when there is sufficient water in the soil and the soil temperature is 15°C or higher at a depth of 10 cm.
- A temperature of 27 to 30°C is required for optimum growth and development.
- Flower initiation and the development of flower primordia are delayed with increased day and night temperatures.
- It is grown as a *Kharif* crop in northern India. In western and southern parts of the country it is grown as a Rabi crop.
- The minimum temperature for the germination of sorghum seeds is 7-10 °C.
- Flowering is hastened by short days and delayed by long days.
- Heading in sorghum is influenced by temperature as well as photo period.
- Sorghum varieties vary in their sensitivity to both temperature and photoperiod.

Soils:

- Sorghum is grown in a variety of soils in India.
- Soils with clay loam or loam texture havinggood water retention capacity are best suited for sorghum cultivation.

- It does well in pH range of 6.0-8.5 as it tolerates considerable salinity and alkalinity.

Hybrids/varieties:

- **Varieties:** CSV 4, CSV 6, CO-24, CO-25, CO-26, GJ 38, GJ 39, CSV 14R, CSV 216R (PhuleYashoda), CSV 18 (SPV 1595) and M 35-1.
- **Hybrids:** CSH 1, CSH 2, CSH 5, CSH 9, CSH 10, CSH 11, CSH 12, CSH 14.

CROPPING SYSTEM

North India:

- Sorghum-wheat
- Sorghum-wheat-moong
- Sorghum-pea
- Sorghum-gram
- Sorghum-potato-wheat

South India:

- Sorghum-cotton
- Sorghum-tobacco
- Groundnut - sorghum
- Sorghum-ragi-groundnut
- Sorghum-cotton-groundnut

Field Preparation:

- Sorghum requires a well prepared seed bed for good crop establishment. Proper tillage reduces weeds by killing the germinating seedlings and burying deep the weed seeds.
- One deep ploughing with mould board plough in summer followed by 3 to 4 harrowing to maintain weed free conditions.
- **Seed rate:** 12-15 kg per hectare
- **Spacing:** Row to row 45 cm and plant to plant 15 cm

Method of sowing:

- Broadcasting
- Behind the plough
- Bullock drawn seed drills
- Tractor drown seed drill

Time of sowing:

- *Kharif*: June-July
- *Rabi*: Mid September – Mid October
- Summer: Mid January – Mid February

Fertilizer management:

- Application of 10 tons/ha FYM at the last ploughing and 40 kg N/ha fertilizer is advised.
- In the absence of FYM, 80 kg of N and 40 kg P2O5/hectare is recommended.
- One half i.e 40 kg N and full P2O5 is to be applied at sowing, while remaining 40 kg N is to be applied 30-40 days after sowing. In case of light soils with low rainfall, 60kg N and 30 kg P_2O_5 is recommended.

Water management:

- Usually sorghum is grown as a rainfed crop. The irrigation should however be provided whenever, rains are not received.
- At the time of flowering and grain filling stages, the crop requires more water.
- At no stage, the plants should be allowed to wilt.
- Suitable drainage conditions should be provided for the removal of excess rain water from the field.

Weed management:

- Both grassy and broad leaved weeds grow with sorghum crop.
- In case the weeds are not brought under control at right time, there is 20-60 per cent reduction in yield.
- Sorghum is infested with *Echinocolacrusgulli, Eleusineindica, Setariaglauca, Cyrepusrotundus, Sorghum halepans, Cynodondactylon.*
- Weeds should be removed with the help of Khurpi or hand hoe when crop is about three weeks old.
- In case manual weeding is not possible use Atrazine at the rate of 0.5 to 1.0 kg active ingredient per hectare.

DISEASE MANAGEMENT

Grain mold

Damage:

- Grain molds are severe during the years of prolonged rainfall at the time of grain maturity.
- It results in discoloration of grain, but severity of infection reduces grain weight and size leading to considerable loss of yields even up to 100%;
- Reduces germination and acceptability of the harvested grain, nutritive value and market price.
- The toxins produced are harmful to animals.

Control measures:

- Spraying three times with Captan (0.3%) + Dithane M 45 (0.3%) at 10 days interval from flowering period can also control grain molds.

Charcoal Rot in sorghum

Infected Roots:

- The charcoal rot fungi infects roots of plants growing under adverse environmental conditions, particularly moisture stress and high temperature. Infected roots show water-soaked lesions that turn brown or black.

Sorghum lodging due to Charcoal Rot:

- Affected stalks are soft or spongy at the base and tend to lodge. Lodging is the most apparent symptom of charcoal rot.

Management:

- Maintaining soil moisture through irrigation, if possible, during the post- flowering period can minimize charcoal rot infestation.
- A balanced fertilizer program is beneficial as with high levels of nitrogen application with low levels of potassium may lead to charcoal rot.
- Growing of drought tolerant, lodging resistant, and no senescing types of sorghum like CSV 17, SPV 462 etc. can reduce yield losses from charcoal rot infestations.

Insect management

Shoot fly:

- *Damage symptoms:* It is a seedling pest and normally occurs in the 1st 4th week after germination.
- Maggot feeds on the growing tip causing wilting of leaf and later drying of central leaf giving a typical appearance of 'dead heart' symptoms.

Management:

- Under moderate levels of infestation, a mixture of 60% treated and 40% untreated seed could be used.
- Besides, any of the granular formulations of Furadan 3G or Phorate 10 G at the time of sowing as soil application in the seed furrows @ 20 kg/ha can also effectively check the pest incidence.
- In case soil granular application is not done, damage can be minimized by spraying seedling at 7 and 14 days stages with Endosulfan @ 2 ml/ liter water.

Stem borer

Damage symptoms:

- It infests the crop from 2nd week till maturity. Initially, the larvae feed on the upper surface of whorl leaves leaving the lower surface intact as transparent windows.
- As the severity of the feeding increases, blend of punctures and scratches of epidermal feeding appears prominently.
- Sometimes 'dead heart' symptoms also develop in younger plants due to early attack.
- Subsequently, the larvae bore into the stem resulting in extensive stem tunneling.
- Peduncle tunneling results in either breakage or complete or partial chaffy panicles

Management:

- Effective control of the borer can be achieved by application of any of the following insecticides in to the whorl i.e. Endosulfan 4G/4D, Carbaryl 3G, Malathion 10D or Furadan 3 G @ 8 12 kg/ha at 20 and 35 days after emergence.
- The treatment should only be given after ascertaining the infestation levels as evidenced

Harvesting and processing:

- When the crop matures the leaves turn yellow and present a dried up appearance.
- The grains are hard and firm.
- At this stage, harvest the crop by cutting the earheads separately.
- Cut the straw after a week, allow it to dry and then stack.
- In the case of tall varieties, cut the stem at 10 to 15 cm above ground level and afterwards separate the earheads and stack the straw.
- Dry the earheads.
- Thresh using a mechanical thresher or by drawing a stone roller over the earheads or by using cattle and dry the produce and store

Yield:

- 50 quintals of grain
- 100-125 quintals of dry stover from hectare of crop.

REFERENCES

https://www.dreamstime.com › Illustrations

https://www.gettyimages.com/illustrations/sorghum

https://pngtree.com/so/sorghum
https://www.shutterstock.com/.../cartoon-image-sorghum-plant-179808314
https://www.shutterstock.com/search/sorghum+shell
https://www.amazon.com/Sorghum-Sandals-Cartoon.../dp/B07KDHC3JB
https://www.123rf.com/photo_12969269_3d-render-of-cartoon-character-.

Index

A

Acid-Declined Cotton seed, 9

B

Bajra, 8
Barley, 7
Basal tillers, 86
Bengal Monosex Tilapia Hatchery, 129

C

Carrot, 10
Chilli, 142-148
    beta carotene, 145
    capsaicinoids, 146
    colour measurements, 145
    determination of ascorbic acid, 145
    determination of ph, 145
    determination of water activity, 145
    dried chilli, 143
    drying method, 144
        freeze drying, 144
        hot air oven, 144
        microwave oven, 144
        sun drying, 144
    evaluation of physical and chemical quality, 145
    freeze drying (FD) method, 146
    introduction, 142
    measurable quality attributes, 142
    methodology of drying, 142-148
    raw material, 143
    scovilled organoleptic test, 146
    total phenolic content, 145
Chilly, 10
Clarias batrachus, 155
Conversion of sorghum biomass feed stocks, 91
Corcyra cephalonica, 99
Crown roots of the sorghum, 87
Cucurbit seeds, 10

D

Dey, Shipa Rani, 83, 142, 168, 180

F

Fertilizer and irrigation, 4
Food and Crop Storage Technology, 168-179
    advantages of cold storage, 174
    aeration method, 173
    agric./bio-material, 175
    barn, shelf & pit, 172
    classification of
        dryers, 176
        storage types, 169-171
    drying, 175
    environmental factors, 171
    essential properties of air, 176
    improved crib, 173
    introduction, 168
    level of technology, 174
    material of construction, 173
    microorganism, 171
    modern storage structures, 172
    – structures, 171
    parameters for modern storage structures, 175

plastic containers, guard, polythene bag &earthen pot, 172
rhombus & traditional crib, 172
silo, 173
solar dryer, 177
storage, 168
– types, 169
structural stability, 174
traditional structures, 171, 172
types of drying rates, 177
Fumigation, 71

G

Garg, Meghna, 29
Genetic engineering, 41
Genetically modified (GM) oilseed crops, 29
Ghosh, Subrato, 128, 149
Gopalakrishnan, G., 1
Groundnut, 9

H

Harvest Index in sorghum, 88
Hatchery Seed Production Technology, 128-141
Adhikari Scientific Hatchery and Fish Centre, 135
description of Bengal hatchery, 129-130
feed for tilapia fry in hapa, 132-134
fry transport and sale, 130
grow-out farming of monosex tilapia, 137-138
important features in monosex tilapia fry production, 137
maintenance of broodfishes, 135
red monosex tilapia, 138
reproductive biology of *Oreochromis niloticus*, 131
transportation and sale of fry from Adhikari Hatchery, 136
High seed germination, 95
Homogeneity, 3, 4

I

Isolation of seed, 13, 14

K

Krantz anatomy, 87
Kumar, Prasann, 83, 142, 168, 180

L

Labeo bata, 155, 156
Labeo calbasu, 155
Leaf Area Index, 88

M

Maize, 8
Major Seed Oils and their Significance, 29-47
algae and marine phytoplankton, 31
Arachidonic Acid (AA), 40
canola seed, 38
erucic acid oils, 41
fat composition analysis of mustard oil, 32
fatty acids (FAs), 30
gamma-linolenic acid (GLA), 38
high arachidonic and eicosapentaenoic acid oils, 40
– oleic acid oils, 36
– omega-3 long-chain polyunsaturated fatty acids (lc-pufas) oils, 37
– palmitic acid oils, 32-33
– ricinoleic acid oils, 41
– stearic acid oils, 33
– unusual monoenoic fatty acid oils, 35
introduction, 29
lipids, 30
low very long chain saturated fatty acids, 33
– -density lipoprotein (ldl), 36
natural sources of mufas, 31
omega-3 fatty acid, 37
petroselinic acid, 36
polyunsaturated fatty acids (PUFAs), 30, 32
Mature panicle of the sorghum, 89
Monoenoic fatty acids, 35

Mustard oil, 32
Mystus vittatus, 157

N

Natural sources of MUFAs, 31
Nile Tilapia, 128
Notopterus chitala, 149-167

O

Oleic acid, 35, 36
Ompak pabda, 157
Oreochromis niloticus, 128-141

P

Paddy, 6
Poor storage condition, 96
Post harvest losses in India, 95
Processing of seeds, 3

R

Rai, P.K., 29
Recirculatory Aquaculture System (RAS), 158, 159, 161
Removal of external materials, 13
Rhyzopertha dominica, 99

S

Saturated fatty acids (SFAs), 33
Seed moisture content (MC), 101
Seed Preservation Techniques, 95-127
  addition of cryoprotectant, 125
  advanced seed preservation techniques, 98
  advantages of the use of silica gel, 116
  basic requirements, 104
  benefits of modified atmosphere storage, 102
  black box system, 114
  Ca under normal atmospheric pressure, 103
  CO_2 atmospheres, 104
  coloured saturation indicators, 117
  controlled atmosphere storage, 102
  – atmospheres, 103
  cryopreservation, 121-123
    advantages of
  cryoprotectants, 125
  desiccant, 116
  dry room or drying chamber/cabinet, 116
  freezing, 125
    thawing/rewarming, 125
    vitrification, 125
    washing, reculture/regeneration, 125
  fungi and mycotoxins production, 102
  good storage environment, 96
  hand operated vacuum packing system for seed storage, 120
  hermetic storage, 106-108
  introduction, 95
  low oxygen atmospheres, 104
  methods for creating and maintaining modified atmosphere, 99
  modified atmosphere storage, 98
  Nitrogen atmosphere, 105-106
  nutrient changes, 102
  permafrost storage, 109
  principle, 99
  principles of hermetic seed storage, 108-109
  procedures for establishing controlled atmospheres, 105
  role of vacuum sealing in extending seed life, 119
  saturated salts, 117
  seed banking at low temperatures, 122, 123-125
  – deterioration during storage, 97
  – moisture content, 97
  – viability, 101
  sensitivity of seeds, 96
  storability of seeds, 96
  suitable containers, 119
  svalbard global seed vault, 110-114
  types of desiccants, 116

– – hermetic storage systems, 109
ultra dry storage, 114-116
– drying with silica gel, 116
vacuum-sealing, 119
technologies for, 120
– storage, 118-119
Seed processing, 1-28
aspiration, 17
auxiliary building, 12
cleaning, 15
colour separator, 19
– sorter, 19
conveying, 12
electronic colour, 19
– colour sorter, 20
equipment, 14
air screen cleaner cum grader, 15
debearders, 15
huller scarifier, 15
maize sheller, 15
pre cleaning, 14
pre conditioning, 14
scalper, 14
fire-fighting equipment, 12
flutted roller, 18
general sequence of processing, 6
grading, 17
heterogeneous, 4
importance, 1-28
inclination of the screen, 18
indented cylinder separator, 20
introduction, 1
key to efficient plant layout, 11
layout plan for construction of a seed processing plant, 10
magnetic separator, 25
matching capacity, 12
materials removed during seed processing, 4, 5
needle separator, 27
physical characteristics used to separate seeds, 13
planning, 13
pre-conditioning and pre cleaning, 13
principles and objectives, 3
processing area, 11
processing sequence, 12
acid-declined cotton seed, 9
bajra, 8
barley, 7
cucurbit seeds, 10
groundnut, 9
maize, 8
paddy, 6
tomato, chilly, carrot, 10
wheat, 7
purposes of seed processing, 3
rate of vibration of sieve, 18
receiving-cum-drying platform, 11
requirement in seed processing, 4
roll mill or dodder mill or velvet roll mill,
scalping, 17
screen dams, 18
seed movement/basic steps in seed processing plant, 5
– processing plant building, 11
– processing, 2
separating action, 27
sequence, 1-28
– of operation in seed processing, 5
specific gravity separator, 22
spiral separator, 24
type of layouts, 12
combined designs, 13
multistorey, 12
single storey plant, 12
types of seed cleaner cum grader, 18
upgrading, 18
working principle, 17

Seed Production of *Notopterus Chitala* and other Fishes, 149-167
- Bengal Fish Fest 2019 at ICAR-CIFE Kolkata, 163-167
- different components of hatchery, 150
- Dooars Aquaculture Farm, 159
- experience on *N. chitala* seed production, 155
- Fish Farming, 149-167
- fish farming in RAS facility, 158
- – seed production, 151
- grow-out fish farming, 152
- growth of fishes, 160
- mode of functioning of RAS, 159
- Odla fish seed hatchery, 149-167
- potential and prospect of RAS
- Recirculatory Aquaculture System, 149-167
- seed production of major carps, 157
- Sri Laksmikanta Barman, 149-167
- steady progress in aquaculture, 152
- strategies on doubling fish production, 162
- tanks, 151
- Ulupi Matsya Unnayan Prakalpa, 155
- warmwater and coldwater finfish, 153

Seed storage, 48-82
- abiotic factors, 53, 57
- activated clay seed treatment, 73
- activity of organisms associated with seeds in storage, 60
- *Agrason, 71*
- attack by microorganisms and their Control, 82
- biotic factors, 53, 54
- bulk (open) storage, 62
- care and preparation before storage, 70
- carryover seeds, 62
- classification of packing materials or containers, 64
- construction features for good seed warehouse, 68
- control of birds and microorganisms, 81
- controlled storage, 62
- deteriorative changes in seed and their consequences, 66
- dry, cool conditions during storage, 59
- effect of provenance, 54
- factors affecting seed longevity, 53
- foundation stock and enforcement seed sample, 62
- fumigation of the godown, 71
- fungicide, 71
- gas during storage, 58
- general principles of seed storage, 52
- genetic makeup of seed, 54
- germplasm seed storage, 62
- halogenation products or halogen mixture, 73
- Harringtons Thumb Rule, 58
- high quality seed store better than low quality seed, 67
- Indicator device, 79
- indigenous methods of rat control, 81
- initial seed quality, 54
- inorganic non-mercurials, 72
- insect traps for storage godown, 78
- insecticide treatments, 72
- intermediate seeds, 61
- introduction, 48
- longevity of deed is a characteristic of the species or variety, 66
- losses in the course of grain storage, 73
- maintenance of seed vigour and viability, 49
- maintenance of store house hygiene, 75
  - aluminium phosphide, 76
  - chemicals, 75
  - methyl bromide, 76
  - phosphine, 75
  - prophylatic treatment of seeds, 75

management of insect pests of seeds, 74
control of insect pests, 74
curative measures, 74
non-chemical control measures, 74
preventive measures, 74
mechanical traps, 80
microflora, insects and mites, 57
moisture and vapour
pervious containers, 64
proof containers, 65
moisture impervious but vapour pervious containers, 65
natural products used in storage, 77
neem products in pest control, 77
other plant products in pest control, 78
wood ash in storage pest control, 78
objective of seed storage, 49
organic mercurials, 72
organic non-mercurials (e.g.) Bavistin, 72
organo mercurials, 71
orthodox Seeds, 60
other measures for pest and disease control, 76
fumigation
other plant products in pest control, 78
packaging material, 59
purpose of seed storage, 49
rat proofing, 80
recalcitrant seeds, 61
relative humidity, 57
rodent control, 79
rodent management in store houses, 81
sanitation in storage, 58
seed moisture content, 54
– packaging in relation to seed storage, 63
– selection for extended storability, 67
– storage, 49
– – in relation to seed deterioration, 65
– treatment, 71
selection and maintenance of storage godown, 71
stages of seed storage, 50
steps in seed storage, 50
storage conditions, 63
– from harvest until planting, 52
– godown and their maintenance, 68
– – sanitation, 70
– insect management, 75
– of commercial seeds, 61
– on plan, 51
– pests and management, 73
temperature, 58
TNAU 2 in 1 model trap, 79
automatic insect removal bin, 79
insect probe trap, 78
pit fall trap, 79
types of seed storage, 60
wood ash in storage pest control, 78
Sharma, Anubhuti, 29
Soil, 4
Sorghum, 83-94, 180-189
area and distribution, 181
biomass accumulation, 88
canopy of the sorghum, 88
classification of sorghum, 182
climatic requirements, 184
differentiation of panicle and their growth, 89
disease management, 186
charcoal rot in sorghum, 187
grain mold, 186
dormancy, 84
fertilizer management, 186
field preparation, 185
grains in a panicle, 89
growth of roots, 87

– stages of sorghum, 184
harvest index, 88
harvesting and processing, 188
hybrids/varieties, 185
inflorescence, 183
insect management, 187
shoot fly, 187
stem borer, 188
introduction, 180
introduction, 83
leaf structure and its role in sorghum, 87
leaves, 183
method of sowing, 185
nutrient composition of sorghum, 181
origin and history, 181
packages, 180-189
photoperiodic response, 86
plant height, 86
practices, 180-189
root system, 183
seed germination, 84
seedling establishment, 84, 85
soils, 184
sorghum poisoning, 183
stem, 183
taxonomic position, 181
temperature, 89
tillering, 86
time of sowing, 185
water management, 186
weed management, 186
yield, 188
Sridevi, R., 1, 48, 95
Stalks of the sorghum, 90, 91
Stearic acid, 33
Storage temperature, 95

T

Tilapia fry, 130
Tomato, 10

V

Vacuum sealing of seeds, 119
Vegetable oils, 38
Very long chain saturated fatty acids (VLSFA), 29, 33
Vigour of seed, 96

W

Wheat, 7

Z

Zeolites, 116
Zinc-aluminium alloy sheets, 159

* * * * * *